Withdrawing from Iraq

Alternative Schedules, Associated Risks, and Mitigating Strategies

Walter L. Perry, Stuart E. Johnson, Keith Crane,

David C. Gompert, John Gordon IV, Robert E. Hunter,

Dalia Dassa Kaye, Terrence K. Kelly, Eric Peltz, Howard J. Shatz

Prepared for the Office of the Secretary of Defense
Approved for public release; distribution unlimited

NATIONAL DEFENSE RESEARCH INSTITUTE

The research described in this report was prepared for the Office of the Secretary of Defense (OSD) and conducted in the RAND National Defense Research Institute, a federally funded research and development center sponsored by the OSD, the Joint Staff, the Unified Combatant Commands, the Department of the Navy, the Marine Corps, the defense agencies, and the defense Intelligence Community under Contract W74V8H-06-C-0002.

Library of Congress Cataloging-in-Publication Data is available for this publication.

978-0-8330-4772-4

The RAND Corporation is a nonprofit research organization providing objective analysis and effective solutions that address the challenges facing the public and private sectors around the world. RAND's publications do not necessarily reflect the opinions of its research clients and sponsors.

RAND® is a registered trademark.

Cover photo: The Iraqi flag flutters as a soldier of the 5th Squadron, 4th Cavalry regiment, salutes during the transfer ceremony of the JSS Ghazaliyah IV security station to full Iraqi Security Forces control in the Ghazaliyah district of Baghdad on February 14, 2009. Ahmad Al-Rubaye/AFP/Getty Images

Published 2009 by the RAND Corporation
1776 Main Street, P.O. Box 2138, Santa Monica, CA 90407-2138
1200 South Hayes Street, Arlington, VA 22202-5050
4570 Fifth Avenue, Suite 600, Pittsburgh, PA 15213-2665
RAND URL: http://www.rand.org/
To order RAND documents or to obtain additional information, contact
Distribution Services: Telephone: (310) 451-7002;
Fax: (310) 451-6915; Email: order@rand.org

Preface

Security has improved dramatically in Iraq since 2007; both the U.S. and the Iraqi governments want to see the U.S. presence reduced and have the Iraqis assume a greater role in providing for public security. These developments have brought the United States to a critical juncture in Iraq. The emerging challenge is to continue a withdrawal of U.S. forces while preserving security and stability in the country and in the region. With this in mind, the U.S. Congress provided resources in the fiscal year 2009 Defense Appropriations Act for an independent study to assess alternative schedules to draw down U.S. forces and effect the transition to Iraqi forces providing for the nation's security. This study assesses the feasibility of three such plans and makes recommendations designed to reduce the risks attendant on withdrawal; these recommendations are, for the most part, relevant whichever drawdown schedule is ultimately met. The analysis supporting this report was completed in May 2009, and the illustrative schedules all assume implementation decisions having been made in time for implementation in May, if not earlier. To the extent that such decisions are made later, the schedules would likely be pushed back accordingly. We recognize that any drawdown schedule that calls for U.S. forces remaining in Iraq beyond the end of December 2011 would require renegotiating the Security Agreement between the United States and Iraq.

The RAND Corporation National Defense Research Institute was asked to conduct this study. This report documents the study findings. It describes alternative drawdown schedules and analyzes how internal Iraqi security and stability and regional political and military issues might affect and be affected by these plans. It should interest senior members of the Obama administration, including policymakers in the Departments of Defense and State, members of Congress, and military planners and operators.

This research was sponsored by the Principal Deputy Assistant Secretary of Defense for International Security Affairs and conducted within the International Security and Defense Policy Center (ISDP) of the RAND National Defense Research Institute (NDRI), a federally funded research and development center sponsored by the Office of the Secretary of Defense, the Joint Staff, the Unified Combatant Commands, the Department of the Navy, the Marine Corps, the defense agencies, and the defense Intelligence Community.

For more information on RAND's International Security and Defense Policy Center, contact the Director, James Dobbins, who can be reached by email at dobbins@rand.org; by phone at 703-413-1100, extension 5134; or by mail at the RAND Corporation, 1200 South Hayes Street, Arlington, Virginia 22202-5050. More information about RAND is available at www.rand.org.

Contents

Figures

Tables

Summary

In late 2008, Congress asked the Department of Defense to have the RAND Corporation assess the feasibility of two alternative schedules for the drawdown of U.S. forces in Iraq. Since then, the Obama administration has announced a timeline for the drawdown of U.S. forces. This report accordingly looks at three alternative schedules, one matching the administration's intentions, one somewhat faster, and another slower; judges the risks associated with each; and recommends ways to reduce those risks.

The Alternatives

We consider three alternatives: one in which combat units are drawn down in 12 months, one in which combat units are drawn down in 16 months, and a third one that retains some combat units for 32 months. In each alternative, all U.S. military forces will be withdrawn from Iraq by the end of December 2011, in accordance with the Security Agreement between Iraq and the United States.[1] We assume a start date of May 1, 2009, for all three alternatives.

The 16-month alternative is our version of how the administration's August 2010 goal might be achieved. In addition, we offer two additional drawdown schedules: one faster than the administration's and another slower. We include these additional alternatives to consider the feasibility of altering the administration's withdrawal framework in the event a faster drawdown is desired or if risks to the security of the departing U.S. forces or the Iraqi population require a slower-paced drawdown.

We recognize, however, that the selected schedule will become the basis for personnel and logistics planning. Although attempting to substantially alter the selected schedule once a drawdown schedule has been selected is possible, doing so would likely entail major financial and readiness costs. Abruptly switching from one alternative schedule to another would also have detrimental effects on security and diplomacy in

---

[1]   Agreement Between the United States of America and the Republic of Iraq on the Withdrawal of United States Forces from Iraq and the Organization of Their Activities During Their Temporary Presence in Iraq, signed in Baghdad on November 17, 2008.

Iraq and the region, greatly increasing the probability that some of the risks discussed in Chapters Four, Five, and Six of this monograph will arise. We did not examine these costs in our study.

The force remaining after the drawdown of combat units varies with each alternative. In alternative 1, the force is referred to as the *residual force*. This force consists of enablers, support personnel, and trainers. Its mission is to advise and assist the Iraqi Security Forces (ISF) and to protect ongoing U.S. civilian and military efforts within Iraq. In alternative 2, the force remaining after combat units have departed is referred to as the *transition force*. It is composed of advise and assist brigades (AABs) supplemented by additional training, enabling, and support personnel. Its mission is to advise and assist the ISF, to conduct counterterrorism missions in coordination with the ISF, and to protect ongoing U.S. civilian and military efforts within Iraq. In alternative 3, combat units remain through the end of the Security Agreement period, along with enablers, trainers, and support forces.

Alternative 1: Combat Units Depart by April 30, 2010

In this alternative, all U.S. combat units will depart within 12 months of the start of the drawdown (May 1, 2009). The departure of combat units will leave 44,000 U.S. troops, who will subsequently be drawn down. This force will consist of units that perform key enabling functions and training for the ISF as well as the support forces necessary to sustain these forces (to include base support) and support limited ISF counterterrorism operations. This residual force will depart no later than December 2011, a departure date in line with the Security Agreement between the United States and Iraq. The following describe alternative 1:

- **Rationale:** This alternative offers the administration an option to remove all combat units early if desired. Although at present there appears to be no reason to expedite the drawdown in this way, conditions may change: For example, U.S. forces may be needed to support conflicts elsewhere in the world, the Iraqi government may call for a faster removal of U.S. forces in response to a changing political climate in Iraq, or the economic situation in the United States may dictate the need to reduce costs by bringing our forces home early.
- **Planning:** Initiating this plan would normally take 90 days to allow for the necessary planning. However, the planning conducted as part of the current plan can provide for the initial redeployments in this alternative, cutting the lead-time requirement by about 30 days to a decision in early June. Additional planning that is necessary can take place as the initial units begin to redeploy.
- **ISF support:** Under this alternative, the ability to partner U.S. combat units with their ISF counterparts for training purposes will end in April 2010. However, the full, predrawdown complement of trainers (3,500) will remain in the residual force through April 2011. These trainers comprise the mobile training

teams (MTTs), and they conduct much of the training of the Iraqi Army. There are 16,500 enablers available to support ISF operations through the end of April 2011; the enablers will then draw down through the end of the Security Agreement period in December 2011.

- **Security:** Because of the short timeframe to draw down all combat units from Iraq in this alternative, the number of combat units available through February 2010 to help secure the Iraqi election process is fewer than in alternative 2.[2] Compared with 2003, when many U.S. Army support units were not prepared to provide their own security, these units are now better trained and armed to protect themselves. This may reduce the need for U.S. combat units to be present in Iraq to provide force protection to support forces.
- **Unforeseen contingencies:** After April 2010, the ability of the remaining forces to engage in combat operations is greatly reduced. Contingency operations will likely be conducted primarily by the ISF.
- **Leaving Iraq:** Combat units will depart at a sharp pace from May 2009 through April 2010. Once the combat units have departed, the remaining forces will draw down through December 31, 2011. By the end of December 2011, the last U.S. military personnel will have departed and all U.S. bases will have been closed or transferred to the Government of Iraq (GoI).

To mitigate some of the potential risks, the United States could take the following measures:

- Reassign some U.S. personnel from combat units to MTTs and other organizations to train the ISF.
- Base U.S. combat units (e.g., two combat brigades) in a nearby nation, such as Kuwait, to provide a quick-reaction capability. (Understandably, this would require a negotiated agreement between the United States and Kuwait, but if successful, it would provide a good hedge against risks generated by the departure of combat units from Iraq.)
- Shift some security functions and ISF training inside Iraq to contractors.
- Leave behind some U.S. equipment in the combat units for the ISF for training and future operations.

Alternative 2: Mission of U.S. Forces Changes After August 2010

This alternative is RAND's interpretation of the administration's goal to change the mission in Iraq from combat operations to advising and assisting the ISF after all combat units have departed in August 2010. The U.S. force presence will drop to

---

[2] By the Iraqi election process we mean the elections in December 2009 through the seating of the newly elected Iraqi government sometime in February 2010.

50,000 troops by that time, and the remaining forces will constitute a transition force. It will consist of AABs and additional training, enabling, and support personnel. The following describe alternative 2:

- **Rationale:** This alternative reflects the essentials of the administration's goal for withdrawing from Iraq. Our view is that the President is attempting to fulfill his promise to "responsibly remove our combat brigades [from Iraq]."[3] Sixteen months is seen by the administration to constitute sufficient time for an orderly, secure drawdown.
- **Planning:** The initial portion of this plan is exactly the same as in alternative 1. Consequently, to execute the initial phase as described in this report would require a decision in early June 2009. The remainder of the drawdown would not require accelerated planning.
- **ISF support:** The ability to partner U.S. AABs with their ISF counterparts for training purposes will continue, almost to the end of the Security Agreement period. The number of trainers remaining in the transition force remains constant at 3,500 (predrawdown levels) until February 2010. Brigades currently slated to replace units in Iraq will be configured as AABs. Therefore, fewer trainers may be required as these units replace redeploying units. The enablers remain at predrawdown levels until May 2010 and then begin to fall off as some of the enabling activities are assumed by the AABs. Because the AABs retain most of their combat equipment, they will also be able to partner with the Iraqi Army for training purposes.
- **Security:** The initial drawdown of 12,000 personnel leaves approximately 12 combat brigades in Iraq in November 2009 to provide security for the December national elections. Further force reductions are then halted until February 2010. This will provide the "robust force" GEN Raymond Odierno, Commander, Multi-National Force–Iraq (MNF-I), needs to ensure a safe election process. After August 2010, we assume approximately six AABs will be available in the transition force along with a small number of other security forces.
- **Unforeseen contingencies:** In addition to providing a security force to protect U.S. military and civilian personnel still in Iraq, the AABs can also serve as a contingency force because of their ability to resume combat missions rather easily.
- **Leaving Iraq:** From May through October 2009, approximately 12,000 combat and support forces will depart from Iraq. The 130,000 remaining personnel will stay until February 2010, at which time the drawdown resumes. Once the combat units depart, the military mission will change to assisting and advising the ISF. In this alternative, by May 2011, the total number of troops will have dropped to roughly 35,000. This provides ample time to draw down the rest of the force by

---

[3] Obama, 2009a.

December 2011. The pace of that withdrawal will depend on the situation on the ground at that time.

The drawdown/re-roling of U.S. combat units from Iraq by September 2010 will have some effect on the security of the remaining forces (depending on the evolving security situation). However, unlike alternative 1, in this alternative, the creation of the AABs retains the ability of the U.S. forces to partner with and train the ISF and provide additional security if required. In addition, the AABs will provide a significant hedge against the possibility that violence could reemerge and threaten the U.S. personnel who remain in Iraq. The risk-mitigating measures described in alternative 1, such as shifting personnel in combat units to perform ISF training and shifting security functions to contractors, are not necessary in this alternative.

Alternative 3: Maintain Combat and Noncombat Units Through December 2011

In this alternative, combat units organized as brigade combat teams (BCTs) remain in Iraq until the December 2011 departure deadline. This alternative adds flexibility by not requiring a fixed date for the removal of combat units and changing the mission of the remaining force before the end of the Security Agreement period in December 2011. Also, it does not require the re-roling of BCTs at any time in the drawdown process. In addition, the longer drawdown schedule provides more flexibility in sequencing the departure of combat units. With additional time, it is easier to plan for the removal of units from relatively secure areas first.

- **Rationale:** This alternative provides the most flexibility. If some or all of the potential risk factors described in detail in the body of this report come to pass, the retention of some combat units to the end of December 2011 allows the command in Iraq the opportunity to respond militarily. In addition, this alternative provides a better opportunity for the command to sequence the redeployment of combat units consistent with security requirements throughout Iraq.
- **Planning:** As in alternative 1, initiating this plan would normally take 90 days given the estimated planning lead time. However, the planning conducted as part of the current plan can provide for the initial redeployments in this alternative, cutting the lead-time requirement by about 30 days to a decision in early June. Additional planning that is necessary can take place as the initial units begin to redeploy.
- **ISF support:** The ability to partner U.S. combat units with their ISF counterparts for training purposes will continue almost to the end of the Security Agreement period, but at an increasingly reduced number. As in alternative 1, the number of trainers in the force (in MTTs) remains at approximately 3,500 until the beginning of May 2011. Unlike alternative 2, in this alternative rotational units will not be configured as AABs, and trainers will be needed longer. Enablers remain

at their predrawdown level until February 2010, and their drawdown rate starts slowly from then.

- **Security:** The initial drawdown in this alternative is approximately five BCTs with their associated support elements. This will demonstrate to the Iraqi population that the U.S. is fulfilling its commitment to leave Iraq in a more dramatic way than in alternative 2. However, it also means that the number of combat brigades available to secure the election process in December 2009 and through the seating of the new government will be three fewer than in alternative 2. The fact that there will still be three combat brigades in Iraq in March 2011 in this alternative ensures a capable remaining force.

- **Leaving Iraq:** This alternative draws down approximately five BCTs and their associated support personnel and equipment before the Iraqi national elections to demonstrate U.S. resolve to remove its forces from Iraq as agreed. Once the drawdown resumes in February 2010, we assume a linear drawdown through the end of 2011, the end of the Security Agreement period. The remaining nine BCTs will depart at an average rate of approximately one BCT every two months. As in alternative 2, the exact drawdown rate will depend on the security conditions in the country at the time. However, the absence of a deadline for the removal of all combat units except the December 2011 deadline gives the command in Iraq the ability to implement a flexible sequenced redeployment based on the security situation in various parts of the country.

- **Unforeseen Contingencies:** The remaining BCTs in this alternative are not configured as AABs and their mission does not change. Hence they are fully capable of responding to contingencies.

Unlike alternative 1, U.S. support forces, trainers, and enablers in alternative 3 will be less dependent on the ISF for their security because some U.S. combat units will remain until almost the end of the drawdown. The remaining BCTs will be able to continue partnering with the ISF units almost to the end of the Security Agreement period as well. This implies that there will be no need to take the various risk-mitigating steps described in alternative 1. However, with this alternative come the costs of supporting a large contingent of U.S. forces in Iraq for longer than in alternatives 1 and 2. It also incurs the opportunity costs of not being able to use the forces elsewhere.

Also, the maintenance of a large U.S. force in Iraq through the summer of 2011 may lead some Iraqis to conclude that the United States is continuing its occupation of the country. Therefore, a risk mitigation step in this alternative could be to develop an information campaign to explain why U.S. combat units are remaining through the full Security Agreement period.

Additional Drawdown Factors

We next focus on the other factors that must be considered in implementing any draw-down plan. These include such procedural issues as unit rotation schedules, the phasing of the drawdown, and the geographical sequencing of unit withdrawal. In addition, we describe the evolution of the ISF, and how the outcome of the Security Agreement referendum might affect the U.S. drawdown.

Unit Rotation Schedules

To the extent possible, the drawdown in each of our alternatives would be accomplished through the non-replacement of redeploying units. This is what is contemplated by the MNF-I as it plans its drawdown. To a large degree, the pattern has been to rotate the entire military force in terms of units about every 12 months. However, the drawdown and the overall U.S. military presence differ from rotating units in and out of Iraq. Units take only part of their equipment to the theater, receiving the rest in Iraq from a pool of equipment referred to as Theater Provided Equipment (TPE), which remains in Iraq. This equipment will have to be withdrawn in any drawdown. If a unit redeploy-ing is not to be replaced, then all of its equipment will have to be removed, creating a considerable burden on the logistics system.

Sequencing the Drawdown

The sequencing of the departure of U.S. forces from Iraq needs to take into account the varying security levels around the country. The tension between the GoI and the quasi-independent Kurdish northern portion of the country suggests that U.S. forces should depart at a somewhat slower rate from that region. Similarly, due to the critical-ity of Baghdad, U.S. forces should depart the capital at a slower rate compared with other portions of the country. However, given the fragile peace in most of the country, the MNF-I must remain flexible enough to respond to a changing security situation. The report includes a proposed sequence, summarized below, based on current security conditions. All alternatives discussed above should take sequencing into account as the combat units draw down, but alternative 3 provides the commanders on the ground the most flexibility.

Status of the Iraqi Security Forces

Two Iraqi organizations are central to Iraq's ability to establish a stable and secure coun-try: the Iraqi military and the National Police (NP). Therefore, the projected improve-ment in their proficiency in the months leading up to December 2011 is central to the drawdown schedule for U.S. forces engaged in training these forces. As of December 2008, approximately two-thirds of the Iraqi Army was at the upper levels of readiness. The NP's overall readiness is significantly lower. Several factors can affect the pace of improving and maintaining ISF readiness: the number of U.S. trainers, the presence of U.S. combat units and enablers, and the rate at which the forces improve.

The Security Agreement Referendum

The Security Agreement allows for a popular referendum to endorse its terms; the target date for holding this referendum is July 2009. Were the agreement to be rejected, U.S. forces would be obliged to withdraw within 12 months. This would undercut the deliberate planning envisioned by the MNF-I for the drawdown and eventual complete withdrawal of U.S. forces, and it would obviate all three of the alternative drawdown schedules presented above. It would also drive the command into an intensive withdrawal process that is barely attainable under the best of circumstances. However, interviews with Iraqi and MNF-I officials indicate that the prospect of the Security Agreement referendum being defeated—or even taking place at all—is low for three reasons: (1) a legislative framework has to be developed for the referendum to take place, (2) even if the referendum is held, there is no indication that the agreement would be rejected, and (3) even if the referendum is held, it would likely be delayed by at least several months, during which time the command would be moving forward with its own withdrawal preparations so that the 12-month deadline would be that much less demanding.

Logistics Considerations

To determine the feasibility of each of the alternative drawdown schedules, we estimated the amount of time it would take to redeploy U.S. military forces and their equipment from Iraq onto ships for movement out of the region. We also estimated the amount of time it would take to close or transfer bases. This entailed determining how much has to be moved, the redeployment throughput capacity and routes, and the time required to complete base closure. To mitigate timeline risk, especially where alternatives are just barely feasible, we also developed some risk-mitigation actions that would reduce the risk of bottlenecks developing and, in some cases, could increase the speed of withdrawal, if desired.

Drawdown consists of two major elements: the movement of units and their equipment out of Iraq and the closure of bases. Some contract support personnel and their equipment will likely be drawn down as the combat units withdraw, but there is flexibility in the degree to which this needs to occur by the combat unit drawdown target dates. It will also be economical to donate some or perhaps much of the contractors' government-owned equipment. Thus, the alternatives create two overlapping phases: (1) the redeployment of combat units and associated support units and (2) the redeployment of units and the closure (or transfer) of bases. The requirements for "phase 1" activities are more immediate and need to be started sooner. These activities are very demanding and may involve bottlenecks.

The redeployment of units consists of moving equipment and personnel and pre-paring them for transit out of the region. We further divide moving unit equipment, including items procured specifically for current operations, into the following two broad categories: (1) military vehicles and (2) all other items, most of which are trans-ported in containers. Capacity for moving units out of Iraq appears to be sufficient for each of the three alternatives. However, the aggressive portions of the drawdown schedules (or of any other compressed drawdown plan) require very high-capacity uti-lization. With high-capacity utilization, very small amounts of process variability or disruptions can create delays. Generally, there are three ways to increase or "protect" capacity for redeploying units:

- actions that either increase capacity or provide low-cost ways to help ensure assumed capacity is achieved
- actions that reduce demands for transportation and on base closure or that shift movement from peak periods to smooth out workload
- actions that shift demand from military convoys and processing facilities to alter-native modes, providers, and routes.

Although redeploying units from Iraq presents a large, demanding logistics prob-lem requiring significant resources, logistics capabilities are unlikely to constrain oper-ational and strategic drawdown planning with respect to the flow of forces out of Iraq provided that a decision to draw down combat units is made at least a year before the withdrawal deadline. While all three alternatives are logistically feasible, any fur-ther delay in the start of a fast-paced redeployment schedule later than February 2010 for alternative 2 will make the achievement of the August 2010 deadline doubtful. However, to hedge against logistics execution risk, there is a wide variety of options across the three categories just mentioned either to increase capacity or to ensure that process-throughput capabilities meet expectations. Only one of these mitigating actions, however, "self-redeployment" of units, could allow for a couple of additional months of delay in initiating a large-scale drawdown alternative while preserving the ability to keep the August 2010 target date for the withdrawal of combat units.

Large base-closure and transfer requirements could impose a long-lead require-ment on overall drawdown planning. But closing or transferring large bases should—given early enough start dates—be possible within both the timeframe called for in the Security Agreement and any other timeframes the administration and the military have publicly discussed.

Stability and Security Issues

Three principal categories of dangers may threaten Iraq's internal security and stability during and after the drawdown of U.S. forces:

- extremists, who reject the emerging political order and would use violence to drive Iraq back into chaos
- mainstream armed opposition groups, who now participate in the political order but have the capability and my be tempted to turn to force to gain political advantage and control of resources
- politicized ISF, characterized by the GoI's growing heavy-handedness and potential use of the ISF to crush political rivals or a coup.

U.S. drawdown plans and risk-mitigation policies should focus primarily on keeping the major actors in the political process and preventing them from wanting to use force rather than on the more likely but less important threats of extremism and terrorism. The U.S. government will need to make a sober assessment of the ways in which the GoI and the ISF could play harmful as well as helpful roles in improving security and stability in Iraq.

Extremists have been weakened politically and militarily but will likely continue to attack U.S. forces and others. Less likely but far more consequential is the risk that one or more of Iraq's main factions may abandon peaceful political pursuit of goals in favor of violence. U.S. withdrawal of combat units could make this more likely insofar as opposition groups see greater opportunity or need to resort to force, especially if the ruling regime and its forces continue to grow in power. However, this problem may not disappear by December 2011, and the United States should be prepared to maintain its honest broker/mediator role without a large military force on the ground.

A more authoritarian GoI, with a more muscular ISF as its partner, puppet, or puppet-master, would likely be resisted by militias tied to the Sunni, the Kurds, and excluded Shi'a political factions. The resumption of armed resistance on the part of the Sunni or stepped-up encroachment by the Kurds could spawn greater concentration and abuse of power by ruling Shi'a parties. The likelihood of the ISF being used to oppress or coerce the Sunni population is mitigated by both the fact that the ISF are mixing ethnic groups (at least Sunni and Shi'a Arabs) in their major formations and the fact that most of the experienced officers are Sunni. This should act as a brake on the ISF coercing the Sunni minority and provoking a violent response. While not likely, a spiral of more-violent opposition and harsher authoritarianism could imperil Iraq's new order and important U.S. interests.

The likelihood and severity of extremist violence is, for the most part, insensitive to the speed of the U.S. drawdown. In contrast, because U.S. forces have helped to moderate the behavior of the main opposition groups and their forces—i.e., al-Sadr and Jaysh al-Mahdi (JAM), the Sunni and the Sons of Iraq (SoI), and the Kurds and the *Peshmerga*—and of the GoI and the ISF, the speed of combat force withdrawal could affect the decisions and actions of these organizations. Moreover, because these actors control significant armed power, the decision to pursue violence by one or more of them would be more consequential for Iraq's security and U.S. interests than would extremist violence. It follows that drawdown planning should be shaped by how the drawdown could affect these actors' choices.

Rapid withdrawal of combat units would likely not increase the danger of JAM violence because al-Sadr is substantially weakened politically and JAM itself is already overmatched by the ISF; under these conditions, reverting to violence would entail major costs. It follows that a rapid withdrawal of combat units from predominantly Shi'a areas would not markedly increase insecurity and instability in these parts of Iraq. Moreover, early withdrawal from the Shi'a south could be welcomed by al-Maliki and al-Da'wa, who could claim yet another success. Finally, with a moderate to high risk of direct attack on U.S. forces in areas where Iranian-supported Special Groups operate, and given the fact that the U.S. "occupation" is one of the rallying points for opposition groups, there could be security and political advantages in the early departure of U.S. combat units.

A slower withdrawal would be indicated for Sunni and mixed-Arab areas. The SoI trust the U.S. military more than they do the GoI and the ISF. A rapid U.S. departure could make them feel, and actually be, vulnerable to government neglect or oppression. Moreover, assuming that the Sunni realize that the ISF are steadily gaining a fighting advantage over Sunni fighters, they will be less inclined to resort to force with the passage of time. U.S. forces could leave western Iraq, which is largely Sunni, fairly rapidly without endangering stability. A more gradual departure of U.S. forces from mixed Sunni-Shi'a areas could provide the time needed to settle the future of the SoI, continue to promote Sunni-Shi'a reconciliation, and leave the ISF better positioned to counter a new insurgency. The most important of these mixed-Arab areas are Baghdad and its belts. A small number of U.S. forces should remain in those areas for some time.

The greatest threat to stability would be an Arab-Kurdish conflict, which could arise from a potentially dangerous combination of unsettled issues. The status of Kirkuk is still contentious. The Kurds regard this important city and oil-rich region to be traditionally part of their territory. Continued Kurdish encroachment into this and other contested areas could lead to conflict that could be started by an incident that, though minor itself, unleashes a chain of uncontrollable events and eventually leads to conflict. Tensions could rise to a dangerous level if the Kurds are marginalized in the GoI and in the ISF. A Sunni-Shi'a Arab alliance that manifests itself in a federal government that excludes Kurdish parties or in a de facto exclusion of Kurds from ISF units outside of the Kurdish region could create conditions for conflict over the contested areas. If the Kurds also conclude that their military position relative to the ISF will deteriorate, eventually leaving Kurdistan vulnerable, they could deduce that the next few years present the best, and last, opportunity to secure the long-term freedom, safety, and prosperity of Iraqi Kurds, including by obtaining Kirkuk and other disputed areas. The departure of U.S. forces from contested areas in the north could leave the Kurds feeling less secure yet less constrained. Accordingly, maintaining significant U.S. forces in this area for some time, while transitioning to an embedded presence, would be prudent.

Although violent extremists, such as al-Qaeda in Iraq (AQI) and Special Groups, have been too weakened to derail Iraq's political process, they can be expected to threaten departing and remaining U.S. military and civilian personnel during the drawdown. Both groups would like to be able to claim that they caused the United States to retreat. The AQI threat is likely to be concentrated in Mosul and southward through Baghdad and to take the form of suicide bombings. The Special Group threat is likely to be concentrated in Baghdad and southward through Basra and to take the form of attacks involving improvised explosive devices, rockets, mortars, or small arms.

This analysis of Iraq's internal security and stability suggests a time-tailored withdrawal: first from the Shi'a south and the Sunni west; then from the mixed center in and around Baghdad, leaving a few forces in key areas; and finally from the contested north and the few places in Baghdad where forces remain. Maintaining a presence through either embedded personnel or a stand-alone entity to act as honest broker and mediator will likely prove more critical in the north than maintaining large numbers of combat forces. Arguably, combat forces play a more critical role in contested areas around Baghdad, and in Mosul (due to the lingering AQI presence); nonetheless, they must be out of Iraqi cities by mid-2009. Maintaining some forces as a deterrent in mixed areas until the new government is established seems wise.

This analysis suggests that forces in the south and west could be extracted as soon as feasible. Forces in and around Baghdad and Iraq's north could be extracted gradually, with the pace governed to some extent by events such as continued Sunni-Shi'a (SoI-GoI) progress. When combat units are removed from the center and the north in particular, a significant training and advisory mission should replace them. Noncombat forces would remain through the Security Agreement timeframe (and perhaps longer if the Iraqis so desire).

Regional Issues

Our analysis focuses on five of Iraq's regional neighbors with respect to how the withdrawal might affect them and vice versa: Iran, Saudi Arabia, Syria, Turkey, and Israel. The first four play the largest roles in their ability to affect the withdrawal positively or negatively. Although Israel is not a major player with respect to the drawdown, its regional actions and the effect of the drawdown on Iran's regional role will affect broader U.S. regional interests.

Jordan and Kuwait also border Iraq, but we did not single them out for analysis because neither of these countries has the level of capability or motivation to intervene in Iraqi affairs that is possessed by the other four states. To the extent that they do possess these capabilities or motivations, we expect such intervention to largely align with U.S. interests. That said, because the drawdown can exacerbate the Iraqi refugee challenge within Jordan, we consider that aspect of the drawdown's effect on Jordan in our discussion of mitigation measures.

Taking our analyses of individual countries into account, we arrive at the following summary conclusions for U.S. withdrawal in general, and not for individual withdrawal alternatives.

The withdrawal's effect on the region need not harm U.S. interests. While the Middle East will continue to face a number of serious challenges in the wake of the U.S. drawdown from Iraq, many of these challenges will either have existed or grown with the presence of U.S. forces in Iraq or have existed independently of a U.S. presence in Iraq. Moreover, the withdrawal's effect on key regional challenges, such as the spread of terrorism, is likely to be marginal. A U.S. drawdown may even improve the prospects for more-extensive regional and international cooperation on counterterrorism efforts. It could also enhance the development of a regional security structure that could, in time, reduce the requirement imposed on the United States to provide security. The withdrawal could also improve the prospect of garnering greater regional support, particularly from wealthy Gulf states, to contribute more resources to promote Iraqi stability and to support international organizations assisting with the Iraqi refugee populations.

Overt military intervention by Iraq's neighbors (except Turkey) is less likely than covert, unconventional, or political efforts to exert influence. To the extent that destabilizing scenarios in Iraq lead Iraq's neighbors to intervene, we find an important distinction between the types of intervention we can expect. While a Turkish intervention, if it occurred, would likely be overt, conventional, and specific to the Kurdish question, the other three critical actors (Iran, Saudi Arabia, and Syria) are more likely to intervene in a manner that is covert, unconventional, and more broadly aimed at cultivating general influence within Iraq.

The nature and future evolution of the GoI and the political reconciliation process in Iraq are more critical than effects produced by the drawdown. The most critical factor in shaping future regional calculations toward Iraq has much less to do with the U.S. drawdown than with how the Iraqi system itself evolves. If the Iraqi state is viewed as developing along sectarian lines with a government in Baghdad dominated by Shi'a, this will likely antagonize the Sunni states that border Iraq. At the same time, if Iraq were to be seen as remaining very much subject to U.S. influence, this would antagonize the Iranians and increase their determination to meddle in Iraq. Consequently, the evolution of a politically inclusive yet independent and nationally oriented Iraq that is stable enough to maintain internal security but not strong enough to threaten its neighbors again will be most conducive to (1) maintaining a balance of influence within the region and (2) reducing the risk of external intervention. Promoting such a balance will be a central consideration for U.S. security assistance to the Iraqi state.

The consequences of a U.S. drawdown from Iraq are understandably viewed by Iraq's neighbors primarily through their own domestic prisms. The Kurdish risk is a problem because of the significant Kurdish population in Turkey; to a lesser degree, Iran and Syria see the Kurds as a potential risk to their own domestic stability. Similarly, concerns over the spread of sectarianism worry Arab neighbors because of minority (or, in some cases, majority) Shi'a populations in their own countries that are perceived as a challenge to ruling regimes and thus are often marginalized and repressed, whether in the eastern provinces of Saudi Arabia or in small Gulf states, such as Bahrain.

Continued U.S.-Iranian hostility will significantly increase the costs and risks associated with drawdown, particularly if the hostility intensifies. Given Iranian interests in Iraq, a successful U.S. drawdown and a stabilizing outcome for Iraq are more likely to benefit from cooperation or coordination with the Iranians as opposed to their active opposition. Iran has at times during the U.S. occupation sought to use levers within Iraq—including lethal force—against the United States. This occurred primarily during periods of high tension between the United States and Iran. It is worth attempting to reduce such tensions through a U.S-Iranian engagement process with the aim of inducing Iran to support a reduction of violence in Iraq and the maintenance of stability. There is no guarantee that Iran would cooperate, although it might do so if it believes it would gain influence by assuming the role of a protector of Shi'a interests. Such an engagement process would have to take place across the full range of U.S.-Iranian issues. It is most unlikely that Iran would cooperate with the United States in Iraq if other elements of the relationship were still at a high level of tension, or if Iran perceived itself to be under imminent threat (e.g., from Israel).

In any event, uncertainties about regional security on the part of U.S. friends and partners, notably Israel and Gulf Cooperation Council countries, call for the continued presence of U.S. military and other assets in or near the region for the purpose of providing security reassurance and (possibly) security guarantees. In addition, the U.S. departure from Iraq may provide an opening to launch new cooperative forums and a new security structure for the Persian Gulf region, although such efforts would be difficult to implement and would require significant investment by the United States and other Western countries.

Major Findings

This report contains many detailed observations on areas related to the three alternatives for the drawdown of U.S. forces from Iraq. Here, we list the major findings we drew from our analysis:

- **Drawdown timelines.** The United States can meet the drawdown timelines for the April 30, 2010, August 31, 2010, and December 31, 2011, drawdown dates. There are logistical risks associated with the April 30, 2010, and August 31, 2010, deadlines that can be mitigated.
- **Arab-Kurdish armed conflict.** The greatest threat to Iraqi stability and security comes from an Arab-Kurdish armed conflict over contested areas.
- **Iran.** Iran has limited but significant potential and incentive to destabilize Iraq, regardless of the timing of U.S. withdrawal. Its actions will be significantly influenced by the overall state of U.S.-Iranian relations.
- **The ISF.** The development, professionalism, and accountability of the ISF are critical to the country's long-term stability.
- **Reconciliation and development.** The success of the U.S. drawdown will require continued efforts, by the United States and others, to promote reconciliation and development within Iraq.

Recommendations

As part of our analysis, we identified measures that would smooth the drawdown of U.S. forces or mitigate some of the potentially detrimental consequences of the drawdown discussed in the report's chapters. We group those consequences into three risk categories: (1) risks to U.S. forces during the drawdown, (2) risks to Iraqi security and stability resulting from the withdrawal of U.S. forces, and (3) risks to regional political and military stability. The body of the report describes ways to mitigate a number of related issues (e.g., refugees, populations at risk). Below, we summarize mitigation measures in the form of recommendations focused on issues that pose the most risk in the three categories just described.

Arab-Kurdish Conflict

The Kurdistan Regional Government's (KRG's) aspirations for greater autonomy and its desire to incorporate more territory into the KRG endanger Iraq's unity and could spark serious internal conflict or provoke a response from one of Iraq's neighbors. The future status of Kirkuk and other disputed territories presents the most serious threat to internal stability in Iraq. These issues are unlikely to be fully resolved by 2011, and this area is therefore likely to remain a dangerous flashpoint after the last U.S. troops depart. Consequently, we recommend

- phasing the withdrawal of combat units so that those nearest the contested areas are the last to leave. The United States must be careful not to create false expectations among Kurdish leaders that U.S. troops might remain after December 31, 2011.

- exploring the possibility of a UN peacekeeping or military observer force moving into the Kirkuk/Arab border areas once all U.S. troops depart.
- coordinating diplomatic strategies for the region with Turkey and, if possible, Iran and Syria.

Iranian Subversion

Iran, operating largely through client organizations or operatives in Iraq, has the capability to cause considerable mischief. Whether it has the wish to do so remains a question. In many ways, its interests in Iraq align with those of the United States, and it is not clear that Iran would wish to delay the U.S. withdrawal in any case. Consequently, we recommend that the United States

- ameliorate this issue by opening a dialogue with Iran, perhaps making bilateral relations contingent on Iranian behavior in Iraq
- increase its surveillance of Iranian-supported groups in Iraq and bolster efforts to disrupt Iranian clients in Iraq by stemming the flow of money to them.

The Sons of Iraq Return to Violence

The SoI were instrumental in reversing the spiral of violence in Sunni areas and at one point numbered about 100,000 fighters. They remain numerous and well equipped. Should the SoI become frustrated with the rate and degree to which they are being incorporated into Iraqi society, they have the potential to cause serious destabilization in Iraqi society. Consequently, we recommend that the United States

- employ diplomatic efforts aimed at ensuring that the GoI meets its commitments vis-à-vis the SoI
- seek ways to train the SoI and provide them new economic opportunities
- work with the GoI to forestall any destabilizing local measures, such as forced disarmament or local discrimination in housing or other benefits.

The Iraqi Security Forces

In many ways, the future of Iraq rests on the skill of its security forces, particularly the Army and the NP. If they are unable or unwilling to preserve the gains made in security and stability, the country could slide back into chaos. While these forces are much improved, they still have serious shortcomings, especially in such enabling capabilities as long-range fires and air support and logistics. Consequently, we recommend that the United States

- keep the U.S. personnel embedded with Iraqi security organizations in the country for as long as possible

- encourage the Iraqi Army to transfer its operations centers to the Iraqi police organizations so that they can assume the internal security duties that are properly their responsibility
- consider recasting its rules on foreign military sales so that the Iraqis do not have to deliver full payment up front, at least as long as oil prices remain low
- consider increasing funding for Iraqi officers to train in the United States as a way of improving the professionalism of Iraqi military leaders
- encourage the Iraqi Army to shift some of its forces from combat units to logistics to begin development of the supply capabilities it sorely needs.

Acknowledgments

A report of this scope cannot be assembled without the assistance of many people and organizations. We gratefully acknowledge the assistance of the individuals and organizations listed below. They gave unstintingly of their time, and their expertise and candor made invaluable contributions to this report. More people helped us than we can name, but we recognize that their support was every bit as useful. Finally, we wish to note that not all the people acknowledged here will agree with the conclusions we reached and the recommendations we make.

Iraqi Citizens

Dr. Mowaffak Al-Rubaie, National Security Advisor
Ambassador Samir Shakir Al-Sumaydi, Iraqi Ambassador to the United States
General Nasier A. Abadi, Joint HQ VCOS
LTG Hussein al-Awadi, Commander, National Police
MoI Deputy Minister Maj. Gen. Ayden Kahled
Quabad Talabani, Kurdish Regional Government Representative

U.S. Embassy Iraq

Ambassador Thomas Krajeski
Mr. Chris Crowley, USAID Director
Mr. Thomas R. Delaney, USAID Deputy Director
Ms. Phyllis Powers, Office of Provincial Affairs Director
Mr. Mike Dodman, Economic Counselor
Mr. Michael Corbin, Political-Military Counselor
Maj Gen (Ret.) William Lynch, JSPA Director
Mr. Alex Mistri, JSPA Deputy Director
Mr. Jim Wallar, Treasury Attaché

U.S. Military Organizations and Contractors

Maj Gen Robert R. Allardice, USAF, CENTCOM J-5
CJ5 RDML David Buss, MNF-I
MG Kenneth S. Dowd, CENTCOM J-4
Maj Gen Ken Glueck, USMC, Chief of Staff, MNF-I
LTG Frank Helmick, Commanding General, MNSTC-I
BG Peter Lennon, CDDOC, Commander, CENTCOM Deployment and Distribution
 Operations Center
GEN Raymond Odierno, Commanding General, MNF-I
CJ9 MG David Perkins, MNF-I
BG Jim Rogers, Commander, 1st TSC
BG Kurt Stein, CJ1/4/8, MNF-I
BG John F. Wharton, ARCENT G4/CG AMC–South West Asia, 3rd Army/Army
 Central Command
COL Robin Akin, MNF-I, CJ1/4/8 Logistics
Mr. Don Anderson, AMC/LOGCAP, AMC–South West Asia
Ms. Jody Baker, Transportation Specialist, SDDC
CPT Keri A. Bell, 311th ESC
LTC Donald Blue, 420th Movement Control Battalion
CW5 Marvin Booker, Joint Munitions Planner
COL Robert Buehler, OIF Strategic Planner
LTC Monica Burnhauser, MNF-I CJ1/4/8
Maj Shawn Campbell, Chief, Joint Services Branch
LTC Steven T. Clauser, 311th ESC
LTC Matt Coon, USMC, J3 Plans, Iraq and Afghan N. distribution
COL Mike Culpepper, C5 Chief of Plans, MNC-I
LTC Joe Davisson, USAF, J3 Fusion Cell, TRANSCOM
LTC Randy Delong, Supply & Sustainment Chief, Class I, III, IX, 1st TSC SPO
LTC Millicent Dill, Joint Deployment Distribution Operations Chief, MNC-I
Mr. Bruce Don, MNF-I CJ1/4/8, Reposture Plans/Ops
COL Edward Dorman, MNC-I C4
LTC Kevin Dunlop, J-5, Political Military Planner, Iraq
CDR Rachel Fant, CCJ4-P
LTC Marty Garner, S3, 1186th TTSB, KNB
Mr. Redding Hobby, Deputy CENTCOM CJ4
COL Mike Hughes, Chief of Staff, AMC–South West Asia
MAJ Irene Isenberg, 311th Expeditionary Support Command
LTC Ross Johnson, Deputy SPO Class VII, 1st TSC SPO
COL Mark Kehrer, Commander's Initiative Group, MNF-I
LTC Janet Kirkton, CJ-5 Staff, MNSTC-I

COL Richard Koucheravy, CJ-5 Chief of Staff, MNF-I
Col Christopher J. Kulas, USAF, TRANSCOM LNO to CENTCOM & SOCOM
Mr. Johnny M. Lanctot, Contract Specialist, TRANSCOM TCAQ-I
COL Judith Lemire, Support Operations Officer, 1st TSC
LTC Gary McClendon, ARCENT G4 Sustainment Ops Division
Col Jim Meersman, CDOC, CENTCOM Deployment and Distribution Operations Center
Col Michael Meese, Director, MNF-I Commander's Initiative Group
LTC Vernon M. Miranda, XO, CENTCOM J4
LTC George Pack, Chief Mobility Branch, 1st TSC SPO
Mr. Lawrence J. Pleis III, Logistics Plans, CENTCOM CJ4-P Kuwait
LTC Colice D. Powell, Distribution Chief, 1st TSC SPO
MSG Christopher Reeves, Navy Logistics Support Group
LTC Joan M. Smith, Logistics Planner, MNF-I CJ1/4/8
Ms. Joyce Taylor, AMC–South West Asia
LTC Charlester White, ARCENT C4, Chief of Operations
CMDR Roger F. Wilbur, Chief of Operations, NAVELSG FWD HQ, Navy Logistics Support Group
COL Stanley H. Wolosz, Commander, 595th Terminal Transfer Group (SDDC)
Ms. Kanika S. Wrice, Honeywell Technology Solutions Inc., Reports Manager ARCENT G-4 Asset Visibility

Other Organizations

U.S. Marine Corps Intelligence Activity, Middle East Branch
The Institute for National Security Studies, Tel Aviv

Reviewers of This Report

Finally, we appreciate the thorough and thoughtful reviews of our four reviewers: RAND colleagues Lynn Davis and John Dumond, Michael O'Hanlon of the Brookings Institution, and Major General William Nash (USA, ret.). In addition, RAND colleague Richard Neu reviewed Appendix C. Their efforts greatly improved the report.

Abbreviations

AAB	advise and assist brigade
AMC	U.S. Army Materiel Command
AQ	al-Qaeda
AQI	al-Qaeda in Iraq
ARCENT	U.S. Army Central Command
ARI	automatic return item
BCT	brigade combat team
CAI	Customs and Agricultural Inspection
CENTCOM	U.S. Central Command
CET	convoy escort team
COIN	counterinsurgency
CONUS	continental United States
CSC	convoy support center
CSH	combat support hospital
DoD	U.S. Department of Defense
DoS	U.S. Department of State
EFP	explosively formed penetrator
ESC	Expeditionary Support Command
FB	flatbed
FOB	forward operating base

FPS	Facilities Protection Service
GCC	Gulf Cooperation Council
GoI	Government of Iraq
HET	heavy equipment transporter
HQ	headquarters
IED	improvised explosive device
IMET	International Military Education and Training
IPS	Iraqi Police Service
IRR	Iraqi Railroad
ISCI	Islamic Supreme Council of Iraq
ISF	Iraqi Security Forces
ISR	intelligence, surveillance, and reconnaissance
ITN	Iraqi Truck Network
JAM	Jaysh al-Mahdi
KCIA	Kuwait City International Airport
K-crossing	Khabari crossing
KNB	Kuwait Naval Base
KRG	Kurdistan Regional Government
mbpd	million barrels per day
MNC-I	Multi-National Corps–Iraq
MND	Multi-National Division
MNF-I	Multi-National Force–Iraq
MoD	Ministry of Defense
MoDM	Ministry of Displacement and Migration
MoI	Ministry of Interior
MRAP	Mine Resistant Ambush Protected vehicle
MTT	mobile training team

NP	National Police
PKK	Partiya Karker Kurdistan [Kurdistan Worker's Party]
PRT	Provincial Reconstruction Team
PUK	Patriotic Union of Kurdistan
QAP	al-Qaeda on the Arabian Peninsula
RPG	rocket-propelled grenade
SDDC	Surface Deployment and Distribution Command
SFA	Strategic Framework Agreement
SOF	special operations forces
SoI	Sons of Iraq
TPE	Theater Provided Equipment
TRANSCOM	U.S. Transportation Command
TSC	Theater Support Command
UN	United Nations
UNHCR	UN High Commissioner for Refugees
USAID	U.S. Agency for International Development
USM-I	U.S. Mission–Iraq

CHAPTER ONE

Introduction[1]

Following its successful invasion of Iraq and removal of Saddam Hussein, the United States found itself unprepared for the security and reconstruction challenges that followed. It was slow to recognize and even slower to respond to violent resistance to the occupation and the new political order. By the time sovereign authority was returned from the Coalition Provisional Authority to the Iraqi Interim Government in mid-2004, Iraq was a country at war with itself on two fronts: a Sunni insurgency stoked by foreign jihadis and an attempt by Shi'a militant Muqtada al-Sadr and his Jaysh al-Mahdi (JAM) to gain political power by force. By 2006, Sunni suicide bombers and Shi'a death squads operated wherever Sunni and Shi'a lived in proximity, especially in Baghdad.

Only when the United States changed strategy in 2007 did Iraq pull out of its descent into civil war. A Sunni backlash by tribal sheikhs and ex-insurgent Sons of Iraq (SoI) against the wanton terror of al-Qaeda in Iraq (AQI) was facilitated by U.S. payments. Thirty thousand additional U.S. troops using proper counterinsurgency (COIN) tactics were able to stop most sectarian killing in Baghdad. Meanwhile, al-Sadr ordered a JAM ceasefire.

Politically, Nuri al-Maliki, an obscure politician from the Shi'a al-Da'wa Party, proved to be a surprisingly effective and tough prime minister. Facing rule by a Shi'a-Kurdish coalition, the Sunni came to see the end of their domination of Iraq as irreversible, involvement in the political process as essential, and participation in government as important. As a result, all major factions—Sunni, mainstream Shi'a parties (i.e., al-Da'wa and the Islamic Supreme Council of Iraq [ISCI]), and the Kurdish bloc—now pursue their respective interests through peaceful politics. Still, these interests clash: The Shi'a are determined to consolidate majority power over the national government, the security forces, and the country's resources (mainly oil revenues); the Sunni want to dilute Shi'a national power and govern in predominantly Sunni provinces; the Kurds want to increase the self-sufficiency and possibly the size of the lands under the control of the Kurdistan Regional Government (KRG).

---

[1] In addition to the authors listed on the cover of this report, the following individuals contributed to the writing of this chapter: Jerry M. Sollinger, Jessica Hart, K. Scott McMahon, and Howard J. Shatz.

The tenuous cooperation of the major ethnosectarian factions, along with the improved capabilities and performance of Iraqi Security Forces (ISF), has left such violent extremists as AQI and the Iran-backed "Special Groups" isolated politically and weakened militarily. The December 2008 agreement between the Iraqi and U.S. governments on the status and withdrawal of U.S. forces within three years has further undercut fringe groups and strengthened the Iraqi government's hand. Although most Iraqis welcome the U.S. military's departure, there is some apprehension in all quarters about the effects of President Barack Obama's decision to withdraw all combat units by August 2010.

Iraq's political uncertainty is complicated by an economic downturn owing mainly to the low price of the country's main source of income, oil. Following several flush years when the price of oil was high, lower oil prices mean that government spending, infrastructure projects, private investment, employment, and resources for ISF enhancement will suffer. Although Iraq is no longer at war with itself, its capacity to succeed in peace is limited.

In sum, Iraq is a fledgling democracy in which politics aligns with sect and ethnicity; a federal state whose constituent elements and communities have different visions of their roles in that state; an economy blessed by but excessively dependent on fossil resources; and a country surrounded by others—i.e., Iran, Turkey, and Sunni Arab countries—with different and not entirely helpful agendas. This is the starting point of this report on the implications and ways to mitigate the risks of U.S. force withdrawal.

The Purpose of This Report

The purpose of this report is to assess the feasibility of several alternative drawdown schedules; assess the risks attendant, to varying degrees, on all these schedules; and recommend ways to reduce such risks. Therefore, the report's recommendations are for the most part relevant regardless of which schedule is ultimately met. We consider three alternatives: one in which combat units are drawn down in 12 months, one in which combat units are drawn down in 16 months, and a third one that retains some combat units over 32 months. In all three alternatives, all U.S. forces are scheduled to withdraw from Iraq by December 31, 2011, in accordance with the Security Agreement between Iraq and the United States.[2] All alternatives assume for the purpose of this discussion a start date of May 1, 2009.

Why Three Alternatives?

The President has announced that the U.S. mission in Iraq will change from combat operations to advising and assisting by the end of August 2010, and the military com-

---

[2]   Agreement Between the United States of America and the Republic of Iraq on the Withdrawal of United States Forces from Iraq and the Organization of Their Activities During Their Temporary Presence in Iraq, signed in Baghdad on November 17, 2008.

mand in Iraq is developing a plan to achieve this goal. This is the 16-month alternative, and, in Chapter Two, we provide our version of how the August 2010 goal might be achieved. In addition, we offer two additional drawdown schedules: one faster than the administration's and another slower. The reason for including these is to assess the feasibility of altering the administration's withdrawal framework in the event that a faster drawdown is desired or if risks to the security of the departing U.S. forces and/or the Iraqi population require a slower-paced drawdown.

The Effects of the Drawdown

This report also considers internal security and stability issues both during and after the drawdown of U.S. forces, identifying direct threats to U.S. forces, other dangers that threaten the security and stability of Iraq, and specific risks that could be mitigated. It also considers the drawdown from a regional perspective, including how such states as Iran, Syria, and Turkey might view and react to the removal of U.S. forces from Iraq. This report analyzes the drawdown alternatives with respect to the demands they place on the logistics system and the capability of that system to meet those demands. This analysis goes beyond the movement of troops and equipment out of the country and also discusses the closure or transfer of U.S. bases in Iraq. Finally, the report analyzes the ways in which various risks that could arise as a result of the U.S. withdrawal process could be mitigated.

Methodology

Many of the topics discussed in this report required nonquantitative research methods. The exceptions are the analysis of drawdown alternatives (Chapter Two) and the discussion of logistical constraints (Chapter Three). The methodologies used to generate the information in these two chapters are outlined in the chapters themselves or, in the case of the assessment of alternatives, in Appendix B. For the other chapters, the study team relied on

- extensive personal experience of the RAND study team working in and studying Iraq
- interviews with key U.S. and Iraqi personnel and analysts and government officials from other countries in the Middle East
- official documents and other English-language and Arabic-language source documents.

At the White House, the team interviewed personnel at the National Security Council. Within the U.S. Department of Defense (DoD), the team interviewed key officials in the Office of the Secretary of Defense, the Joint Staff, U.S. Central Command (CENTCOM), and, in Iraq, the Multi-National Force–Iraq (MNF-I) and other military and civilian defense organizations. The team also consulted with other study groups, such as the CENTCOM Assessment Team.

At the U.S. Department of State (DoS), the team interviewed personnel at the bureau of International Narcotics and Law Enforcement Affairs, the U.S. Agency for International Development (USAID), the office of Near East Affairs, and the U.S. Embassy Baghdad.

The research team also met with several of the intelligence community organizations, such as the Central Intelligence Agency and the Defense Intelligence Agency.

RAND also consulted with prominent Iraqis, including the Iraqi ambassador to the United States and the Iraqi National Security Advisor (and several of their assistants). We also consulted with a representative of the KRG, as well as senior members of the Iraqi armed forces, the National Police (NP), and the Iraqi Police Service (IPS).

The team researching the effect of the drawdown on the region interviewed several regional and local expert analysts and government officials as well as religious clerics based in the Middle East (specifically, in Bahrain, the United Arab Emirates, Israel, Jordan, and Lebanon).

The team also consulted international organizations, such as the UN High Commissioner for Refugees (UNHCR), as well as members of academic institutions and private research organizations (specifically, The Brookings Institution and Mary Washington University).

Chapter Six on mitigating risks draws on prior RAND analysis of the effectiveness of U.S. policies in Iraq, RAND work on postconflict nation-building, analyses of U.S. policies and developments in Iraq conducted for the U.S. Mission in Baghdad from 2004 to 2009, and the personal experiences of the project team in Iraq. The project team responsible for Chapter Six has over 40 months of on-the-ground experience in Iraq and includes a number of members who have served in Iraq in support of the U.S. military, the Coalition Provisional Authority, and the U.S. Embassy Baghdad. Chapter Six draws on a wide range of surveys of Iraqi living conditions and attitudes and also uses surveys and interviews with U.S. military personnel concerning the effectiveness of various nonlethal tactics. The chapter also draws on interviews with Iraqi government officials as well as British, other European, and U.S. officials involved in the Iraq operation.

Throughout the report, we use different terms to refer to the removal of forces from Iraq. Each has a different meaning, and we define them here. *Withdrawal* refers to an outcome—i.e., the complete removal of all U.S. forces, or all combat units, from Iraq. *Drawdown* refers to the process of removing forces from Iraq. Eventually, drawdown may lead to withdrawal. *Redeployment* also refers to the process of removing forces from Iraq, but it has a more technical meaning and refers primarily to the logistics considerations attendant on the process of moving soldiers and equipment at a measured pace in accordance with specified procedures. Redeployment does not necessarily mean deployment to another theater.

About This Report

The ensuing chapters of this report are organized in the following way. Chapter Two describes the three withdrawal alternatives. For each, it describes the plan, what that plan implies, and what mitigating steps might be taken to offset associated risks. Chapter Three discusses the logistical feasibility and implications of each plan and describes some operational-level steps that could be taken to reduce the risk posed by some of the plans or their particular aspects. Chapter Four takes up the issues of security and stability in Iraq. Chapter Five examines the regional issues relevant to the withdrawal, focusing on the nations in the surrounding region that are most likely to affect and be affected by the withdrawal. Chapter Six describes various risks that could affect the drawdown process and what can be done to mitigate them. Chapter Seven presents the major findings and recommendations of the research.

The report has three appendixes. Appendix A provides the legislative language that authorized this study. Appendix B describes the formulas we used in calculating the capacities of the system.

Appendix C describes some of the economic and advisory issues that may affect Iraq's ability to function as a government, the risks these issues pose, and some approaches to mitigating these risks. Although the economic issues addressed in this appendix are generally unaffected by the withdrawal of U.S. forces from Iraq, when discussing the report with various government officials, there was considerable interest in the subject. Concern was expressed about the ability of the Iraqi government to (1) continue supporting the development of a competent military and (2) continue to integrate former Sunni insurgents into the military and other government positions. In addition, because the appendix reports on the economics of oil in Iraq, repayment of the Iraqi debt to other nations, and support for the Iraqi economy and governance, important policy questions relevant to these topics are included in the appendix.

CHAPTER TWO

Drawdown Scheduling[1]

The Obama administration has announced a timeline for the removal of all U.S. forces from Iraq, and GEN Raymond Odierno, the commander of the MNF-I, has outlined his plan to achieve the administration's goal.[2] The administration has announced that by August 2010, the U.S. mission in Iraq will change from combat operations to advising and assisting the ISF. In this chapter, we illustrate how such a plan might be implemented, and we discuss two additional, and bounding, alternatives: drawdown of combat units by April 30, 2010, and drawdown of combat and noncombat units by December 2011. Although drawdown schedules in this report depict specific patterns, it is understood that, in their planning process, commanders will make schedule judgments based on the security situation and conditions that might adversely affect the drawdown.

In this chapter, we set the stage by outlining the administration's goals for withdrawing U.S. forces from Iraq; we then focus on the issues that must be considered in implementing the MNF-I's plan (or any drawdown plan). These include such procedural issues as unit rotation schedules, the phasing of the drawdown, and the geographical sequencing of unit withdrawal.[3] In addition, we describe the evolution of the ISF, and how the outcome of the Security Agreement referendum might affect the U.S. drawdown. In subsequent chapters, we discuss logistics considerations of the drawdown and its effect on the nations in the region and on Iraq's internal stability and security.

---

[1] In addition to the authors listed on the cover of this report, the following individuals contributed to the writing of this chapter: Rebecca Bouchebel, Jessica Hart, Timothy Jackson, David M. Oaks, Lowell Schwartz, Douglas Shontz, Shivan Siran, and Peter Wilson.

[2] Obama, 2009a; Odierno, 2009a.

[3] We omit base closure and transfer here. These topics are discussed more fully in Chapter Three and Appendix B.

Ending the Combat Mission in Iraq

In remarks delivered at Camp Lejeune on February 27, 2009, President Obama announced that the United States' combat mission in Iraq will end by August 31, 2010. He pledged to remove all combat brigades from Iraq by that date and to change the mission from combat to "supporting the Iraqi Government and its Security Forces as they take the absolute lead in securing their country."[4] To accomplish this new mission, the President announced that

> we will retain a transitional force to carry out three distinct functions: training, equipping, and advising Iraqi Security Forces as long as they remain non-sectarian; conducting targeted counter-terrorism missions; and protecting our ongoing civilian and military efforts within Iraq. Initially, this force will likely be made up of 35–50,000 U.S. troops. Through this period of transition, we will carry out further redeployments. And under the Status of Forces Agreement with the Iraqi government, I intend to remove all U.S. troops from Iraq by the end of 2011. We will complete this transition to Iraqi responsibility, and we will bring our troops home with the honor that they have earned.[5]

In his letter to MNF-I personnel, GEN Odierno outlined how he intends to operate within this framework:

> Our Joint Campaign Plan sets out how we are transitioning from a primary focus on population security to one focused on building Iraqi capacity to achieve sustainable stability. Following an initial drawdown over the next six months, *our forces will remain at the robust level through the critical time leading up to and immediately following Iraq's national elections in late-2009/early-2010.* As of 31 August 2010 our combat mission in Iraq will end. U.S. forces will be composed of a transition force that consists of a single headquarters, several Advisory and Assistance Brigades, and appropriate supporting forces. *The mission of our transition force will be to train, equip and advise professional Iraqi Security Forces; to conduct coordinated counter-terrorism missions; and to protect our ongoing civilian and military efforts within Iraq.*[6]

This plan calls for the temporary conversion of combat brigades into advise and assist brigades (AABs, referred to as "re-roled" brigades in the force descriptions below) that would continue to work with the ISF and assume control of the U.S. trainers who are currently embedded with the ISF.

---

[4] Obama, 2009a.

[5] Obama, 2009a.

[6] Odierno, 2009a (emphasis added).

Iraqi Security Forces

Training the ISF is a primary mission of U.S. forces in Iraq. As combat units depart, the remaining forces will continue this mission. Therefore, the rate at which the remaining trainers draw down is, in part, dependent on the ability of the ISF to operate as a competent force on its own. In Chapter Four, we discuss the internal security risks associated with a weakened or incapable ISF, and in Chapter Six, we offer mitigation measures to address these risks. In this chapter, we focus on the U.S. military resources devoted to training the ISF and especially the Iraqi Army to become a competent and professional force.

Two Iraqi organizations are central to Iraq's ability to establish a stable and secure country: the Iraqi military and the NP.[7] Therefore, the projected improvement in the proficiency of these forces in the months leading up to the end of the Security Agreement in December 2011 is central to the drawdown schedule for U.S. forces engaged in training the military and the police. The ISF are nearing their end strength of 650,000, a considerable force by any standard. The ISF draw from all groups in Iraq, to include several Sunni groups, and their quality is mixed.[8]

Continued improvement in the Iraqi Army combat, infrastructure, and special operations battalions at a rate similar to that reported during 2008 should permit the gradual drawdown of U.S. trainers, although the exact drawdown rate is not clear. As of December 2008, approximately two-thirds of the Iraqi Army was at the upper levels of readiness (i.e., Tier 1 or Tier 2), with the remaining units (i.e., those at Tier 3 or Tier 4) needing considerably more training.[9]

The Joint Staff has estimated that the Iraqi Army can adequately maintain internal security provided that 80 percent of its units are at Tier 1 or Tier 2. During 2008, the number of Tier 1 or Tier 2 units increased at the rate of more than one battalion per month.[10] The Iraqi Army could reach the 80-percent level of readiness or better by the end of 2011 if it continues to improve at this rate.

The NP are assessed in a similar manner, but their overall readiness is considerably lower. The police appear to have significantly increased the number of Tier 2 units between January 2007 and October 2008, but the data do not indicate a predictable rate of improvement that can be extrapolated through the end of 2011.

---

[7] The NP are similar to Italy's carabinieri. The IPS operates at the province level.

[8] See Chapter Four for a more detailed discussion of the ISF. Chapter Six discusses the risks associated with the development of the ISF and proposes mitigation measures.

[9] U.S. Department of Defense, 2008. Tier 1 implies that a unit is capable of planning, executing, and sustaining COIN operations. Tier 2 implies that a unit is capable of doing the same, but with coalition support and enablers. Tier 3 implies that a unit is partially capable of conducting COIN operations with coalition units. Tier 4 units are incapable of conducting COIN operations.

[10] Interview with staff from the Joint Staff, Strategic Plans and Policy, Political-Military Planning Division, February 3, 2009.

Two factors affect the pace of improving and maintaining ISF readiness:

- **The number of U.S. trainers.** Achieving the 80-percent goal means maintaining the balance between retaining trainers in sufficient numbers and the imperative to draw down forces as quickly as possible.
- **The presence of U.S. combat units.** Iraqi Army units at Tier 1 or Tier 2 rely to some extent on being partnered with U.S. combat units. The U.S. drawdown will affect both improving and sustaining readiness.

U.S. Military Forces in Iraq

Discussions about the drawdown of U.S. forces from Iraq typically focus on several types of forces. For the purpose of the analysis in this report, we divide U.S. military forces in Iraq into five categories:

- **combat units:** U.S. Army and U.S. Marine Corps ground maneuver forces, specifically Army brigade combat teams (BCTs), Marine regimental combat teams, and Army Apache attack helicopter units. Organic to these units are some combat support and combat service support units. For simplicity, throughout the rest of this report, we refer to these brigade-size units as BCTs or simply combat brigades.
- **re-roled combat units:** combat units whose mission changes. The administration's goal is to change the missions of some number of combat brigades from combat to advising and assisting Iraqi forces as of the end of August 2010. These brigades will be augmented with training personnel from the mobile training teams (MTTs) and redesignated as AABs. They will retain much of their equipment and personnel; principally their mission will change. Along with a single overall headquarters and appropriate supporting forces, these units will comprise what MNF-I refers to as the *transition force*.[11]
- **enablers:** units that support U.S. combat units and also provide key enabling capabilities for the ISF. These capabilities include intelligence, information, electronic warfare, psychological operations, technical reconnaissance, U.S. Air Force elements, special operations, and civil affairs.

---

[11] In response to queries, the DoD issued the following definition of AABs:

"Advisory and Assistance Brigades are Army Brigades specifically task-organized to conduct stability missions, including training and assistance, capacity building, and support to interagency development efforts. AAB's, like all deployed units, will retain the capability for self-defense. They will differ substantially from the combat brigades in the scope and nature of their operations, in how they are manned and trained, and commanders will adjust the numbers and types of equipment and personnel as their mission dictates."

Communication with staff from the Office of the Under Secretary of Defense for Policy, April 28, 2009.

- **trainers of the ISF:** military personnel who are embedded with Iraqi forces in MTTs. There are 300 of these teams associated with Iraqi units from the division level down to the battalion level. Each team has approximately ten personnel, the precise number depending on the type of Iraqi unit with which the team is associated. Other U.S. personnel and units in Iraq also train the ISF through the Multi-National Security Transition Command–Iraq and partnerships that have developed between U.S. combat units and Iraqi Army forces. The administration's goal is to transition most of these functions to the AABs by the end of August 2010.
- **support personnel:** units that carry out support functions for combat units and the enabling and training forces. They include military police, medical, transportation, supply, maintenance, engineering, support aviation, support headquarters, and other units.

In alternative 1 below, the force remaining in Iraq after the drawdown of combat units is referred to as the *residual force*. This force consists of enablers, support personnel, and trainers. Its mission is to advise and assist the ISF and to protect ongoing U.S. civilian and military efforts within Iraq. In alternative 2, the force remaining in Iraq after most combat units have departed is referred to as the *transition force*. It is composed of AABs supplemented by additional training, enabling, and support personnel. Its mission is to advise and assist the ISF, to conduct counterterrorism missions under the ISF's lead, and to protect ongoing U.S. civilian and military efforts within Iraq. In alternative 3, combat units remain through the end of the Security Agreement period in addition to enablers, trainers, and support forces.

Sequencing the Withdrawal of U.S. Combat and Support Forces

In the drawdown alternatives reported in this study, the departure of U.S. forces from Iraq takes into account the varying levels of political integration and security around the country. Given the tension between the Government of Iraq (GoI) and the quasi-independent Kurdish northern portion of the country, U.S. forces depart in our drawdown alternatives at a somewhat slower rate from that part of the country, since the presence of the U.S. military helps reduce the probability of violence between GoI forces and Kurdish groups.[12] Similarly, due to the criticality of Baghdad, each of our alternatives has U.S. forces departing the capital at a slower rate than those in the western and southern portions of the country, where the security situation has improved dramatically in the past year.

---

[12] A discussion of the consequences of a Kurd-Arab confrontation in the contested areas in Iraq is included in Chapter Four.

However, as GEN Odierno has stated, the situation in Iraq can change rapidly, and the MNF-I must remain flexible enough to respond to a changing security situation.[13] All alternatives should take sequencing into account as the combat units draw down, but alternative 3 provides the commanders on the ground the most flexibility. In Chapter Four, we also discuss several "dangers" that could threaten the relative calm that exists in Iraq today as U.S. forces draw down and that in turn could affect the sequencing of combat units redeploying from Iraq.

Implementation and the Rotation Schedule

To the extent possible, the drawdown in each of our alternatives would be accomplished through the non-replacement of redeploying units. This is what is contemplated by the MNF-I as it plans its drawdown. To a large degree, the pattern has been to rotate the entire military force in terms of units about every 12 months. Thus, the number of military personnel to move out with units during a year of drawdown in any of the alternatives below will be less than has been the case in these one-year rotational cycles.

However, the drawdown and the overall U.S. military presence differs from the rotation of units into and out of Iraq. Units take only part of their equipment to the theater, receiving the rest in Iraq from a pool of equipment referred to as Theater Provided Equipment (TPE), which remains in Iraq. This equipment will have to be withdrawn in any drawdown. If a unit redeploying is not to be replaced, then all of its equipment will have to be removed, creating a considerable burden on the logistics system.

Although we did not explicitly account for each rotating unit during the drawdown schedule reported for each alternative, the personnel amounts included in the figures in this chapter show the personnel and BCTs remaining at the start of the month—whether because of the removal of forces or the non-replacement of units.[14]

The Security Agreement Referendum

The Security Agreement allows for a popular referendum to endorse its terms, targeted for July 2009. Were the agreement to be rejected, U.S. forces would be obliged to withdraw within 12 months. This would undercut the deliberate planning envisioned by the MNF-I for the drawdown and eventual complete withdrawal of U.S. forces, and it would obviate all three of the alternative drawdown schedules presented in this chap-

---

[13] Odierno, 2009b.

[14] A more detailed discussion of the implications of the rotation cycle on the drawdown schedule can be found in Chapter Three.

ter. It would drive the command into an intensive withdrawal process that is barely attainable under the best of circumstances and would severely limit the command's ability to provide adequate training to the ISF and to effect base transfer and closure to the standard the United States and Iraq are adhering to today.

That said, interviews with Iraqi and MNF-I officials indicate that the prospect of the Security Agreement referendum being defeated, or taking place at all, is unlikely for three reasons:

- A legislative framework has to be developed for the referendum to take place. The Iraqi parliament has not begun to develop this framework and there is no indication of this being a high priority of any of the major political parties.
- Even if held, there is no indication that the Security Agreement would be rejected. The major parties are either supportive of the agreement or have not made opposition to the agreement a prominent part of their political strategy.
- If held at all, the referendum would at the very least be delayed by several months. In the meantime, the command would be moving forward with its own withdrawal preparations so that the 12-month deadline would be that much less severe.

In Chapter Six, a number of measures are suggested to avoid creating a climate in which popular support for holding the referendum (and then rejecting the Security Agreement) could be increased.

Three Alternatives

In the congressional action described in Appendix A, Congress called for an independent and objective study of 12- and 18-month timelines for the complete withdrawal of all U.S. forces from Iraq. Additionally, the United States and Iraq concluded the Security Agreement that calls for the withdrawal of all U.S. military forces by the end of 2011. Consequently, this study considers three alternatives: one for the drawdown of all combat units from Iraq in 12 months, a second for changing the mission of combat units to advising and assisting after a 16-month period (the administration's goal), and a third, retaining some combat units over a 32-month period. In each alternative, all U.S. military forces depart Iraq by December 31, 2011. We have constructed the alternatives to be responsive to broad military and nonmilitary drawdown goals.

The alternative drawdown schedules presented here are essentially mutually exclusive. That is, once the government directs one of these or another alternative schedule, that schedule will become the basis for personnel and logistics planning. Attempting to substantially alter the selected schedule would likely entail major financial and readiness costs. In addition, abruptly switching from one alternative schedule to another would have detrimental effects on security and diplomacy in Iraq and the region, greatly increasing the probability that some of the risks discussed in Chapters Four, Five, and Six of the monograph will arise. We did not examine these costs and other effects in our study.

In this section, we present the rationale for each alternative, how each is defined, and finally, how they compare.

Rationale

The most distinguishing feature of each alternative is the timeline for the drawdown of combat units from Iraq and the subsequent removal of the remaining force. Alternative 1 calls for the complete removal of combat units from Iraq by April 30, 2010, and the continued drawdown of the residual force through the end of December 2011. In alternative 2, all combat units depart by the end of August 2010. At that time, the mission of the U.S. forces in Iraq changes from combat operations to advising and assisting the ISF. AABs will comprise part of the transition force, which will be subsequently withdrawn by the end of December 2011. In alternative 3, some combat and noncombat units will remain in Iraq through December 2011.

Alternative 1. This alternative offers the administration the option to remove all combat units earlier than in alternative 2 if desired. Although at present there appears to be no reason to expedite the drawdown in this way, conditions may change: For example, U.S. forces may be needed to support conflicts elsewhere in the world, the Iraqi government may call for a faster removal of U.S. forces in response to a changing political climate in Iraq, or the economic situation in the United States may dictate the need to reduce costs by bringing our forces home early.

Alternative 2. This alternative reflects the essentials of the administration's goal for withdrawing from Iraq. By drawing down all combat units in roughly 16 months, our view is that the President is attempting to fulfill his promise to "responsibly remove our combat brigades [from Iraq]."[15] Sixteen months is seen by the administration as sufficient time for an orderly, secure drawdown. In addition, because the transition force is partly comprised of re-roled AABs, this alternative provides a transition force that can both provide support to the ISF and respond to unforeseen contingencies.

Alternative 3. By taking advantage of the entire Security Agreement period to withdraw all combat and noncombat units from Iraq, this alternative provides the most flexibility. If some or all of the events described in Chapter Four, which outlines risks, come to pass, the retention of some combat units to the end of December 2011 would allow the command in Iraq the opportunity to respond militarily. In addition, unforeseen contingencies might arise, such as tensions with Iraq's neighbors or a collapse of the Iraqi government. This alternative also provides a better opportunity for the command to sequence the redeployment of combat units consistent with security requirements throughout Iraq.

---

[15] Obama, 2009a.

Defining the Alternatives

We defined alternatives in terms of a number of their characteristics. In addition to their most distinguishing feature, the drawdown schedule, several other characteristics allow us to both define the alternatives and compare them. These are (1) the type and amount of planning needed, (2) the level of support for the ISF, (3) the security available to the Iraqi population and remaining U.S. military and civilians, (4) the need to demonstrate U.S. resolve in leaving Iraq, and (5) the ability to respond to unforeseen contingencies.

Planning. As is discussed more fully in Chapter Three, planning for the removal of U.S. forces from an active combat theater can take time. The actual drawdown of units requires a minimum of 90 days for planning because considerable coordination must take place to determine the sequencing of departing forces, to ensure that transportation is available, and to make decisions concerning the disposition of unit property. This would be the amount of time needed to add units to current redeployment plans.

ISF Support. As mentioned, one of the primary missions of U.S. forces in Iraq is to train the ISF. This includes formal training by the MTTs, as well as unit partnering, in which a U.S. combat unit mentors a comparable Iraqi unit. As combat and training units draw down, the opportunity to accomplish either diminishes.

Security. The MNF-I has expressed concern about the security of the Iraqi population during the December 2009 national elections and the subsequent seating of the new government.[16] Although exactly when the government will be seated is not known, the command in Iraq speculates that this will occur in March.[17] The objective is to help ensure that voting is safe and the transition of power peaceful. Establishing the conditions for a peaceful election process requires some combat presence in Iraq. Each alternative then is defined in part by its ability to balance the size of the drawdown in the first six months, with the need to provide security for the election through the seating of the new government.

Leaving Iraq. The security needs and the need to deal with unforeseen contingencies are balanced by the requirement that the United States is seen to be serious about removing its forces from Iraq consistent with the Security Agreement. By summer 2009, U.S. forces are committed to leaving bases that are in cities. In addition, it is important that they are also seen to be departing Iraq.

Dealing with Unforeseen Contingencies. In the event that sectarian violence reignites or hostile fringe groups threaten the secutiry of U.S. and Iraqi forces, some combat capability will be required. In addition, some combat capability will be needed to support ISF counterterrorism missions as spelled out by the President in his speech at Camp Lejeune, North Carolina, in February 2009.

A more detailed discussion of the three alternative drawdown schedules follows. We first introduce each alternative in terms of the highlights of its drawdown schedule,

---

[16] Prior to the publication of this report, the GoI postponed the elections to the end of January 2010.

[17] Interview with MNF-I staff, Baghdad, February 2009.

to include figures that depict the number of troops and combat brigades remaining at various intervals. Next, we define each alternative in terms of the characteristics discussed above, to include a discussion of the drawdown plan. Although depicted on the figures and mentioned briefly in the drawdown schedule, a more detailed discussion of the drawdown of the remaining forces is included in Appendix B. Finally, we present the implications of each alternative and offer possible risk-mitigation steps where applicable.

Alternative 1: Combat Units Depart by April 30, 2010

In this alternative, all U.S. combat units will depart within 12 months of the start of the drawdown. Units will depart at roughly even intervals beginning at a sharp pace by August 2009, given a decision to do so by early June. After U.S. combat units have departed, approximately 44,000 U.S. troops will remain in Iraq. This force will consist of units that perform key enabling functions and training for the ISF, as well as the support forces necessary to sustain these units (to include base support) and to support limited ISF counterterrorism operations. This residual force will depart no later than December 31, 2011, a departure date in line with the Security Agreement between the United States and Iraq. Figure 2.1 depicts the drawdown schedule for this alternative.[18] The numbers in the bars are the number of combat brigades remaining at the start of the month depicted, with the exception of December 2011. In that case, we are referring to the end of the month.

Planning

While initiating this plan would normally take 90 days given the estimated planning lead time, some planning has already been done. Consequently, the planning lead time can be reduced by about a month or so, requiring a decision in early June 2009, with additional redeployments building upon existing plans, which would be used to initiate the drawdown.

ISF Support

With this alternative, the ability to partner U.S. combat units with their ISF counterparts for training purposes, which has facilitated the improved level of readiness of the ISF (and particularly the Iraqi Army), will end. The number of trainers remaining in the residual force (in MTTs) remains at 3,500 through the beginning of May 2011.[19] The number decreases linearly from that time to December 2011. The training support provided by the MTTs therefore remains at or close to predrawdown levels for most

---

[18] Data used to generate this figure are included in Tables B.1 and B.4 in Appendix B.

[19] Details can be found in Appendix B.

Figure 2.1
Alternative 1: Combat Units Depart by April 30, 2010

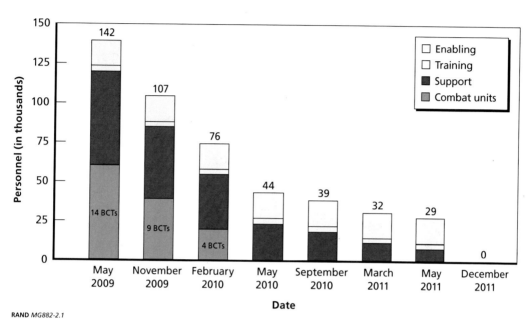

RAND MG882-2.1

of the time the residual force remains in Iraq. This makes up, in part, for the inability to partner with the ISF after May 2010. Nevertheless, there is still a risk that training will be deficient.

The enablers available to support ISF operations also remain at predrawdown levels at 16,500 through the end of April 2011, when a linear drawdown to December 2011 begins. This also provides the Iraqi military with the enabling support it needs till almost the end of the Security Agreement period.[20]

Security

Because of the short timeframe to draw down all combat units from Iraq in alternative 1, the number of combat units available to help secure the Iraqi election process is less than in the other two alternatives. By elections in December 2009, nine combat brigades will be available, a force comparable to the nine combat brigades available in alternative 3 but less than the 12 combat brigades and AABs available in alternative 2. However, by February 2010, there will be approximately four remaining. Alternatives 2 and 3 provide for a substantially larger combat force through February 2010.

The security of remaining U.S. military personnel may be affected, depending on the security situation in Iraq. Compared with 2003, when many U.S. Army support units were not prepared to provide their own security, these units are now better trained

---

[20] Details can be found in Appendix B.

and armed to protect themselves. This may reduce the need for U.S. combat units to be present in Iraq to provide force protection to support forces. However, in the event of a renewal of large-scale violence, the support units will not be prepared for sustained offensive combat operations of the type commonly conducted until mid-2007. Support forces draw down to 24,000 personnel, of which 3,600 are security forces, by the end of April 2010, and then reduce to 9,000 (of which 1,300 are security forces) by the end of April 2011, at which time they draw down linearly to December 2011.[21]

Leaving Iraq

Combat units will depart from August 2009 through the end of April 2010. In Figure 2.1, the force level at the top of the bar is the number of personnel in Iraq as of the first of the month depicted below the bar. The first bar depicts the approximate composition of the 142,000 U.S. military personnel at the start of the drawdown in the four force categories: enabling, training, support, and combat. Subsequent bars show the mix of forces in Iraq at intervals consistent with the other two alternatives until the end of the drawdown.

Once the combat units have departed, the remaining forces will draw down through December 31, 2011, as indicated. By the end of December 2011, the last U.S. military personnel will have departed and all U.S. bases will have been closed or transferred to the GoI. By the end of the first 12 months, approximately 98,000 U.S. military personnel will have departed, leaving roughly 44,000 U.S. military personnel still in Iraq. A rapid drawdown of this nature will signal to the Iraqi population that the United States is serious about removing its forces from Iraq in the spirit of the Security Agreement.

Unforeseen Contingencies

This is perhaps the weakest part of this alternative. After April 2010, the ability of the residual force to engage in combat operations is greatly reduced. The best the security force contingent is able to do with any success is to protect the remaining U.S. military and civilian personnel. Dealing with some of the contingencies discussed in Chapter Four will have to be relegated to the ISF.

Mitigation Measures

In presenting the next two alternatives, we discuss the implications of adopting the alternatives in terms of the need to mitigate the risks we highlighted for alternative 1. In this section, we acknowledge the inherent risks of alternative 1 and offer some mitigation measures. To mitigate some of the potential risks, the U.S. government and/or the command in Iraq could take the following measures:

---

[21] Details can be found in Appendix B.

- Reassign some U.S. personnel from combat units into MTTs and other organizations to train the ISF. This would compensate, in part, for the lack of partnering after May 2010.
- Base U.S. combat units (e.g., two combat brigades) in a nearby nation, such as Kuwait, to provide a quick-reaction capability in the event that a situation emerges in Iraq that the ISF with the remaining U.S. forces cannot handle on their own. Understandably, this would require a negotiated agreement between the United States and Kuwait, but if successful, it would provide a good hedge against the risks generated by the departure of combat units from Iraq. The United States already has several bases in Kuwait that could temporarily house one or more combat brigades. Kuwait seems unlikely, however, to accept the deployment of significant numbers of U.S. troops for any length of time, making this at best a rather temporary expedient.
- Shift some security functions and ISF training inside Iraq to contractors. This could be a problem for both the DoD and the DoS. In the latter's case, a number of DoS-managed Provincial Reconstruction Teams (PRTs) depend on the U.S. military for logistics support and, importantly, protection. If the U.S. military departs from the vicinity of a PRT that should remain open for a longer period, there may be a need to increase the amount of contractor-provided security for that location until the PRT is finally closed.
- Leave behind some U.S. equipment (e.g., Mine Resistant Ambush Protected [MRAP] vehicles) in the combat units for the ISF for training and future operations.

Alternative 2: Mission of U.S. Forces Changes After August 2010

This alternative is RAND's interpretation of the administration's goal, announced by President Obama in February 2009. After the combat units depart in August 2010, the mission of U.S. forces will change from combat to assisting and advising the ISF. The U.S. force presence will drop to 50,000 troops by the end of August. The remaining forces constitute the transition force announced by GEN Odierno, and it will consist of AABs and additional training, enabling, and support personnel. In this alternative, we assume that the 50,000 personnel remaining at the start of September 2010 will draw down to 35,000 by May 2011 and linearly thereafter to the end of December 2011, in line with the Security Agreement. The alternative described in this section is not an official plan proposed by the military command in Iraq; the concept of that plan was briefed to the Joint Staff in May 2009. Instead, much of the following discussion of this alternative is RAND's interpretation of how this plan might actually be implemented. For example, we assume that the drawdown of U.S. forces will resume in February 2010 in order to achieve the August 2010 target of 50,000 troops. However, CENTCOM and the administration might elect to wait longer after the elections before resuming the drawdown of U.S. troops. Figure 2.2 illustrates RAND's interpretation of how the drawdown might be conducted under this alternative.[22]

Planning

This alternative is close to the plan the command intends to implement, and therefore, we assume that planning for the removal of combat units is currently under way, if not already complete. We expect that very little additional planning would be necessary except to deal with unforeseen contingencies.

ISF Support

In this alternative, the ability to partner U.S. AABs with their ISF counterparts for training purposes will continue almost to the end of the Security Agreement period. The number of trainers (again in the MTTs) remaining in the transition force begins to drop in February 2010, with 1,000 remaining in May 2011.[23] Brigades currently slated to replace units in Iraq will be configured as AABs.[24] These replacement brigades continue to arrive in Iraq during 2010 and 2011 as part of the normal unit rotations and will be configured as AABs. In Figure 2.2, the process of introducing AABs is shown

Figure 2.2
Alternative 2: Mission of U.S. Forces Changes After August 2010

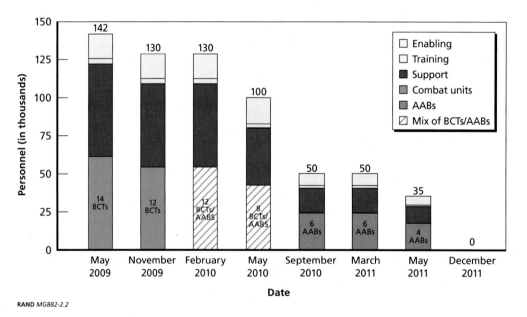

RAND MG882-2.2

---

[22] Data used to generate this figure are included in Tables B.2 and B.5 in Appendix B.

[23] Details can be found in Appendix B.

[24] As of this writing, the first unit being trained as an AAB is undergoing field exercises at Ft. Polk, La. (communication with staff from the Office of the Under Secretary of Defense for Policy, April 28, 2009).

to begin roughly in February 2010. Consequently, they will begin to take over part of the training mission. The number of trainers drops to 2,000 by September 1, 2010, when the transition force will consist of approximately six AABs.

The number of enablers available remains at 16,500 until the beginning of May 2010 and then begins to fall off. By the beginning of September 2010, it drops off to 8,000 and stays at this level until the beginning of May 2011, at which time it decreases linearly until the end of December 2011. Maintaining a force this size is necessary to provide the enabling support not available from the AABs.[25]

Because the AABs retain most of their combat equipment, they will also be able to partner with the Iraqi Army units, as is the case today.

Security

The initial drawdown in alternative 2 is 12,000 personnel. The command in Iraq has stated that this constitutes two combat brigades and associated support forces. This drawdown will leave approximately 12 combat brigades in Iraq in November 2009 to provide security for the December national elections. Further force reductions are then halted until February 2010.

After August 2010, approximately six AABs will be available in the transition force along with 16,000 support forces, 2,100 of which are security forces.[26] This will constitute the security force available to protect the remaining U.S. military and civilian personnel. The fact that the AABs retain most of their combat equipment provides the transition force with considerable combat capability if needed.[27]

Leaving Iraq

From May through October 2009, approximately 12,000 military personnel will depart from Iraq as planned. The 130,000 remaining will stay until February 2010. This means waiting until February 2010 to resume the drawdown and reduce the presence to 50,000 troops by the end of August 2010. To achieve this will require drawing down 80,000 troops and associated equipment in seven months.

Once the combat units depart, the transition force will consist of AABs and other support forces, enablers, and trainers. The military mission will change from conducting combat operations to assisting and advising the ISF. Although not explicitly stated by the MNF-I, it is likely that a large portion of this transition force will remain as long as possible. In this interpretation, by May 2011, the total number of troops will have dropped to roughly 35,000. In Figure 2.2, we depict the AABs and other forces as remaining through May 2011. This provides ample time to draw down the rest of

---

[25] Details can be found in Appendix B.

[26] See Table B.5 in Appendix B.

[27] Details can be found in Appendix B.

the force by December 2011. The pace of that withdrawal will depend on the situation on the ground at that time.

Unforeseen Contingencies

In addition to providing a security force to protect U.S. military and civilian personnel still in Iraq, the AABs can also serve as a contingency force because of their ability to resume combat missions rather easily. Clearly, the transition force in alternative 2 is considerably more capable than the residual force in alternative 1 in terms of its ability to take on combat missions if needed.

Implications of This Alternative

The drawdown/re-roling of U.S. combat units from Iraq by September 2010 will have some effect on the security of the remaining forces (depending on the evolving security situation). However, unlike in alternative 1, the creation of the AABs in alternative 2 retains the ability of the U.S. forces to partner with and train the ISF and to provide additional security if required. In addition, the AABs would provide a significant hedge against the possibility that violence could reemerge and threaten the U.S. personnel who remain in Iraq.

Compared with alternative 1, this alternative provides the United States with a clearer picture of the internal situation in Iraq at the time the combat units depart, so there may not be a need to position U.S. combat units in nearby countries. The other risk-mitigation measures described in alternative 1, such as shifting personnel in combat units to perform ISF training and shifting security functions to contractors, are not necessary in this alternative. The issue of whether and what equipment will transfer to the Iraqis would be determined based on ISF capabilities and needs.

Alternative 3: Maintain Combat and Noncombat Units Through December 2011

In this alternative, combat units organized as BCTs remain in Iraq until the December 2011 departure deadline. This alternative adds flexibility by not requiring a fixed date for the removal of combat units and by not changing the mission of the remaining force before the end of the Security Agreement period in December 2011. In addition, it does not require the re-roling of BCTs at any time in the drawdown process. The longer drawdown schedule in this alternative provides more flexibility in sequencing the departure of combat units. With additional time, it is easier to plan for the removal of units from relatively secure areas first. Figure 2.3 depicts the drawdown schedule for this alternative.[28] The numbers in the bars are the number of combat brigades remaining at the start of the month depicted.

Planning

The rapid, initial drawdown of combat units through the end of October 2009 is exactly the same as in alternative 1. So again, while initiating this plan would normally take 90 days given the estimated planning lead time, some planning has already been done, somewhat reducing the necessary planning lead time. Nevertheless, a decision would still need to be made by early June 2009.

ISF Support

As in alternative 2, the ability to partner U.S. combat units with their ISF counterparts for training purposes will continue almost to the end of the Security Agreement period, but involving reduced numbers of U.S. troops. To compensate, the number of trainers in the force (in MTTs) remains at approximately 3,500 until May 2011.[29] After that date, the trainers draw down through December 2011.

Figure 2.3
Alternative 3: Maintain Combat and Noncombat Units Through December 2011

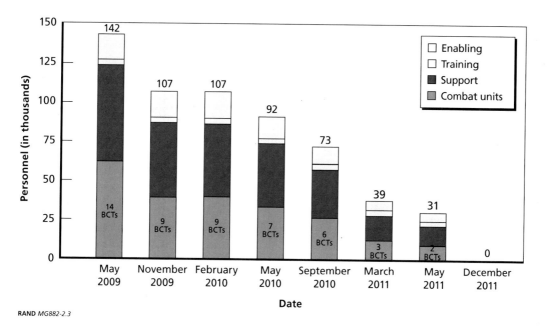

RAND *MG882-2.3*

---

[28] Data used to generate this figure are included in Tables B.3 and B.6 in Appendix B.

[29] Details can be found in Appendix B.

The full complement of 16,500 enablers remains up to February 2010. However, their number drops to 11,000 in September 2010 and 6,000 in March 2011.[30]

Security

The initial drawdown in this alternative, as in alternative 1, is 35,000 personnel, or approximately five BCTs with associated support elements. This is three BCTs and 23,000 troops more than in alternative 2. Thus, this alternative is able to demonstrate to the Iraqi population that the United States is fulfilling its commitment to leave Iraq in a more-dramatic way than in alternative 2. However, it also means that the number of combat brigades available to secure the election process in December and through the seating of the new government will be three less (at nine BCTs) than in alternative 2 (at 12 BCTs).

The security forces accounted for in the support-force category start from a force of 6,400 in May 2009. By the end of October, the force is at 5,800, and it remains at that level through the election process (i.e., elections and seating of the government). Security forces begin drawing down again in February 2010, with 1,900 remaining in March 2011. This is only slightly lower than the security forces in alternative 2. However, the fact that there will still be three combat brigades in Iraq in March 2011 under this alternative ensures a capable remaining force, as is the case in alternative 2 with the remaining AABs.[31]

Leaving Iraq

This alternative consists of three phases. As in the previous two alternatives, alternative 3 takes into account political events in Iraq in the coming year. National elections are currently scheduled for December 2009, and this alternative draws down approximately five BCTs and their associated support personnel and equipment (roughly 35,000 personnel and equipment) before that date to demonstrate to the Iraqis that the United States is willing to reduce its profile in Iraq, thereby making the remaining combat and other forces more acceptable to the Iraqis. The second phase is the pause in the drawdown to secure the election process. Once the drawdown resumes in February 2010, we assume a linear drawdown through the end of 2011, the end of the Security Agreement period. The remaining nine BCTs will depart at an average rate of approximately one BCT every two months.

Unforeseen Contingencies

As does alternative 2, this alternative provides a larger security force to protect U.S. military and civilian personnel still in Iraq than alternative 1. The remaining BCTs are not configured as AABs, however, and their mission does not change. Hence they are

---

[30] Details can be found in Appendix B.

[31] Details can be found in Appendix B.

fully capable of responding to contingencies. The major difference between the transition force AABs in alternative 2 and the remaining BCTs in this alternative is that the BCTs continue to function as combat units throughout the time they remain in Iraq. Whereas the AABs need to change their mission to deal with contingencies, the BCTs do not.

Implications of This Alternative

Unlike alternative 1, in alternative 3, U.S. support forces, trainers, and enablers will be less dependent on the ISF for their security because some U.S. combat units will remain until almost the end of the drawdown. As in alternative 2, the remaining BCTs will be able to continue partnering with ISF units almost to the end of the Security Agreement period. Because U.S. combat units will be available inside Iraq until the Security Agreement deadline for withdrawal, there will be no need to take the various risk-mitigation steps described in alternative 1. However, with this alternative come the costs of supporting a large contingent of U.S. forces in Iraq for longer than alternatives 1 and 2.

Also, the maintenance of a large U.S. force in Iraq through the summer of 2011 may lead some Iraqis to conclude that the United States is planning to continue its occupation of the country indefinitely. This posture could lend credence to disruptive political actors in Iraq who argue the United States has no intention of withdrawing its military forces. Therefore, a risk-mitigation step in this alternative could be to develop an information campaign to explain why U.S. combat units are remaining through the full Security Agreement period.

Conclusion

Alternative 1 provides for a rapid removal of all U.S. combat units from Iraq at the expense of providing a smaller force to support security through the seating of the newly elected Iraqi government. The rapid removal of U.S. combat units will demonstrate to the Iraqi people that the U.S. military is indeed withdrawing from Iraq, and it supports the desire in the United States to end the U.S. military involvement in Iraq. The residual force remaining after April 2010 will provide the training and enabling capability to support the ISF. However, if the security situation deteriorates, it is not clear that the support forces will be able to provide adequate protection.

Alternative 2 offers a slower-paced drawdown of U.S. combat units, and it provides a greater combat capability to support the December 2009 elections through the seating of the new government than alternative 1. Because the transition force that will be left in Iraq after August 2010 consists of combat brigades re-roled as AABs, the command is able to hedge against the reignition of conflict in Iraq. Although the AABs will likely be more dispersed than the combat brigades, they will still retain nearly the full complement of BCT equipment. In addition, the AABs are able to continue training the ISF through the end of the Security Agreement period by partnering with ISF units—something not possible under alternative 1. However, the slow drawdown of combat units under this alternative risks imparting to the Iraqis the impression that the United States is deliberately delaying departure and intends to continue to occupy their country. In addition, the re-roling of combat brigades while allowing the units to retain almost all of their combat equipment may be seen as yet another indication that the United States intends to continue its occupation of Iraq.

Alternative 3 presents a more flexible drawdown schedule, but at the cost of supporting a large contingent of U.S. forces in Iraq for longer than alternatives 1 and 2. Although this option calls for the departure of more combat units before the election than does alternative 2, the size of the combat force remaining through the seating of the new government remains at nine BCTs. The security of the remaining force is better accounted for in that combat units remain in Iraq through December 2011. This also allows for the remaining combat brigades to partner with ISF units as in alternative 2, thus improving the ability to train the ISF. However, if combat units were to remain in Iraq through the entire Security Agreement period, it may also appear, as in alternative 2, that the United States intends to continue to occupy Iraq. In addition, it is contrary to the administration's stated goal of altering the mission of the remaining combat units. However, as the command in Iraq has said repeatedly, the calm the country has experienced in late 2008 and early 2009 is very fragile, and events in Baghdad in the spring of 2009 bear this out. An alternative that allows for retaining combat units in Iraq beyond the August 2010 goal set by the administration provides the flexibility needed to confront this potential instability and to sequence the departure of combat units consistent with the security situation throughout Iraq.

Shortfalls in the Iraqi Armed Forces' Capability Beyond 2011

Officials from the MNF-I responsible for training the ISF maintain that, although Iraqi forces are steadily improving, there are a number of key shortfalls in their operational capabilities that are likely to persist beyond 2011. The three most prominent, currently filled by the U.S. military's enabling forces, are

- a very limited capability to provide logistical support to sustain sizable forces in the field
- no capability to provide precision close air support
- a very limited ability to execute airborne intelligence, surveillance, and reconnaissance (ISR) operations.

Developing logistical support capacity is the most straightforward of these shortfalls to remedy. After 2011, the United States, with the consent of the Iraqi government, could maintain some type of security assistance to Iraq through its embassy, as the U.S. government does with other countries in the region. Ongoing training of the Iraqi military to help it upgrade its logistical support capability could be made a priority of that program and, if it is, steady progress in this area can be expected.

The latter two shortfalls will take longer to remedy. Iraq has begun the process of purchasing F-16 aircraft from the United States. Details have yet to be finalized, though the Iraqi Air Force would like to purchase approximately 100 F-16 aircraft by 2020. That said, the time between delivery of the first F-16 aircraft—2012 at the earliest—and the establishment of the first operational squadron could well stretch to 2020 or beyond. Not only must a cadre of pilots be recruited and trained, but a logistical support infrastructure needs to be established. Both must largely be built from the ground up.[32]

Aerial ISR is more challenging yet, and for the foreseeable future, Iraq will lack this capability, which would be a valuable force multiplier in the event of invasion or serious insurgency.

So, for some time after 2011, if Iraq is threatened with external aggression or a large-scale insurgency, it will have to either do without precision close air support and aerial ISR or request assistance from the United States or elsewhere. To that end, the United States could keep some combat aircraft and some unmanned aerial vehicles in the region that could deploy rapidly into Iraq if requested by the GoI.

---

[32] Multi-National Security Transition Command–Iraq, 2009.

CHAPTER THREE

Logistics Factors and Constraints Affecting the Drawdown[1]

In this chapter, we estimate the amount of time it will take to redeploy U.S. military forces from Iraq onto ships for movement out of the region, and we discuss bounds on how long it will take to completely eliminate a U.S. military presence in Iraq (including bases).[2] While units and other resources could be and have been moved directly from Iraq to Afghanistan, this analysis considers the out-of-region case because it demands additional processing steps to accommodate customs and agricultural cleanliness inspections. We first estimate the drawdown capabilities and then apply these estimates to the three alternatives described in Chapter Two to assess their logistical feasibility. Assessing the logistical feasibility of options entails determining how much has to be moved out of the region by category, the throughput capacity of redeployment processes and routes, and the length of time it takes to complete the base closure and transfer processes. Finally, we identify risk-mitigation actions: resources, policies, and diplomatic agreements that would reduce the risk of logistics bottlenecks developing and, in some cases, increase the speed of the drawdown. We assume a deliberate, controlled drawdown that ensures safety, security, property accountability, and the perception of an orderly redeployment process.

Drawdown consists of two major elements: the movement of combat units and associated support units out of Iraq and the closure or transfer of bases along with the full elimination of a U.S. military presence in Iraq. Alternative 1 demands the drawdown of combat units by the end of April 2010. In alternative 2, combat units are withdrawn, although some are re-roled as AABs. Both alternatives 1 and 2 also involve the associated closure or transfer of smaller bases and include the initial stages of drawing down the largest bases. Some contract support personnel and their equipment will likely be drawn down as the combat units are redeployed, but there is flexibility in the degree to which this needs to occur by the combat unit drawdown target dates

---

[1] In addition to the authors listed on the cover of this report, the following individuals contributed to the writing of this chapter: Rick Eden, Lionel A. Galway, John Halliday, David M. Oaks, and Paul Sorensen.

[2] The estimates presented in this chapter are based on extensive interviews, site visits to key redeployment nodes in Kuwait, and a large number of briefings and other documents provided by the key organizations involved in redeployment.

specified in alternatives 1 and 2. All alternatives require a complete drawdown of the military presence, including both the drawdown of supporting contractors and their equipment and the closure or transfer of all bases, by December 31, 2011 (the end of the Security Agreement period).

In some respects, the alternatives create two overlapping drawdown phases: first, the redeployment of combat units and associated support units and second, the redeployment of the enabling and training units, the movement or transfer of base property, the phase-out of contract support, and base closure or transfer. The requirements for "phase 1" activities are more immediate, need to be started sooner, are often thought to be demanding (because they involve several redeployment-process bottlenecks), are much better understood, and are the focus of redeployment-timing commitments. Among the potential process bottlenecks, we did find that the convoy capacity to move equipment out of Iraq is likely to be the tightest limiting factor given current policies and resources, but there are also a number of ways that this constraint could be alleviated, which will be discussed in the risk-mitigation section of this chapter. The information available to assess "phase 2" activities is much less mature. For these reasons, the bulk of this chapter focuses on the drawdown of military units.

The redeployment of units consists of moving equipment and personnel and preparing them for transit out of the region. We further divide moving unit equipment, including items procured specifically for current operations, into the following two broad categories that place different demands on the redeployment system: (1) military vehicles and (2) all other items, most of which are transported in containers. Another category of equipment, primarily facility-oriented items or non-unit equipment that is not military specific, consists of items that will remain in Iraq or elsewhere in the region.[3] Equipment that will be sold or turned over to Iraq obviously does not have to be moved out of the country, thereby reducing the burden on redeployment resources. Assets to be redistributed in the region also consume fewer redeployment-process resources because they typically do not have to go through the same shipment-preparation processes needed for transport to the United States.

Drawdown Processes

We first frame the drawdown problem by placing it in the context of the normal pattern of force rotations. To a large degree, this pattern has been to rotate the entire military

---

[3] Some items are simply not economical to ship, with their transportation costs (or transportation-plus-refurbishment costs) exceeding the item's residual value after use. In some cases, such costs even exceed the price of a new item. Other restrictions preclude importation of some equipment into the United States. Two examples of such equipment are canvas products, such as tents, that present agricultural risks, and items not produced in accordance with U.S. regulations, such as the commercial sport utility vehicles being used in Iraq.

force in terms of units about every 12 months.[4] Thus, the number of military personnel to move out with units during a year of drawdown in any of the considered alternatives will be less than has been the case in the "normal" one-year rotational cycles.

However, drawing down U.S. military forces and the overall U.S. military presence differs in several respects from the process of rotating units into and out of Iraq. For military units, the amount of equipment to be moved out during drawdown will increase compared with normal rotations because rotating units take only part of their equipment into and out of the theater, receiving the rest in Iraq from a pool of equipment that stays in country. On average, these units bring only about 30 percent of their military vehicles, although this portion includes vehicles (such as tanks and other combat maneuver vehicles) that are the most redeployment-resource intensive. For the alternatives, therefore, the most important difference vis-à-vis normal rotations is the increased outflow of military vehicles, with more closure or transfer of smaller bases also occurring. For the complete drawdown called for by the end of December 2011, the new requirements beyond current force rotations are the reduction of the contract workforce, the removal of equipment and real property from bases that do not belong to units, the removal of equipment used by contractors, and the closure or transfer of bases. Note, however, that the vast bulk of nonmilitary equipment and property is expected to remain in Iraq.

Planning the Redeployment of a Unit

The first part of redeployment planning involves determining which units will redeploy when. Once the decision is made to redeploy a unit, coordination begins among a large number of organizations. They determine what materiel will be shipped to the unit's home station, what equipment will be shipped to centralized equipment repair and refurbishment locations, and what property will be donated to the Iraqis. Then, they determine transportation requirements and schedule trucking, aircraft, shipping, and the use of washracks. Currently, initial coordination starts about 160 days before movement. However, if the equipment- and materiel-disposition processes were streamlined and standardized, this process might be collapsed to less than 90 days, with the focus on transportation and other redeployment-resource (e.g., washrack) planning and scheduling.

Moving U.S. Military Personnel Out of the Region

When a unit redeploys, a portion of the unit helps prepare the unit's equipment for shipment. The remainder of the unit's personnel can depart the theater earlier. As their equipment moves out of a base, personnel are moved to the airfield nearest to their base in Iraq. From there, military aircraft fly them to Ali Al Salem Air Base in Kuwait. Then

---

[4]   For most of Operation Iraqi Freedom, this has been the dominant pattern, but some units rotate more frequently, and there have been periods during which tours were extended.

they move to Camp Buehring, Kuwait, to prepare for movement home. From Buehring, they move to Kuwait City International Airport for flights to the United States by commercial charter aircraft. In total, about 142,000 military personnel in Iraq must be moved and redeployed using this process.

There are also about 100,000 non-Iraqi contractor support personnel—28,000 from the United States and 72,000 third-country nationals brought in by the contractors.[5] However, contractors are responsible for their own movement, and other transportation options are open to them. For example, some U.S. contract personnel can and do use commercial air charter service from Baghdad to Kuwait.

Moving Military Vehicles from the Region

Redeploying military vehicles from Iraq to the United States or other permanent U.S. military bases is, compared with operations to move other equipment, the most resource intensive.[6] We assume that all military vehicles will be redeployed, including MRAPs and other such vehicles procured for current operations that are not on standard unit authorization documents. Using data provided by U.S. Army Central Command (ARCENT), we estimate that there are 45,000 military vehicles in Iraq across the services. Figure 3.1 shows the overall flow of this equipment from bases to shipping. This section explains the process and resources required to effect this flow.

To date, vehicles have been moved from Iraq to Kuwait by military-managed truck convoys, although the majority of the convoy personnel and trucking are contractors and commercial vehicles. Military convoys consist of three main types of assets: military trucks, commercial trucks, and convoy escort vehicles for force protection. Heavy equipment transporters (HETs), which are military and commercial "lowboy" tractor-trailers capable of carrying very heavy loads, are necessary to move heavier tracked vehicles, such as tanks and Bradley Fighting Vehicles, and some larger wheeled vehicles. There are also two categories of HETs: those that can handle the weight of M1A1/M1A2 tanks and those that cannot. Most but not all of the tank-capable HETs in use in theater are military vehicles, and the lower-capacity HETs are commercially provided. Flatbed (FB) trailers transport other vehicles. Most FB trailers in use by ARCENT, whose units are responsible for theater-level convoys, are provided through contractor support. Besides providing transport capacity, military HETs and FB trailers with military communication capabilities are interspersed with commercial trucks to help provide convoy command and control to ensure that the convoy stays together and maintains the correct spacing between vehicles.

Each convoy of 30 trucks is also considered by the military to require convoy escort teams (CETs) consisting of four military vehicles; less-secure areas require CETs

---

[5]   Another 63,000 Iraqis serve in contract support positions.

[6]   Most equipment not needed for other operations will go back to the United States, given the current U.S. basing posture.

Figure 3.1
Equipment Flow from Iraq to Kuwait

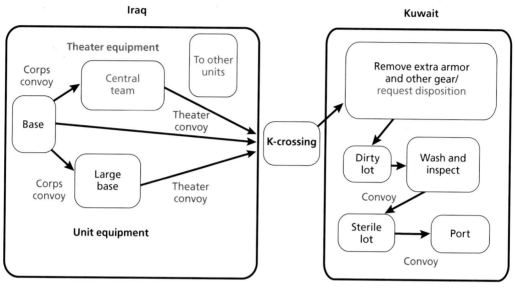

with six or more vehicles. CETs remain with the convoys until they drop off their loads in Kuwait. The CET requirement does not apply if an Iraqi trucking firm provides the convoy, an option discussed later in this chapter. If the unit is located at a sufficiently large base—i.e., one that can accommodate two full convoys on base—convoys provided by the 311th Expeditionary Support Command (ESC) in Kuwait pick up the vehicles and bring them to Kuwait. Otherwise, 3rd ESC trucks in Iraq generally transport the vehicles to a larger base, where they are picked up by theater trucks.

Besides convoy capacity, the throughput potential of movement through Iraq and Kuwait is affected by which roads the convoys are allowed to use, the hours of permissible convoy movement, and the capacity of convoy support centers (CSCs) or "truck stops." CSCs are necessary because all redeployment routes require multiple days of transit. CSCs provide sleeping quarters, food and water, fuel, and maintenance capabilities. The number of convoys they can host is limited by their storage and throughput capacities.

Generally, convoy movement is planned to occur at night, both for security reasons and to leave roads available for local use, which minimizes U.S. military interference in Iraqi and Kuwaiti life. Road conditions affect movement speed and, in some locations, whether two-way HET traffic is feasible. The feasibility of two-way traffic is crucial on some routes because these routes also serve as deployment routes for incoming units during force rotations and as supply-delivery routes (e.g., for food and parts sent to units in Iraq). Permissible road use is driven by security conditions and agreements with the governments of Iraq and Kuwait. Route clearance, which is the removal of mines and improvised explosive devices (IEDs) along roads by engineers using special route-clearance capabilities and equipment, must be conducted before military convoys begin using a new route in Iraq. Afterward, a combination of surveillance and active patrolling ensures continued clearance and safety.

The redeployment route for military vehicles entails crossing the border from Iraq into Kuwait. This involves a checkpoint and a customs inspection. The primary purpose of the inspection is to prevent contraband from entering Kuwait. As shown in Figure 3.1, all redeployment convoys currently transit a route that takes them through the Khabari crossing (the so-called K-crossing), where the customs inspection takes place. The route from the K-crossing to staging areas in Kuwait is relatively narrow and can handle only one-way HET traffic. This requires that convoys be metered onto the road to and from the K-crossing from the north and south, producing a potential chokepoint that must be considered when evaluating convoy capacity.

Currently, redeployment convoys move vehicles to one of two locations in Kuwait for shipment preparation. If U.S. Army organizations have TPE that is no longer needed in Iraq, they transfer these items to U.S. Army Materiel Command (AMC) teams in Iraq; Army BCTs also transfer automatic return items (ARIs) to these teams.[7] To date, however, much of the TPE has stayed in Iraq, transferring from outgoing to incoming units. Convoys deliver the "excess" TPE and ARIs to a temporary storage and staging yard in Camp Arifjan. Convoys deliver the remaining vehicles that are returning home with a redeploying unit to a staging yard at Kuwait Naval Base (KNB). These rules are likely to change once large-scale drawdown begins and most equipment is being sent home. All U.S. Marine Corps unit vehicles being returned to a home station or a Marine Corps depot are sent to KNB. See Figure 3.2 for a map of Kuwait.

The next stage in the process removes reactive armor and slat armor, any remaining communication equipment, and other vehicle "accessories." This work is most intensive in the case of tracked vehicles (such as tanks), most of which are sent to Arifjan as ARIs. After removing the appropriate items from the vehicles, either the unit or AMC moves them to washracks, where the vehicles are thoroughly cleaned in accordance with tight agricultural inspection standards. When cleaning is complete, customs and agricultural inspectors check the vehicles, and any additional necessary

---

[7]   TPE consists of equipment that remains in theater across force rotations. It includes (1) items that units do not have in their standard designs but which have been procured specifically to meet operational needs in Iraq (such as MRAPs) and (2) items that are simply kept in theater for use across multiple force rotations rather than being moved out by one unit and moved in by another. Whether a particular piece of equipment is treated as the latter type of item is driven by equipment shortages across the services or a need to ease the transportation burden. TPE is first checked to see if the equipment is needed elsewhere within the division area or Iraq by a current or incoming unit.

ARIs are items that are always sent to some type of non-unit maintenance refurbishment program after a deployment to be reconditioned if necessary. Other equipment is sent to a non-unit refurbishment program on a conditional basis, or is always refurbished at the local organizational level. ARI equipment is not sent to a unit's home station but rather directly to the refurbishment site.

Figure 3.2
Map of Kuwait

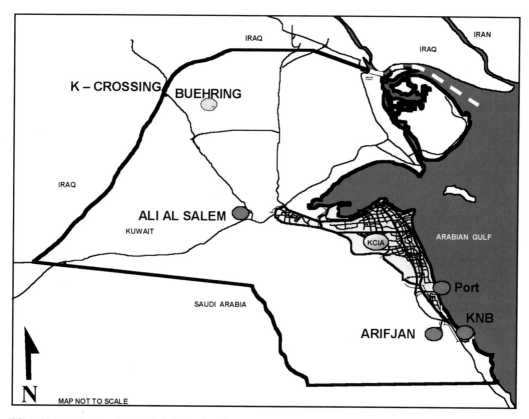

SOURCE: "MNC-Kuwait PDSS Brief," undated.
RAND *MG882-3.2*

cleaning is performed. The customs portion involves looking for contraband, and the agricultural inspection process ensures that the vehicle is completely clean to prevent nonnative plants and animals and other pests from entering the United States. After passing inspection, the vehicles are moved to secure, sterile lots. Unit equipment then moves forward to a staging area at the port in preparation for loading onto a ship. ARIs and TPE must remain in the sterile lots until the instructions about where they should be sent are received; at that time, they too move to the port staging area.

The MNF-I plans to send TPE to Kuwait with unit equipment when a large-scale drawdown commences, and clearly the volume of equipment flowing south per unit will go up because less and less TPE will be needed in Iraq as units leave without being replaced. Thus, ARCENT will likely need to determine a new method for routing units and vehicles to Arifjan rather than KNB to accomodate this increase in volume.

The Surface Deployment and Distribution Command (SDDC) coordinates shipping, including shipping via military large, medium-speed roll-on/roll-off ships and commercial roll-on/roll-off ships, such as auto carriers. An SDDC unit loads or coordinates the loading of a ship at the port.

Military organizations and supporting contractors in Iraq also have an estimated 20,000 nonmilitary vehicles, such as sport utility vehicles. In general, these vehicles do not conform to U.S. specifications, and they are not generally considered economical to bring to the United States. Thus, many may be left in Iraq. Alternatively, sending some to other locations in the region for sale would require fewer resources than transporting them to the United States (due to different customs and cleaning requirements and because there would be no restrictions on the mode or route of transport out of Iraq). Therefore, a movement option could be selected to minimize competition with military-vehicle redeployment processing. Further, with respect to the 12- and 18-month alternatives, which focus on the drawdown of combat units, some or many of these vehicles could be moved later, if movement is deemed necessary.

Base Closure

As units are designated to leave a base and the base becomes unnecessary, an extensive closure or transfer process that has been developed by MNF-I is followed. As the result of process mapping, streamlining, and modeling, the process appears to be well designed and should help ensure a smooth drawdown.

First, the intent to vacate is discussed with the GoI to determine whether it wants to take possession of the base. If not, real estate records are scoured to ensure that the property is returned to the original owner. Property on the base must be inventoried and a determination as to its disposition must be made.

Determining the disposition of base assets proceeds through five options, which are presented in order of preference (from first to last) below:

1. reduce or stop ordering to draw down through consumption (applies to supplies)
2. redistribute within the services, to contractors supporting CENTCOM, or to the DoS U.S. Mission–Iraq (USM-I)
3. transfer to Iraq along with the base
4. transfer to Iraq for use elsewhere
5. discard it.

If the MNF-I determines that materiel is in excess of the needs of the services and the USM-I, the MNF-I is allowed to transfer materiel to Iraq. The MNF-I has established detailed processes and a Web-based tool for establishing whether or not an item is in excess of U.S. need and thus can be transferred to the GoI. For a transfer to Iraq with the base, there is a set dollar threshold for the overall base; for a transfer to Iraq without the base, there is a set dollar threshold per item. For property values above these thresholds, requests for transfer of excess equipment have to be submitted to the Deputy Undersecretary of Defense for Logistics and Materiel Readiness.

Once materiel disposition planning is completed, plans are made and executed to physically move all of the materiel and equipment that is to be redeployed, redistributed, transferred to Iraq for use elsewhere, or discarded. Finally, any necessary environmental cleanup is conducted, with such requirements minimized for those bases being transferred.

Larger bases are akin to small-to-medium–sized cities, housing up to 50,000 military personnel and contractors and with the requisite infrastructure needed to support them and provide the desired quality of life. The infrastructure includes housing, office space, dining facilities, fitness centers, retail outlets, maintenance facilities, industrial operations, and standard utilities. The bases, virtually all buildings on them, and other areas on bases requiring protection are also surrounded by extensive barriers for force protection. Over the years, large numbers of containers have been left on these bases, and their contents have not been fully inventoried. Thus, the total amount of material to be moved from these bases remains uncertain, but the process entails either substantial work to determine materiel status with respect to need and transfer or substantial movement needs.

Methodology

Our approach to determining the time required to draw down forces in Iraq and to determining the feasibility of meeting the alternative deadlines was to review plans and assessments developed by the DoD, interview DoD planners, and perform spreadsheet- and simulation-based analyses.

ARCENT, with its dual role as the Coalition Forces Land Component Command, and its executive agent responsibilities for the region and in general, is responsible for theater-level ground transportation and many of the centralized logistics activities. It is also specially designated as the lead or executive agent for redeployment. The 1st Theater Support Command (TSC) and its subordinate units (the 311th ESC [Kuwait] and the 3rd ESC [Iraq]), the MNF-I, the Multi-National Corps–Iraq (MNC-I), the CENTCOM Director of Logistics, U.S. Transportation Command (TRANSCOM), the Defense Logistics Agency, AMC, and the other DoD logistics organizations involved in drawdown have conducted significant drawdown analysis, planning, and preparation. This work moved into high gear in mid-2007 amid uncertainty and political debate about when a drawdown might occur. The objective was to understand what drawdown options might be feasible and to be prepared for a major reposturing of forces on short notice. In conjunction with planning efforts, several of these organizations created working groups to determine and coordinate cross-organizational issues and keep everyone informed. These efforts produced early estimates of drawdown capabilities and identified a number of processes that could be limiting factors. CENTCOM's report to Congress in September 2007, which was supported by the administration, emphasized staying the course and maintaining a large presence in Iraq, but the working groups stayed in place and held regular and frequent meetings to ensure that long-term preparations would be on track for a drawdown regardless of its start date. Additionally, they began to gradually improve redeployment capabilities, and, as the situation began to improve in Iraq and resulted in reduced demand for some supplies, they began to draw down stocks to ensure that inventories stayed proportionate to demand, thereby preventing excess from building up.

Thus, the throughput capabilities of all of the equipment-movement processes have been assessed by CENTCOM organizations and by TRANSCOM. After we reviewed their analyses and collected data to see where capabilities had changed and assumptions should be changed, we focused our attention both on the processes considered potential bottlenecks and on areas where capabilities seemed to have changed the most. Convoy, washrack, and Customs and Agricultural Inspection (CAI) resources and processes in particular have been considered potential bottlenecks in some past analyses.

Assessment of U.S. Military Personnel Movement Capacity

The throughput capacity of the overall airflow is estimated to be very high in comparison with the potential need. Additionally, Camp Buehring and other camps in Kuwait have large housing capacities. Although achieving a steady flow of personnel redeployment at the maximum rate is unlikely, even half the maximum potential flow rate of personnel is much higher than the need projected in even the most aggressive redeployment scenarios.

The high level of slack capacity in the military's personnel-redeployment system contrasts greatly with equipment-redeployment capabilities and base closure or transfer timelines. This is not to dismiss moving personnel as trivial. Significant planning must go into moving them in a safe, well-coordinated manner. Rather, the point is that by adjusting the level of aircraft used, the throughput capacity can be readily aligned with operational needs. The nodes have the ability to handle high levels of flow, and aircraft are available in sufficient numbers.

Assessment of Convoy Capacity for Military Vehicles and Unit Equipment

Convoy throughput capacity is the most difficult process capacity to estimate because it depends on so many interlinked factors. These include route security and permissible movement windows, route capacity, the availability of CETs, the weather, religious holidays that affect road use, truck availability, CSC capacity, and customs inspections for passage from Iraq into Kuwait.

To make a rough estimate of convoy capacity, we employed a spreadsheet model that determined the number of loads that could be moved per month given the number of trucks available and convoy roundtrip times. To determine the number of loads that will have to be moved, we used (1) the number of military vehicles in Iraq, (2) information about how many vehicles of each type could go on either an HET or an FB trailer, and (3) an estimate of the number of containers needed to move the rest of a unit's equipment. We used a range of roundtrip times and a varying number of containers per unit for sensitivity analysis, basing our assessments on the longest roundtrip times and the highest number of containers used per unit in the sensitivity analysis. Finally, we compared the resulting number of daily convoys with the daily limits permitted by the road from the K-crossing to staging areas in Kuwait. We also developed and employed a simulation model to check the steady-state model. Given the clear options available to add CETs (discussed in the risk-mitigation section of this chapter), we did not specifically consider CETs when determining convoy capacity.

Like ARCENT and the MNF-I, we determined that convoy capacity may be the tightest constraint (based on the number of trucks currently available). Still, although our estimate of convoy surge capacity has a wide band of uncertainty, the lower end should be sufficient to accommodate a nine-month drawdown window for withdrawing all combat units.[8] However, several sources of route- (and thus convoy-) capacity uncertainty present risk and require monitoring. Sandstorms can close roads for several days at a time. Religious holidays affect route operating hours. Permissible road-use hours could change during the Security Agreement period as the U.S. military continues to try to "share the road" and Iraqis desire less U.S. military interference in their lives. Road interdiction could temporarily close routes. Another potential limiting factor is the road in Kuwait that connects facilities with the border crossing: It is only wide enough for one-way HET traffic, requiring convoys to be released in a coordinated fashion from alternate directions. However, we found the number of trucks to be a greater limiting factor than the capacity of this route in Kuwait. Given all of these factors, ARCENT, in conjunction with the MNF-I and the MNC-I, will have to carefully manage route and convoy capacity.

Nevertheless, convoy capacity is also relatively flexible because it does not typically rely on one route and fixed facilities. Rather, it relies on assets that can easily be added in small increments. Additionally, transportation modes and slightly different but similar types of assets can often substitute for each other, a feature that could be exploited to relieve demand on military or military-managed convoys. Further, there are ways to reduce the amount of materiel that has to be moved. Thus, there are three major options for improving the capacity of military convoys relative to the capacity requirement: increasing the capacity of the military convoy system, finding transportation substitutes to reduce the demand on military convoy capacity, and reducing demand altogether. CENTCOM may be able to exercise these options to increase drawdown capabilities or to mitigate the risks associated with problems if capabilities are deemed inadequate. In combination, the options provide some robustness in the face of highly uncertain movement capacity as compared with movement needs. These options are discussed in detail in the final section of this chapter.

---

[8]   This does not include the lead time necessary to plan the redeployment of units. It covers only the physical movement time once such a drawdown begins.

Assessment of Staging and Washrack Capacity

Both Camp Arifjan and KNB have vast staging capacity for vehicles awaiting washracks, and additional land is available. Staging-area capacity is therefore unlikely to become a constraint. Washrack capacity, however, may be more constrained in the short to medium terms because washracks have long-lead construction timing. So, if washrack capacity were tight, it would demand careful attention, since capacity cannot be quickly added. However, there are some ways to mitigate shortages in capacity or at least squeeze out the full potential of available physical assets.

At one time, there were some drainage, pump, and pressure washer issues that were believed to require extensive washrack scheduled maintenance time—up to half of each month under heavy use. However, these issues have been resolved, with generally very high washrack uptime: As of this writing, scheduled maintenance is conducted once per week and completed in 12 hours over the course of a night shift.

One significant issue is that the concrete at Camp Arifjan is almost too thin for heavy tracks, resulting in some breakage. Additionally, the pipes are under the concrete, making pipe repair difficult. A redesign proposal for these washracks to increase pipe accessibility has been developed, and a request for funding is in process. Note that the concrete at KNB is thicker, resulting in higher uptime.

To estimate washrack throughput capacity, we estimated the demand on washracks and the likely amount of time the washracks would be available. The demand estimate is a function of the number of military vehicles (by type) in Iraq and the estimated time required to wash each vehicle type using the conservative end of reported wash times provided by ARCENT. To determine available washrack time, we assumed 24-hour operations, 12 hours of scheduled maintenance per week, and an 80-percent utilization rate during the remaining time. This 80-percent rate reflects downtime and time spent on breaks and meals. We also accounted for days when KNB washracks cannot be used due to ammunition loading and unloading operations at one of the KNB berths.

Given the maintenance findings and reported washrack times, the lower end of the capacity estimate should be more than sufficient for the 12-month alternative. However, different unit types put dramatically different loads on the washracks. In particular, tracks and engineer vehicles require the most wash time. Therefore, it will be important for the U.S. military to meter, to a degree, the flow of heavy BCTs, engineer units, and Stryker BCTs through Kuwait. This flow is likely to be consistent with planning based on operational needs and must be coordinated with the regional drawdown schedule discussed in Chapter Two.

Assessment of Customs and Agricultural Inspection Capacity

Although it is often considered a potential constraint, CAI capacity for military vehicle processing is very flexible. The number of inspectors has been increased since 2007, and a further 70-percent capacity increase is scheduled for mid-2009. Additionally, the requirement for an inspector to escort convoys from the sterile area to the ports has been lifted, with the transportation units now responsible for maintaining positive control. More importantly, there are no prerequisites for training, and the training course is a two-day, 20-hour block of instruction. Either additional military personnel or contractors could be trained. The potential limit or risk is that there are few trainers for the military-unique portion of the course. The rest of the training consists of standard customs and agricultural inspection standards and procedures.

CAIs are also required for containers, but the inspection time is relatively low, and this is not typically considered a constraint. Most containers are inspected before leaving bases in Iraq. In Kuwait, inspectors examine 10 percent of them for quality control, and these inspections occasionally lead to more-intense inspection of problem batches. However, the rate of containers with customs problems—either contraband or paperwork problems—has decreased since the 1st TSC has focused attention on the issue. Because CAI capacity is flexible, we did not calculate the throughput capacity available with current and planned inspectors.

Assessment of Sterile Lot Capacity and Disposition Instructions

After completing a CAI, vehicles are moved to a sterile lot. With coordinated flow, capacity in the lots should be adequate. One factor that is not a problem at present but could become an issue is delay in receiving disposition instructions. For Army TPE and ARIs, AMC must send disposition instructions indicating where to ship the items. Until AMC provides this disposition information, vehicles must remain in the sterile lot. With a relatively low volume of TPE being returned to the continental United States (CONUS), current delays are not problematic. However, with large flows, such delays could cause backups in the sterile lots, which could in turn cause backups in the washracks.

ARCENT and AMC are considering process and information system options for addressing this issue. An alternative or complementary approach would be to eliminate the need for in-country disposition. One such option would be for vehicles to be sent to a standard or the most likely reset location. Another would be to provide disposition, if necessary, en route.

Assessment of Port and Shipping Capacity

SDDC assessments conclude that port throughput and shipping capacity are relatively high and unlikely to become process constraints. Staging area at the port is substantial, and room for expansion is available if Kuwait agrees. Also, if drawdown operations begin to outpace incoming rotations, some portion of the incoming staging area could be used for redeployment. The ability to use commercial shipping provides access to substantial capacity, and commercial ships can use additional berths at the port beyond the two dedicated to the U.S. military. In our review of assessments and site visits, we did not find any reason to question SDDC's conclusions.

Assessment of Base Closure or Transfer Time

In preparation for meeting the requirement for the U.S. military to be out of Iraqi cities, towns, and villages by June 30, 2009 (in accordance with the Security Agreement with Iraq), the MNF-I has identified a number of bases for closure or transfer and has mapped and improved the base closure or transfer process. Through this effort, the MNF-I has established a fairly good estimate of the time required to close smaller operating locations and bases, such as those with a battalion or less, and medium-sized bases, such as those with a brigade: an average of 64 days and 140 days, respectively. Times for a limited sample of recent closures bear out these estimates.

The MNF-I is now conducting the same type of modeling and analysis for large-base closure or transfer, but good estimates of such closure and transfer times are not yet available. However, the time required to close the largest bases is expected to exceed one year. One element of uncertainty is how much non-unit equipment is on the bases and a second is how much of it will have to be moved out.

Recognizing the likely long timelines and looking toward the end date of the Security Agreement, the MNF-I has developed and is continuing to develop plans to reduce the sizes of large bases gradually through closure in phases. Additionally, the MNF-I has canceled all military construction that would not provide substantial benefit before the end of the Security Agreement.

Overall "Baseline" Findings

In terms of moving U.S. military forces out, all units—people and their equipment—could probably be moved out of Iraq and through the ports to shipping in Kuwait in a lower limit of about 12 months, with the combat forces movable in about nine months if flow were continuous without significant disruptions. These estimates use baseline assumptions, the most notable of which are (1) the need to transport military vehicles out of Iraq on trucks instead of driving them to Kuwait and (2) everything going smoothly. Moving even just the combat and associated supporting units out within a 12-month period, however, would require effectively coordinating and intensively managing the process, carefully tracking the planned and actual flow of units through the different redeployment processes, and quickly addressing developing issues. It must also be noted that planners need up to three months' lead time to begin a fast-paced drawdown of units. Thus, getting to the level of residual forces specified in alternatives 1 and 2 would take at least 12 months from the decision to do so (or the start of associated planning). Although unit-movement and transportation plans have not been developed as of this writing for a target combat-force drawdown date of April 30, 2010, the current planning for a limited drawdown in 2009 accounts for some of the planning lead time. Thus, alternative 1 could be achieved if planning for a more aggressive 2009 redeployment schedule were to begin by June 2009.

Alternative 2, which calls for the drawdown of combat units by August 31, 2010, is feasible, but delaying the start of 90 percent of the drawdown until early 2010 as envisioned under this alternative will likely place significant stress on the redeployment system, thereby creating some timeline risk. Any further delay beyond the plan specified in alternative 2 would place achieving the August 2010 deadline for the drawdown of combat units at significant risk. A couple of additional months of delay could be absorbed if units were to drive their wheeled vehicles from Iraq to Kuwait rather than having them be transported out on other trucks, a risk-mitigation measure discussed later in this chapter. It may also be possible to shut down or transfer some large bases by the end of August 2010 if the associated work were to start almost immediately. However, the emphasis vis-à-vis large bases is more likely to be on base "shrinkage" than on complete closure or transfer by August 2010.

For the overall timeline of the complete drawdown called for in alternative 3, the critical path will be the schedule for closing or transferring large bases, unless a large residual force is left in Iraq until almost the end of 2011.[9] The amount of time it will take to close or transfer the largest bases is not yet clear, but is expected to be more than one year. Thus, for a complete drawdown, the minimum lead time for the start of the process is the longest large-base closure time. So, for alternative 3's complete drawdown by the end of 2011, the start date must be backed up accordingly; if the start date is delayed, unit redeployments must begin at the maximum feasible pace by the end of 2010. The initial sharp drawdown would be the same as in alternative 1, so achieving the first portion of the alternative 3 timeline as depicted in this report would require the same June 2009 decision needed for achieving alternative 1.

Mitigating Logistics Risks or Improving Drawdown Capabilities

Capacity for moving units out of Iraq appears to be sufficient for all three alternatives, but the aggressive portions of these drawdown schedules—or of any other compressed drawdown schedule—would require high-capacity utilization, putting a lot of pressure on the system and producing timeline risk. With high-capacity utilization, even small amounts of process variability or disruptions can create delays. So, increasing capacity—i.e., providing some slack—or putting in place options, especially those that are low cost, to quickly resolve problems and temporary bottlenecks would be valuable if plans envision a compressed drawdown window. As this chapter has noted, there are three general means of increasing or protecting redeployment capacity for units:

---

[9]   Disposition of bases must of course be accomplished in the other alternatives as well, but in those cases, the critical path runs through the more rapid drawdown of vehicles and other materiel that is required.

- **Actions that affect capacity.** These are actions that either increase capacity or provide low-cost ways to help ensure that assumed capacity is achieved. Many of these actions either work at the margins to add a little slack capacity or put in place options to help quickly resolve problems or emerging bottlenecks.
- **Actions that reduce demands for movement and on base closure, or actions that shift workload from peak periods to smooth it out.** These actions could dramatically reduce convoy requirements and therefore could have a substantial effect on the maximum unit drawdown rate. Such actions could also reduce base-closure and base-transfer times. For more extended drawdown alternatives and base closure or transfer, these actions could reduce process stress during the final portion of the drawdown period.
- **Actions that shift demand from military convoys and processing facilities to alternative modes and providers.** These actions would be particularly applicable for shipping items transported in containers, thereby freeing up military convoys to move military vehicles.

Affecting Capacity

Convoys. With regard to convoy capacity, ARCENT has already increased the number of commercial trucks, and the contract has surge provisions that allow for additional expansion. Some expansion can occur almost instantaneously, with 100 additional trucks available within three days. Further expansion capability is reported to be quite large if a little more time is available. However, it is not clear how quickly significant numbers of trucks could be added, and the number of such trucks is unclear. A market analysis of the in-country and regional trucking capacity could help answer this question. Through this means or through discussions with the contractor, ARCENT should develop a rough estimate of the maximum increase feasible and the likely lead time required for procuring increasing amounts of capacity.

An increase in the number of commercial trucks could spark a need for more military trucks if the current ratios are maintained to enable the interspersing of military vehicles for convoy command and control. However, other types of military vehicles could be used for this mission, thereby reducing this potential constraint. However, using other types of vehicles would create some inefficiency in the use of routes.

Before transport capacity becomes a bottleneck, CETs are likely to be in short supply. However, available options should remove CET capacity as a constraint. A clear solution is to change a unit's mission to provide CETs. Contingency plans to do so could be developed. We also heard a willingness on the part of the MNF-I to consider using the ISF for convoy security. Further examination of the acceptability of this option should occur, and discussions with the Iraqis should commence if the option is deemed acceptable.

Finally, it is possible that route times and permissions could lead to bottlenecks. Provisional deliberations to expand time windows and routes might begin with Kuwait and should be kept as an option for local Iraqi governments.

An alternative to improving the capacity of routes through Kuwait is increased use of the route through Jordan (e.g., expanding use of this route to include the movement of military vehicles on trucks). CENTCOM is already using the route for containers and has reached agreement to expand flow to include military assets.

Washracks and CAIs. Washracks have been viewed as a potential bottleneck, but our analysis suggests that this should not be the case. Assuming conservative wash times and reasonable utilization, we found that enough capacity exists to wash all of the military vehicles in Iraq in just over six months. Nevertheless, two actions could be taken to protect the capacity that is available. The first is having enough personnel to utilize allocated washrack capacity fully. This requires having two people work on a washrack at any given time, a goal that can be demanding to maintain during 24-hour operations. Typically, the redeploying unit provides the personnel, but contract personnel could also be used to assist. Thus, ARCENT should adopt contingency plans to hire additional contractors to assist units (all such contractors would likely be third-country nationals, who require 60–90 days to complete the security and badge-approval processes). Alternatively, contract personnel could be used to enable military personnel to return home a little more quickly. Second, the project to redesign and repair the Camp Arifjan washracks should be given priority for completion before a drawdown surge.

CAIs have also been cited as a potential bottleneck. Given the flexibility of capacity afforded by the short, 20-hour training requirement for inspectors, CAIs should not in fact become a bottleneck. Although ARCENT is already implementing plans for a substantial increase in capacity, which should provide some slack, effective monitoring and planning should enable capacity to be further adjusted in advance of demand as needed. To respond to any looming shortfalls, ARCENT should develop contingency options, whether for the training of military or contract personnel, that are ready for execution. Improved lighting at the KNB washracks is also necessary for 24-hour inspection operations if CAI becomes a constraint at shorter daily hours.

Agricultural cleanliness standards are rigorous, so inspection can be an iterative process. With variable wash times and multiple, unpredictable iterations, having slack CAI capacity could be valuable during surge operations to prevent delays that tie up washracks, where inspections take place. Another option is to move wheeled and some tracked vehicles off the washracks for inspection, putting them back in the washrack queue when inspection failure occurs. This is not a good option for tanks and Bradley Fighting Vehicles, however, because their engines are removed for washing and inspection.

Reducing Demand on Convoys and on Base Closure or Transfer Time

Demand on movement requirements can be reduced in two ways. The first is to shift demand out of a potential drawdown surge period; the other is to eliminate the need for transportation assets altogether.

Shifting Demand. Shifting demand has already started: As demand has declined, stockpiles of supplies have been carefully reduced to levels that do not exceed need. The next opportunity is to examine units already in Iraq to determine whether they have any equipment, such as some tracked vehicles, that is no longer critical for their changing missions or the changing threat conditions. Any such equipment could be moved out early. This same consideration should be applied to units that continue to rotate into Iraq. Reducing the amount of equipment (especially tracked vehicles) brought into the country will reduce the later drawdown burden by eliminating—not just shifting—some demand.

Another set of ways to shift demand is through phased base closure or transfer, or through reductions that gradually reduce some bases, especially large ones. The MNF-I has already been developing such plans and continues to do so.

Reducing Demand. There are two primary options for reducing demands on transportation assets. The first measure—and the one with the greatest ability to reduce pressure on convoy capacity—is the use of so-called ground assault convoys in which wheeled vehicles "self-redeploy" to Kuwait. In other words, the vehicles would form their own convoys rather than being loaded onto trucks with CETs. However, each military vehicle in such a convoy would require two military personnel, whereas the CET option involves mostly contractor personnel. Because the ground assault convoy alternative puts more military personnel on the road, thereby potentially exposing them to attacks, it is not preferred. Nevertheless, the MNC-I is developing contingency plans in the event that this alternative becomes necessary to meet drawdown timing requirements.

The second potentially significant method of reducing demand on transportation assets involves using economic trade-off analyses to determine the feasibility of leaving items behind or of donating or selling them to the Iraqi government or private sector. In particular, these alternatives should be considered when they prove more economical than transporting an item, a condition often found in the case of large or heavy items of comparatively low value, such as barrier material and containers. The MNF-I should conduct economic trade-off analyses to support blanket rules for the donation or sale of such items.

By law, the military must determine whether an item is in excess of U.S. needs before donating or selling it. However, some items cost more to transport than they are worth. Also, some items are not associated with a standard, formal requirement, so determining excess can be problematic. In some cases, these factors are conflated.

Barrier material, such as concrete t-walls that are 12 feet high or more and are used to surround virtually all U.S. buildings and protect many roads and perimeters, is pervasive in Iraq. Besides being difficult to move, the t-walls would be valuable to Iraq as bases are transferred, whether in their current force protection role or ground up for construction material.

Tens of thousands of shipping containers have been "permanently" left on U.S. bases throughout Iraq to store material and to serve a variety of ad hoc uses, such as office space. It is not clear how many are used to store items or are needed to ship material to the United States. It will likely not be cost-effective to transport those not used for shipping purposes to CONUS. Moreover, many containers are no longer seaworthy. Container prices range between $2,000 and $3,000. Shipping one to CONUS, including transport to and from ports, material handling, security, and ocean shipment, is estimated to cost $6,800. Like the U.S. military, the private sector uses containers for storage, housing, offices, and even storefronts, and they have significant scrap value. Leaving these excess containers behind would therefore benefit Iraq and be economical for the United States. Similarly, the MNF-I has already found it uneconomical to tear down, ship, and reinstall the tens of thousands of containerized housing units that are in Iraq; buying new units would be more economical. There are likely other assets on bases that are similar to these examples.

Such analyses to determine the economic trade-offs associated with moving rather than replacing property would support what is being called "drawdown authority." For certain items or under certain conditions, the MNF-I has requested that the need to establish that items are excess prior to donation be eliminated. For example, the MNF-I has requested such blanket item approval for barrier material. That approval should be expanded to encompass empty containers and any other items that are not economical to ship. The MNF-I's request for condition-based approval involves situations in which the donation of items would help ensure a smooth, stable transition to Iraqi control. The MNF-I believes that the Foreign Assistance Act may provide the statutory authority for drawdown authority. Besides reducing demand for transport, leaving behind such items as barrier material could shorten the base closure or transfer process.

Shifting Demand to Alternative Redeployment Modes—Convoy Substitutes

If convoy capacity becomes tight, shifting demand to alternative transportation modes and routes—particularly with respect to containers—even in small amounts could relieve pressure and allow military vehicles to flow more smoothly. Restrictions on the movement of containers that do not contain sensitive material are much less strict than those that govern military vehicles, a fact that opens up options. In general, containers can be inspected and cleared for shipment at a base, eliminating the need for intensive port washing; they usually just need a rinse, which does not require washrack capabilities. Moreover, they can be shipped without U.S. military security.

The MNF-I and CENTCOM have been developing a number of such alternatives, some of which may be extended to moving military vehicles as well. No single alternative by itself is likely to provide large amounts of capacity, but having the alternatives available can reduce risk if capacity falls short, even temporarily. It is likely that just a little "pressure relief" will be able to relieve shortfalls in capacity. Additionally, taken together, the set of alternatives provides substantial capacity, especially for container movement.

In February 2009, the MNF-I developed a process for using the Iraqi Railroad (IRR) to the port of Umm Qasr from just north of Baghdad, conducting a pilot test with containers. It plans to conduct another test from further north and to continue developing this option. Moving some nonsensitive military vehicles by rail might be an option as well, but the port does not currently have the capability to process vehicles for return to the United States. Therefore, vehicles that arrive at Umm Qasr would have to be moved to washrack facilities in Kuwait. This would, however, reduce convoy turnaround times if the United States could gain approval to use the main highway that runs down the eastern side of Kuwait. Given the other available alternatives, the option to use rail to transport military vehicles should be kept on the table and examined but pushed toward the end of the list in terms of priority.[10]

Within Iraq, the MNF-I and the MNC-I have been encouraging and enabling development of the Iraqi Truck Network (ITN) to "stimulate [the] Iraq trucking industry, improve tribe/province relationships, encourage regional cooperation, and reduce the number of coalition forces escorting convoys."[11] The ITN consists of a consortium of tribes with a single management agency. The ITN is currently operating primarily in the western part of Iraq, but the MNF-I is supporting ITN expansion efforts in the south with the aim of developing an Iraq-wide hub-and-spoke transportation capability. As its capability to move more and more nonsensitive cargo develops, the ITN will preserve increasing amounts of military convoy capacity for vehicles and sensitive cargo. Of note, the ITN also tends to use routes not used by coalition forces, so ITN use could reduce route bottlenecks if they develop.

Commercial carriers have provided limited amounts of what is called door-to-door redeployment service. In these moves, the commercial carrier picks up a customs-certified container or other cargo at an operating base in Iraq and then assumes complete responsibility for its transportation through Iraq and beyond to the final destination. The development of the IRR and the ITN offers additional options for global door-to-door providers to reach into Iraq, potentially increasing the opportunity for such moves, especially if the development of the IRR and the ITN brings down the cost of in-country transportation, which has been quite high. Door-to-door redeployment service is generally limited to containers because with few washracks in Iraq, units cannot thoroughly clean vehicles and achieve CAI clearance on bases in-country.

Currently, commercial convoys are conveying some containers through Jordan for shipment from the port of Aqaba. Jordan has agreed in principle to permit the

---

[10] The rail is light gauge, so it may experience maintenance disruptions under heavy use.

[11] "3rd Expeditionary Support Command Concept of Support," undated.

United States to use this route to withdraw military vehicles as well. These operations would be mostly commercial, involving U.S. customs and agricultural inspectors and oversight personnel and, possibly, military escort personnel if sensitive cargo is sent via the route. Processing these vehicles for shipment to the United States will require improvements to washing and inspection capabilities. Plans for putting in place the necessary capabilities and implementation details are being worked out. For example, Iraqi drivers are prohibited from crossing the border at present, and lifting this constraint is under discussion. This option would increase redeployment-process resources, such as washracks, in addition to relieving demand on military convoys. Even if it does not prove logistically necessary, this option is valuable because it helps build the U.S. relationship with Jordan.

Even if convoy capacity is estimated to be sufficient, to provide a margin of safety and allow for lead times for the development of options, the United States should continue to explore use of these different modes and routes. As these options are employed and developed, capacity should continue to expand, and problems, if detected, will be resolved. With the exception of door-to-door service, each alternative could, as it proves reliable and becomes more developed, potentially be used to transport military vehicles. Whether this will ultimately include combat vehicles, such as tanks, depends on the pending interpretation of the Arms Export Control Act, which will determine whether such items can be shipped outside of positive U.S. control.

Conclusion

Although drawdown presents a large, demanding logistics problem requiring significant resources, logistics capabilities are unlikely to be a constraint on operational and strategic drawdown planning with respect to the flow of forces out of Iraq *provided that a decision to draw down combat units is made at least a year before a deadline*. Capacity is such that most of the operationally and strategically desirable courses of action should be supportable. A wide variety of options to either (1) increase capacity or (2) ensure that process throughput capabilities meet expectations exist to hedge against logistics execution risk. In contrast to force flow, large-base closure and transfer requirements could impose a long-lead requirement on overall drawdown planning. But closing or transferring the larger bases should—given early enough start dates—be possible within the timeframe called for in the Security Agreement and within any timeframes that the administration and the military have publicly discussed.

CHAPTER FOUR

Internal Security and Stability[1]

By every measure, Iraq has become more secure and stable since its paroxysm of violence in 2006–2007. Yet, simply extrapolating this progress into the future could prove erroneous and cause serious mistakes. Iraq is both complex and fluid: The interaction of political forces, the flaring of threats old and new, and the removal of the strongest security force in the country will likely change—and could weaken—Iraq's internal security and stability. While the withdrawal of U.S. forces need not undermine Iraq's security (depending on timing and details), it could expose U.S interests to risks that need to be mitigated.

When violence in Iraq was at its worst, extremists were able to provoke fighting between major Sunni and Shi'a armed factions vying for political control and resources. Consequently, Iraq's nascent post–Saddam Hussein political order was engulfed by violence. Indeed, violence—whether by Sunni insurgents or Muqtada al-Sadr's JAM—was seen as a way to gain political advantage. In turn, extremists—AQI and Shi'a Special Groups (many of them splinters of JAM), for example—exploited the mayhem to continue wanton violence. Figure 4.1 illustrates the sectarian and ethnic divisions in Iraq.

This deadly cycle ended or at least slowed dramatically in 2007–2008 as Sunni tribes turned against AQI, the U.S. troop surge helped curb sectarian killing, and the ISF, supported by coalition forces, suppressed the Special Groups. The main political factions have largely eschewed violence in favor of political involvement to advance their agendas, even cooperating to confront their common concerns, including extremism. Extremists have an undiminished appetite for violence against the Iraqi state, mainstream parties, ordinary Iraqis, and U.S. personnel. But they lack the physical means, popular support, and (for the moment) foreign backing to reignite large-scale factional violence by themselves.

In contrast to the extremists, the major factions possess ample capabilities to again plunge Iraq into civil war and even threaten the survival of the new Iraqi state.

---

[1] In addition to the authors listed on the cover of this report, the following individuals contributed to the writing of this chapter: Omar Al-Shahery, Martha Dunigan, Keith Gierlack, Todd C. Helmus, Renny McPherson, and Olga Oliker.

Figure 4.1
Sectarian and Ethnic Divisions in Iraq

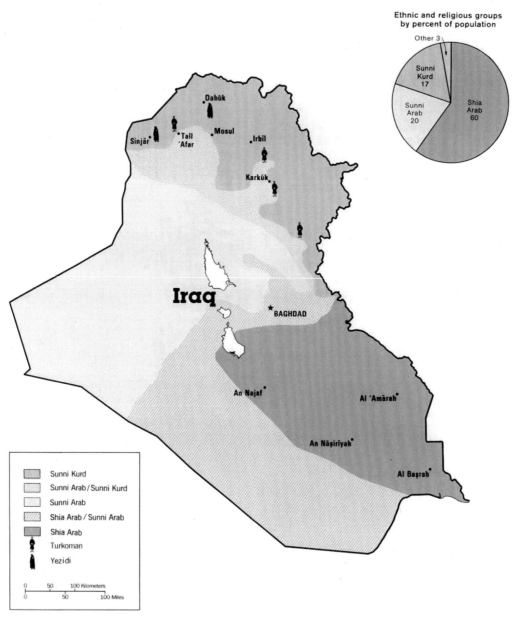

SOURCE: CIA map, provided by the University of Texas Libraries.
RAND *MG882-4.1*

According to some estimates, there are as many as 100,000 SoI,[2] 25,000–40,000 JAM fighters, and 75,000 Kurdish militia members (called the *Peshmerga*).[3] To them, violence is not existential: It is a matter of choice. All main factions now participate, to varying degrees, in Iraqi politics and government. The ISF draw from all groups, also to varying degrees. A political order exists and, though undoubtedly shaky, is increasingly resistant to being torn apart by rejectionists and extremists beyond its fringe. This was evident in the recent provincial elections, in which Sunni participated fully and fruitfully: Al-Maliki's get-tough policies were rewarded by votes, and parties with sectarian platforms were routed by more-moderate and secular ones.[4]

It is now up to leaders of the main Sunni, Shi'a, and Kurdish factions to decide whether to address their differences and compete peacefully or violently. Given Iraq's history of political violence, much of it at the hands of the state, a central factor in their decisions will be the strength, character, and reliability of the ISF—especially the military and the NP.[5] The ISF will soon be the strongest force in the country, not U.S. forces. How this shift from U.S.-led to Iraqi-led security will affect Iraq's future depends on the pace and particulars of the U.S. drawdown, the rate and nature of improvement in ISF capabilities, and the way key political leaders see their options.

As important, and closely related, is whether the Shi'a-led GoI wields its growing political and armed power responsibly, impartially, and constitutionally. Either a pattern of GoI abuse of power or a power vacuum caused by the drawdown of U.S. forces before the ISF can adequately replace them could impel or tempt main opposition groups to choose force over peaceful politics. Thus, two pivotal issues that the United States faces as its forces leave are the strategic choices of the main factions and how the GoI governs and uses the ISF.

With these issues in mind, this chapter presents observations that are important to consider when assessing the U.S. drawdown and analyzes the dangers that could arise during or after the withdrawal of U.S. forces (whether or not those dangers are caused by withdrawal itself). It examines dangers both to Iraq's security and to departing and remaining U.S. personnel; indicates how the pace and particulars of the drawdown could affect or be affected by those dangers; assesses the ability of the ISF to meet

---

[2]   We use the term *SoI* to designate the former Sunni resistance. We understand that the resistance was not homogeneous and was in fact composed of various groups with different goals and agendas. However, for purposes of this analysis, it is sufficient to consider the actions of the Sunni polity and its militant arms as one whole.

[3]   Most *Peshmerga* are now the "internal security forces" of the KRG, which are permitted under Article 121 of Iraq's constitution.

[4]   The one significant exception to this is al-Da'wa, a Shi'a Islamist party.

[5]   One of the principal issues facing Iraqi political and security force leaders in the coming months will be the implementation of the provincial powers law, which places the IPS under the control of the governors rather than the central government. According to interviews with senior Ministry of Interior (MoI) leaders in February 2009, this shift of responsibility from the center to the provinces has not been thought out in detail and is controversial.

Iraq's security challenges; suggests a U.S. approach to ISF enhancement; and identifies risks that should be addressed by U.S. policies, actions, and resources. Options to mitigate risks are addressed in Chapter Six.

The Role of the MNF-I in Promoting Internal Security

From the chapter authors' collective extensive experience in Iraq, from studying the country for several years, and, in particular, from our interviews with senior leaders in the MNF-I and at the U.S. Embassy Baghdad in February 2009, we have developed some insights that form a context for the discussion of the prospects for security and stability in Iraq with the departure of U.S. forces.

First, many of the most challenging problems that the United States faces in Iraq have existed for decades or more. Arab-Kurdish animosity, Sunni-Shi'a animosity, an almost total lack of a trained and capable civil service at the federal and provincial levels, a dysfunctional economy dependent on a badly decaying oil infrastructure, and endemic corruption are among the most critical challenges.

Second, the principal tasks of the MNF-I today are not large-scale combat operations. They are small-scale operations ongoing in various parts of Iraq. Where it is involved in combat, the MNF-I is typically supporting ISF operations rather than leading them. By its very presence, it deters violence on the part of many political actors. Its most critical tasks today are arguably to act as an "honest broker" between competing factions and to serve as a facilitator to help Iraq's government (and, in particular, its security ministries and forces) function. The large-scale dangers highlighted in the next section are kept in check as much or more by the fact that the MNF-I acts in these roles as by its force of arms (although these roles and force are not mutually exclusive).

Dangers

In this section, we categorize the dangers to Iraq's stability and security and discuss each in turn. The dangers comprise groups and their capabilities, the strategic calculations of their leaders, and the events that could precipitate conflict. It is helpful to distinguish three sorts of dangers to Iraq's internal security and stability during and after U.S. force drawdown:

- **extremists,** who reject the emerging political order and would use violence to drive Iraq back into chaos

- **mainstream armed opposition groups,** who now participate in the political order but have the capability and may be tempted to turn to force to gain political advantage and control of resources
- **politicized ISF,** characterized by the GoI's growing heavy-handedness and posible use of the ISF to crush political rivals or a coup.

The first sort of danger is in one important way independent of the departure of U.S. forces: Extremist groups will continue to use violence but are unlikely to pose an existential threat to Iraq unless they can achieve a stroke of catastrophic proportions (e.g., the assassination of a key political or religious leader). Drawdown decisions may present opportunities for extremists to achieve some *tactical* successes, but such decisions probably will not present opportunities for *strategic* successes. The second and third sorts of danger could be affected by when and how U.S. forces depart and by how the United States seeks to preserve and use its influence as the drawdown occurs. These threats are less likely to materialize than the one posed by extremists, but their consequences would be more dire. Further, if current trends among main groups to solve problems through the political process continue, the risk of large-scale violence will be greatly reduced. Broadly speaking, extremists pose greater direct threats to U.S. personnel, while violence between main opposition groups and the GoI poses greater threats to other U.S. interests.

With the prospect and implementation of the drawdown of U.S. forces, the calculations of the principal actors will be heavily influenced by perceptions of a shifting correlation of armed power. Even if none of the actors is looking to start civil war, the behavior of each, their perceptions of each other's motivations, and relationships among them will be shaped by the knowledge of what would happen if a civil war started. In thinking about these leaders, it is useful to understand that few of the major players hold the success of Iraq as their principal motivation. Rather, they are more concerned with their group's and their own personal success.[6]

A key aspect of the calculations of these leaders is the fact that as U.S. forces withdraw and ISF capabilities grow, the ISF will gain advantages over all the other armed forces in Iraq: Shi'a militias, Sunni ex-insurgents, and KRG internal security forces (i.e., the *Peshmerga*). To the extent that U.S. forces have helped contain or deter threats from these forces, the U.S. drawdown could increase their opportunities to use force to achieve their goals, but only insofar as they cannot be contained by the ISF. To the extent that U.S. forces were viewed as providing security, U.S. drawdown could cause a sense of insecurity and create imprudence, especially as the ISF are being steadily improved.

In addition to and possibly aggravating these dangers, the decline in the price of oil and resultant weakening of Iraq's economy could reduce government and pri-

---

[6] See, among many sources, T. Kelly, 2008.

vate investment, increase unemployment, and constrict funding for security, including enhancement of the ISF. This could increase the risk from the first two danger types, in particular.

We turn now to an examination of each of the categories of danger outlined above.

Extremists

If and as Iraq's main groups continue trying to settle their differences politically and manage the country cooperatively, those who reject these groups and this process will remain bent on, or even defined by, violence. Sunni religious extremists (salafi-jihadis), notably AQI, and former Ba'athists could view rapprochement between the Sunni secular mainstream and the Shi'a-led GoI as a reason to escalate terrorism. The final throes of sectarian conflict in Iraq could well be desperate AQI attacks on innocent Shi'a to thwart sectarian accommodation. Although AQI might spare other Sunni in order not to provoke a tribal backlash, it could target U.S. forces and other personnel, GoI officials and symbols, Shi'a leaders, crowded markets, and religious gatherings. Attacks would likely involve car bombs, vest bombs, and IEDs.

Eradicating AQI may exceed ISF capabilities, even with U.S. help, but the AQI threat is more likely to grow weaker rather than stronger. AQI is hampered by a lack of popular support, by restricted movement, and by a dearth of financing. It is now largely confined to Mosul, the Tigris River Valley, and Diyala province. One of its principal causes, and a source of recruiting and fund-raising—the U.S. occupation—is ending. The stream of foreign jihadis, so crucial at the birth of AQI, has become a trickle. Consequently, AQI now relies mainly on Iraqis, increasingly females, to conduct suicide bombings. Unless its "parent," al-Qaeda (AQ), were again to declare Iraq a main theater of global jihad—a prospect that seems unlikely, given two years of failure in Iraq and relative success elsewhere—AQI will have limited means to cause destruction or political upheaval in Iraq. In sum, although violence by AQI will continue, the organization has little ability to increase the level of violence and may lose its appeal with the departure of U.S. forces.

U.S. interest in defeating extremists in Iraq lies not only in the harm these extremists can do there but also in the threats of terror they could pose beyond Iraq into the broader Middle Eastern region, Europe, or the U.S. homeland. With or without U.S. military drawdown, AQI terrorism will likely be confined to Iraq. For Iraq to become a platform for wider jihad would require both increased success of AQI in Iraq (e.g., control of territory) and a reversal of AQ's decision to stress jihad in Afghanistan, Pakistan, and Yemen rather than in Iraq. Neither event seems probable. Improved ISF counterterror forces, complemented by residual U.S. special operations forces (SOF) and ISR in the coming few years, should keep AQI from becoming a base of operations outside of Iraq, even if such measures cannot prevent AQI terrorism in Iraq altogether.

The danger of rejectionist violence is not limited to Sunni jihadis. At least two Shi'a fringe elements could be tempted to resort to force: JAM and the Iranian-sponsored Special Groups. At present, the Sadrist movement appears to be more inclined to pursue politics rather than to use force; therefore, we treat JAM and its political leader, Muqtada al-Sadr, as mainstream political actors while recognizing that they sit somewhat on the fence. How much the Special Groups threaten Iraq's security depends on their capabilities relative to the ISF, Baghdad and Tehran's calculations and political will, and the relationship between the Iraqi and Iranian governments. At present, the GoI appears determined to defeat the Special Groups, and Iran appears unwilling to harm the GoI.[7] Further, since the Special Groups rely on Iran, their actions and capabilities are subject to the diplomatic actions of the GoI, the United States, and other countries and actors.

In our judgment, Sunni and Shi'a extremists outside Iraq's political order will remain violent and will pose some threat to departing and remaining U.S. personnel.[8] Terrorism in Iraq will persist, but it is unlikely to grow, destroy the new political order, induce any main factions to turn to violence, or spill beyond Iraq's border.

Mainstream Armed Opposition Groups

The second danger to Iraq's internal security and stability, and to U.S. interests, would be the decision of one or more mainstream groups to no longer pursue their interests peacefully via the political process. Although this event is less likely than extremist threats, the danger is graver. Any major faction might choose violence out of frustration with electoral results, in response to GoI abuse of power, in order to strengthen its political hand, in response to some unexpected event, or in light of the opportunity presented by the departure of U.S. forces. For example,

- The Sunni could renew armed opposition if the SoI become disaffected with the GoI.
- JAM could try to seize control of population centers if al-Sadr determines this is the best way to expand his political power.
- Kurds could use force to try to secure both what they see as their traditional territory and a self-sufficient Kurdistan, or if they feel isolated and threatened.

---

[7] The most recent examples of this are Tehran's role in ending the fighting in Basra in April 2008 and the decline in the amount of Iranian weaponry found in Iraq since that time (interviews with MNF-I personnel, February 2009).

[8] The threat to U.S. personnel is examined more closely later in this chapter. Some hold that a U.S. withdrawal will make matters worse, since U.S. forces act as a deterrent. Others argue that U.S. forces exacerbate the political situation and provide extremists with targets, and that security will improve when they leave. There is truth in both arguments, but how they balance out is difficult to tell.

The Revival of Armed Sunni Opposition. Sunni violence has greatly diminished since its height as former insurgents have sided with the United States against AQI, as U.S. forces have helped establish SoI units, and as the Sunni political leadership has commenced a transformation that is bringing former resistance leaders into the political process. Furthermore, the ISF are gaining strength, and the Sunni view the national government as less sectarian and more national than before. These trends, if they continue, make the likelihood of large-scale Sunni violence increasingly small—a positive development.

The most likely catalyst of renewed large-scale Sunni armed resistance would be the failure of the GoI (or the Iraqi economy) to provide jobs for the SoI, leaving these ex-insurgents without livelihood and with scores to settle.[9,10] The SoI have sufficient levels of organization and arms to challenge the ISF for control of predominantly Sunni provinces (e.g., al-Anbar) today, but not to gain control of mixed areas that could be contested (e.g., western Baghdad). As time passes and ISF capabilities increase, force will become a less promising and more risky option for the SoI. SoI violence would likely not undermine the loyalty or cohesion of the Iraqi Army or NP, though it could hurt the IPS. This trend will not preclude sporadic violence, nor does it mean that the SoI will bow to the GoI and the ISF if they feel that they and the Sunni in general are being mistreated. Ironically, these former insurgents may not be eager to see U.S. forces depart, because these forces provide the Sunni with protection and have influence with the GoI and the ISF. However, drawdown is less likely to increase the risk of armed Sunni opposition if the SoI are treated fairly by the GoI.

As U.S. forces depart and ISF capabilities improve, the Sunni might perceive a fleeting opportunity to use violence to achieve their goals or defend themselves against the Shi'a-dominated GoI and ISF while they still can. However, since AQI and similar groups are now on the fringe, politics and economics, not religion, are most likely to motivate most Sunni. This increases the possibility of political compromise and negotiated settlements.

A second potential source of Sunni violence is persons formerly affiliated with the Ba'ath Party, who have the potential to affect Sunni politics and Iraq's stability. Although ex-Ba'athists mainly operate from exile, many Sunni still consider them genuine community leaders. The ex-Ba'athists fall into two categories. The first comprises top-level Ba'ath Party hardliners who regard exiled Saddam Hussein lieutenant Izzat

---

[9]   The term *SoI* is a name for a collection of tribal, insurgent, criminal, and other organizations that sided with U.S. forces against AQI. It is not a single entity and so does not respond to a single leader. At the height of the insurgency, Sunni fighters used a variety of small arms, mortars, rockets, and explosive devices, whereas suicide bombings and other terrorist tactics were found predominately in AQI and other Sunni extremist groups. The SoI have been allowed to retain their weapons, although they are not permitted to operate independently of U.S. and Iraqi state forces.

[10] This statement does not argue for the wholesale hiring of the SoI by the GoI or the ISF. There are significant problems with such an approach. However, that discussion is beyond the scope of this report.

al-Duri as the rightful successor to Saddam. These people are unlikely to return to Iraq, and if they did return, we judge that doing so would likely be more a consequence than a cause of renewed broad-based Sunni armed opposition.

The second category—former senior government officials and military officers— is more technocratic than ideological. Many of these people were not in the top four tiers of the Ba'ath Party and thus are eligible to participate in government and politics under current de-Ba'athification laws. They could garner considerable Sunni support. Although efforts to exclude them from public life could make Sunni-Shi'a accommodation less likely and violence more likely, if the Shi'a leadership permits them to take leadership roles, this could further reconciliation.

Sunni representation in key roles in the security forces and ministries may still be a source of tension among the Shi'a even though things have improved, especially because of concerns voiced by several Iraqis and U.S. officials during interviews about an influx of former generals from the pre-2003 Iraqi Army. Statistics on the sectarian makeup of the security forces are hard to come by, but at the time of this writing, only one of fourteen Iraqi Army divisions had a Sunni commander. (Ten command billets are Shi'a, two are Kurdish, and one is vacant.)[11]

On balance, the Sunni are currently leaning increasingly toward involvement in the political order, in government (including at the provincial level), and in the ISF. Having gained political ground, they may also be poised to replace the Kurds in a ruling GoI coalition with the Shi'a. Barring a reversal of these trends, Sunni armed opposition to the GoI looks unlikely and preventable if the SoI are fairly treated by the GoI. The drawdown of U.S. forces need not affect this outlook.[12]

Shi'a Militancy and Fissures. There are many Shi'a militias and other armed groups. These range from the most professional (ISCI's Badr Corps, now mostly integrated into the ISF and government ministries) to the largest (JAM) to smaller but lethal organizations with mostly local reach. Of these groups, we judge JAM to be the principal and most important threat.

The departure of U.S. troops is not al-Sadr's ultimate goal. Rather, it represents the removal of an obstacle to his goal of political power over Iraq's Shi'a and perhaps over Iraq itself.[13] When violence furthers that goal, as it did in 2004–2007, he will use it; when it does not, he will set it aside, as he has done since 2007. Having justified the existence of JAM originally on the basis of the "U.S. occupation," it is unclear how al-Sadr would justify fomenting violence as U.S. forces leave. Meanwhile, al-Sadr's

---

[11] Interview with a former Iraqi Ministry of Defense (MoD) official, March 2009.

[12] Barring an increase in oil revenues in 2009–2010, the GoI will come under pressure to find savings, which could affect SoI jobs and benefits and, thus, the degree to which the SoI are accommodated by the GoI.

[13] See, in particular, Knickmeyer and Raghavan, 2006. Also, a senior Iraqi interviewed for this project opined that al-Sadr's role model is Sayyed Hassan Nasrallah, secretary general of Hezbollah, an opinion widely supported by a broad range of reports.

credentials as a resistance champion have been weakened by his prolonged stay in Qom, and JAM's political and military credibility and potency were weakened by the repercussions of JAM attacks on the ISF in Karbala in 2007 and by ISF actions in Baghdad, Maysan, Karbala, and Basra in 2008.[14] Still, al-Sadr's importance as a demagogue and champion of the socioeconomically depressed Shi'a persists. As long as these Shi'a believe that the mainstream parties and government do not represent them, al-Sadr can disturb the political order and perhaps foment violence. At the same time, it appears increasingly likely that he will use his mobilizing skills peacefully.

We judge that JAM is already overmatched by the ISF and vulnerable. As a result, the Sadrist movement can be expected to stress political agitation, mobilization, and participation over open armed resistance. Although this would not preclude sporadic and low-grade violence, it does suggest that there will be no call for large-scale violence. To succeed in using large-scale violence, JAM would need to either fracture the ISF or cause a large-scale Shi'a uprising (which could in turn fracture or paralyze the ISF). Although fracturing local police is possible and in some places even likely, it is unlikely in the cases of the Iraqi Army and NP. Further, the chance of a large-scale Shi'a uprising is remote if the GoI pays attention to the needs of poor Shi'a in Sadr City, Maysan, and other areas of high Sadrist support. The fact that large-scale Sadrist violence is unlikely is beneficial for the United States in several ways: It reduces direct dangers from this quarter to departing and remaining U.S. personnel; it lowers the risk of intra-Shi'a hostilities and disorder; it removes an excuse for the GoI to tighten and abuse power; and it reduces opportunities for Iran to cause trouble and spread its influence. Although the unlikelihood of large-scale Sadrist violence is far from certain, it suggests that JAM may be a lesser danger as and after U.S. forces depart.

Apart from al-Sadr and JAM, mainstream Shi'a parties could fall into conflict. ISCI has been content to control key ministries (e.g., the MoI until 2007 and Finance even now) as well as key Shi'a provinces (until the provincial elections in 2008), leaving the premiership to what was the weaker al-Da'wa Party. Yet, as al-Maliki grows in confidence and tightens control over central and provincial power, and as ISCI sees its influence deteriorate, it may rethink its position. Its poor showing compared with that of al-Da'wa in the provincial elections might hasten the end of the Shi'a alliance or establish al-Maliki as that alliance's clear leader. ISCI–al-Da'wa tensions could turn violent; in the worst case, ISCI would call on the Badr Corps, and both parties would call on their adherents in the ISF.[15] More likely, however, is that such tensions would manifest themselves in a series of assassinations and bombings. If exploited by other spoilers,

---

[14] JAM is equipped with a variety of small arms, mortars, rockets, and explosive devices. It is large, loosely organized, and not always responsive to al-Sadr's wishes. It is capable of and oriented toward urban fighting and hit-and-run and intimidation tactics.

[15] ISCI control over the MoI forces is much less certain now than in 2006. In particular, Minister Jawad Bolani has done a good job of rooting out party influence, and the NP have made progress in professionalism and efficiency. Assuming that MoI forces are loyal to the GoI, ISCI's armed options are limited.

these events could spread disorder throughout the Shi'a population and Iraq in general. On the other hand, the end of the ISCI–al-Da'wa alliance could lead to a larger role for secular parties,[16] which did better than expected in provincial elections and could begin to erode the preeminence of sect in Iraqi politics. We judge open conflict between ISCI and al-Da'wa unlikely, and if the ISF continue to increase in capabilities and can become a true professional force, they will deter all such party conflicts.

Kurdish Dangers. In modern Iraqi history, the Iraqi Army is the only existential threat the Iraqi Kurds have ever known.[17] Since 2003, the Kurds have followed a two-part strategy: creating an autonomous Kurdistan in Iraq and actively participating in Iraq's national government, policies, and security apparatus. The first strategy is both an end in itself and a hedge against things going awry in the rest of Iraq. KRG President Masoud Barzani emphasizes this aspect. The second strategy is a way to influence what happens in Iraq as a whole, especially because decisions made in Baghdad could affect the Kurds. Iraqi President and Patriotic Union of Kurdistan (PUK) leader Jalal Talabani emphasizes this aspect. Both Barzani and Talabani recognize the need for a dual track. Kurdish participation in Iraqi politics has succeeded thus far because the ruling Shi'a parties needed the Kurdish bloc to form a governing majority. But Kurdish clout in Baghdad is declining as al-Maliki's power increases and the power of ISCI (a strategic partner of the Kurds) decreases. This clout could indeed vanish if a Sunni-Shi'a (Arab) coalition is formed to counter Kurdish expansion.

For those who believe that Kurdish well-being, or even destiny, lies in a strong, safe, autonomous, and self-sufficient Kurdistan that encompasses its "rightful" territory, control over Kirkuk and its oil would assure long-term Kurdish prosperity and security.[18] To attain this control in Kirkuk and other contested areas, Kurds are trying to create facts on the ground through both licit paths (e.g., purchasing land) and illicit means (e.g., intimidation). Success could position them well for a referendum on the disputed areas. It could also position them well should disputes lead to conflict. Figure 4.2 depicts the makeup of the Kurdish-controlled area of Iraq.

Kurds currently feel threatened by two trends: al-Maliki's consolidation of power and the increasing (and planned) capabilities of the ISF. If current trends continue, the balance will tip more in favor of the ISF as time progresses. The exit of U.S. forces will remove what both sides see as the honest broker, and what the Kurds see as a guarantor of their security.

The potential gravity of Arab-Kurdish conflict lies in the fighting capabilities of the two sides and the risk of the breakup of Iraq. The *Peshmerga* are a capable army by regional standards, and their heavy-equipment holdings could grow, especially if the

---

[16] For example, those of Ayad Allawi or Sala al-Mutlaq.

[17] Interview with Ambassador Peter Galbraith, Washington, D.C., January 2004.

[18] The KRG is now largely at the mercy of the GoI in regard to revenues. Even funding for the *Peshmerga* depends on Baghdad.

Figure 4.2
Kurdish-Controlled Areas of Iraq

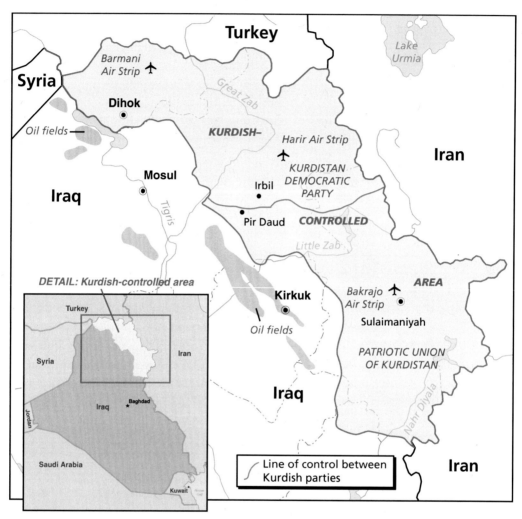

Iraqi Army were to split along ethnic lines. At the same time, the ISF are increasingly capable of conducting demanding operations. Thus, ample forces exist on both sides for large-scale Arab-Kurdish hostilities.

Arab-Kurdish tensions emanate mainly from national political leaders who can modulate tensions to suit their needs.[19] However, a local incident—such as efforts by

---

[19] According to BCT commanders and PRT leaders interviewed in October 2008, and according to MNF-I and U.S. Embassy Baghdad staff interviewed in February 2009, most ISF and *Peshmerga* commanders are inclined to avoid conflict. Furthermore, they assert that the people are generally not in conflict in these areas.

al-Hadba, the victorious party in Ninewah's provincial elections, to drive the Kurds from the province—could trigger fighting.[20] Kurds could also overreact to the loss of political leverage in Baghdad or to local incidents, and they could calculate that they must act before the ISF get too strong. However, the Kurds know that using force to grab Kirkuk or another major territory would likely backfire, costing them the support of the United States and alienating the UN, which has been playing the role of honest broker. A forceful grab at territory would also aggravate Turkey, with which the KRG has recently begun to establish good relations that are central to its continued prosperity.

On the Arab side, the Iraqi prime minister might be inclined to use force to demonstrate his strength of will and win political points for the upcoming national elections. Furthermore, according to many sources, he overestimates the capabilities of the ISF.[21] However, he has the law on his side in that the disputed areas are clearly under the jurisdiction of the central government and non-Kurdish provinces unless a resolution to the Article 140 dispute renders a different outcome.[22]

In sum, a shift in Kurdish strategy away from participation in and with the GoI could be driven by any number of events (e.g., the impending leadership battle in the PUK) that empower the Barzani faction over Talabani's. This in turn could make the Kurds feel more isolated and could intensify Kurdish efforts to increase the wealth, security, and autonomy of Iraqi Kurdistan. Although the Kurds might become more cautious as U.S. forces leave, it is plausible that they will feel impelled to act forcibly while they still can to protect their interests.

Politicized Iraqi Security Forces

As U.S. forces leave, the GoI and the ISF themselves could damage U.S. interests in a secure and stable Iraq if the government abuses power or the military stages a coup. There is a risk that Iraq's political and military leaders could be emboldened by the departure of U.S. forces and their own growing strength to seize control over the political order rather than continue to serve the people. If they do attempt to seize control, there could be violent reactions from the Sunni and the Kurds (neither of whom is prepared to accept Shi'a domination or dictatorship) and perhaps even from other Shi'a parties. There are several variants of a "GoI gone bad" scenario worth anticipating. A common requirement for all such scenarios is the acquiescence of the ISF, in part or in whole, to its politicization.

---

[20] The al-Hadba Party had indicated that it would do this upon taking office (interviews with U.S. government personnel, Baghdad, February 2009). Arab media sources indicate that the Kurds have refused al-Hadba's call for *Peshmerga* forces to be evacuated from the province as a precondition for forming a political alliance. See, for instance, Nuri, 2009.

[21] Interviews with U.S. government personnel, Baghdad, February 2009.

[22] Article 140 of the Iraqi constitution calls for a referendum on Kirkuk and the other disputed territories.

Creeping Authoritarianism. The ruling party could harden and expand its governing powers, operate at or beyond the edge of the constitution (which is fuzzy at best), and use the armed and intelligence instruments at its disposal to intimidate and destroy political opponents. Although countering extremist violence or another such popular cause may be used as a pretext, the regime's chief targets would be its political, sectarian, and ethnic rivals. Another scenario leading to authoritarian government could be brought about by a vote of no confidence in the prime minister. If successful, this would call for a change of government, but al-Maliki might not step down, given his recent success at the polls. Indeed, al-Maliki is already trying to extend his power through the placement of reliable allies in the security forces, the creation of parallel security organs and direct lines of authority through executive decree rather than legislation, and the creation of Tribal Councils across the country.[23] We argue that these events could pose a threat to U.S. interests.

However, it is often difficult to differentiate between legitimate use of force in a violent country and authoritarianism. In the face of extremist attacks and armed opposition from mainstream groups, the GoI should use its power to quell violence and defeat forces that threaten the security of Iraq. But this line is blurred and subjective. Political rivals of the governing party may be hard to distinguish from armed opponents of the state.

Although the line between legitimate uses of power and abuses may be imperfectly clear, two principal signs would indicate that it has been crossed. First is the use of force against parties that oppose the government but do not differ substantially in their tactics from other political parties—if GoI opponents resort to violence, it is harder to argue that using the ISF against them is an abuse of power. Second is the bypassing of established ministerial channels, procedures, and checks and balances for ordering and controlling security operations—an obvious red flag that is already evident.[24] To abuse power in this second way, the ruling party would need either its own armed force (which al-Da'wa does not have) or the acquiescence of a major part of the ISF.

The ISF and Political Power. The leadership of the Iraqi armed forces has traditionally been an identity group itself. Iraqi leaders recognize this threat and the fact that Iraq was prone to coups in the past. To pose such a threat, the ISF (or some major element of the organization) could capture or depose the ruling party or establish itself

---

[23] Although the ostensive goal of creating Tribal Councils is to work with the existing local security infrastructure to ensure law and order, vehement opposition to the councils has emerged from both ISCI and the Kurdish bloc, which interpret them as tools of the al-Da'wa Party meant to influence and perhaps control the population. In response to al-Maliki's introduction of draft legislation to codify the role of the councils in Parliament in November, the Ruling Presidential Council, which is made up of Kurdish, Sunni Islamic Iraqi Party, and Shi'a (i.e., ISCI) members, wrote to the prime minister to call for the cessation of the councils' activities. Leaders of ISCI and the Kurdish Alliance have called the councils illegal. See BBC Monitoring Middle East, 2008.

[24] Of particular concern are steps taken by the prime minister to exercise direct control over forces and operations, to shortcut the cabinet decisionmaking required by the constitution, and to create intelligence and commando capabilities outside the MoD and MoI that report directly to the prime minister.

as the arbiter of political power. The ISF could accomplish this by interfering in politics by either warning or deposing any government that strays from their own interpretation of the constitution. They could also throw their weight behind or against political actors to suit their own definition of national interests and order.

The Iraqi armed forces are now the second strongest armed force in the country, and as U.S. forces leave, they will become the strongest. The United States is making and will continue to make great efforts to improve all the ISF. As the armed forces improve and U.S. forces leave, Iraqi generals will have a growing ability to use force, including for political purposes—a danger exacerbated by weak civilian oversight of the MoD.[25] However, having this capability does not mean it will be used. Whether the shift in armed power will be helpful or harmful to Iraq's security and stability, and to U.S. interests, is a large and difficult question for the United States, and will become all the more so if the Iraqi Army grows more inclined to intervene in politics as U.S. forces leave.

The belief that a more authoritarian Iraqi government would improve security and stability in Iraq and reward U.S. interests could be a dangerous illusion. Major opposition groups, especially the Kurds and the Sunni, would be able and likely determined to resist GoI abuse of power and Shi'a domination. Political leaders, such as KRG President Barzani, Ayad Allawi, and ISCI leaders, from very different groups and parties have made it clear that they would act politically if al-Maliki continues to consolidate power in excess of that permitted by the constitution, and because some of them control large armed groups, they could act violently.[26] Local Sunni leaders interviewed in Iraq in October 2008 also made clear that they would use force to counter an "Iranian government." The danger of large-scale violence could well climb rather than fall if the GoI abuses its power. Although the ISF may eventually become so strong—and Shi'a dominated—that the Sunni and the Kurds must accept Shi'a rule, that day is far off, especially because of economic constraints on the GoI's ability to build powerful armed forces and because of ethnosectarian tensions within the army leadership. In the meantime, to the extent possible, the drawdown of U.S. forces should not empower any trend, including one toward authoritarian government, that could destabilize Iraq.

---

[25] According to interview sources with deep knowledge of the Iraqi general officer corps, this is an accurate description of the senior generals. However, field-grade officers and brigadiers are, according to these sources, likely to be more professional and less conspiratorial in their outlook and character (interviews with experts, Washington, D.C., January 2009, and Baghdad, February 2009).

[26] See, for instance, Mahdi, 2008. Also, in a January 2009 interview with the *L.A. Times*, Barzani noted that "for sure, we will not accept an Iraq ruled by dictatorship" (Parker, 2009).

The Impact of a Weakened Economy

High oil prices until late 2008 allowed Iraq to project a 2009 budget of approximately $90 billion, an amount based on a price of $106 a barrel.[27] But the dramatic fall (about 50 percent) in the price of oil since that time will force sharp cutbacks. Although this shortfall will be partially offset by the GoI's inability to spend all that it budgets, cutbacks will slow investment in reconstruction and funding for security until oil prices recover.

The ongoing failure of the main political groups to agree on a hydrocarbons law and associated revenue-sharing among the provinces reduces prospects for a settlement over Kirkuk and exacerbates Arab-Kurdish tensions.[28] The lack of such an agreement and the central government's indecisiveness about how it will deal with foreign companies deter companies from investing in Iraq's oil industry at the very time when capital and know-how are needed to expand production and increase revenues.

The silver lining in the bleak Iraqi economic and revenue picture is that the crisis will force the GoI to set priorities in the development of the ISF and to stretch out the purchase of modern equipment that could be viewed as threatening by the Kurds (and thus destabilizing) in the near term. Although every nation has the right to maintain the forces needed to counter external threats, the acquisition of such capabilities as long-range fires and high-performance aircraft beyond levels needed to deter external threats could aggravate domestic tensions and hence risks.

Summary of Dangers

U.S. drawdown plans and risk-mitigation policies should be more concerned with keeping the major actors in the political process and away from using force than with the more likely but less dire threats of extremism and terrorism. These goals must include the sober recognition that the GoI and the ISF could play harmful as well as essential roles in Iraq's security and stability.

Extremists have been weakened politically and militarily but, one can assume, will continue violent attacks, including attacks that target U.S. forces and other personnel. Less likely but far more consequential is the danger that one or more of Iraq's main factions could abandon peaceful politics in favor of violence. The drawdown of U.S. forces could make this more likely insofar as opposition groups see a greater opportunity for or a need to resort to force, especially as the ruling regime and its forces grow in power. However, this threat will not disappear before December 2011, and the United States may be able to maintain its honest broker/mediator role without large combat forces on the ground.

A more authoritarian GoI, with a more muscular ISF as its partner, puppet, or puppet master, would likely be resisted with force by the Sunni and the Kurds and,

---

[27] The International Monetary Fund reported in August 2008 that Iraq's growth potential was high due to high global oil prices.

[28] Kirkuk contains up to 13 percent of Iraq's known oil supplies.

possibly, by excluded Shi'a factions. At the same time, the resumption of armed resistance on the part of the Sunni or stepped-up encroachment by the Kurds would be likely to motivate greater GoI seizure and abuse of power. Although it is unlikely, a spiral of more-violent opposition and harsher authoritarianism could imperil Iraq's new order and, with it, important U.S. interests.

Security Needs That Will Remain Unmet After Full U.S. Military Withdrawal

The MNF-I is currently the most powerful force in Iraq, and in important ways, it is the guarantor of Iraqi security. In this section, we consider two aspects of ISF development that are required to fill the security vacuum that could be caused by the departure of U.S. forces. We also consider one mission currently performed by the MNF-I that will remain vital, but that the ISF cannot perform.

When one thinks of the ISF—or any national security forces—three characteristics are important: quantity, quality, and loyalty. With respect to quantity, the ISF are approaching their projected end strength of 650,000 in the Arab part of Iraq; by most measures, this number is more than adequate. The balance between the number of personnel in the armed forces and in the police forces seems reasonable. However, with regard to quality, the ISF are a mixed bag. Some elements—for example, the Iraqi SOF—are well trained and capable, while others—for example, some elements of the Facilities Protection Service (FPS)—are untrained and unreliable. Perhaps the characteristic most critical and difficult to assess is loyalty.

The ISF consists of forces from the MoD (i.e., the Iraqi Army, Air Force, and Navy) and the MoI (principally the IPS and the NP, but also several other forces not discussed in this chapter, such as the Border Police and the FPS). The Counterterrorism Bureau reports directly to the prime minister by executive decree, but its forces were previously part of the MoD. Legislation to make this arrangement permanent has been proposed but is controversial. Other national security agencies, such as the Iraqi National Intelligence Service and the Minister of State for National Security Affairs, play important roles in Iraq but are not central to the discussion of the drawdown of U.S. forces and are therefore not covered here.

The Iraqi Air Force and Navy are in their infancy, and will not be major factors with respect to security and stability in the timeframe of the Security Agreement. However, the future character of the Iraqi Air Force is a critical political issue affecting Arab-Kurdish relations.

A capable Iraqi Army loyal to the Iraqi government and not to any sectarian faction is key to Iraq's stability during the drawdown and after the withdrawal of U.S. forces. As rebuilding began, the Iraqi government originated a combination of local and national divisions, the local ones being the Iraqi Civil Defense Corps divisions, initially conceived as a reserve component force.[29] Of the first ten numbered Iraqi divisions, the even-numbered ones were locally raised and therefore have the ethnosectarian character of their home locations. The odd-numbered divisions are of a national character in that recruits are assigned to divisions after basic training or other assignments without respect to their home locations. The numbered divisions above ten are also national in character. All divisions but the ninth are light infantry (with a few trucks and HMMWVs), and the ninth is lightly mechanized. None has artillery, aviation assets (which are in the Iraqi Air Force), or air defense artillery.

The local divisions have in the past been less effective than the national divisions. For example, in 2006 and 2007, it was very difficult to get units from the local divisions to deploy to Baghdad as part of the Baghdad security efforts because, among several other reasons, they were recruited to defend the nation from outside aggressors and were reportedly therefore unwilling to fight other Iraqis.[30] Further, because the soldiers of these divisions and their families live where they are based, they are subject to local political pressures and violence when deployed near their home locations. For example, the 10th Division in Basra would not fight well against the JAM uprising there in March–April 2008 because the soldiers knew the JAM members (e.g., they were of their own or neighboring tribes and families or were followers of the same religious leaders) and because they feared retaliation against themselves and their families. Similarly, the 2nd Division in northern Iraq is almost entirely Kurdish, and some fear its members are more loyal to the KRG than to the GoI.[31]

NP units, which before 2007 were organized into two divisions and dominated by Shi'a factions loyal to militia leaders, were at one time of local character.[32] Since 2007, however, the leaders of these divisions have been changed and the units retrained, and the NP have grown from two to three divisions, all now of a national character.[33] Although some fear a lingering Shi'a loyalty among NP members, reports from Sunni in Mosul, for example, indicate that the population trusts the NP and views them as reasonably evenhanded.[34] Coalition officials and Iraqi NP leaders indicate that the NP are now a reliable force and are active in most Iraqi provinces outside of Kurdistan.[35]

---

[29] One chapter author's experience in the Coalition Provisional Authority, 2003–2004.

[30] One chapter author's experience in the U.S. Embassy Baghdad, 2006–2007.

[31] Part of the logic in creating a local division in the north was to permit the Kurds to control Iraqi units near Kurdistan, thus mitigating their fear of the Iraqi Army. By the end of the Coalition Provisional Authority, both northern divisions (the 1st and 2nd Divisions) had Kurdish commanders for the same reason.

[32] One chapter author's experience in the U.S. Embassy Baghdad, 2006–2007.

[33] Interviews with NP and MNF-I personnel, Iraq, February 2009.

[34] Interviews with Sunni in Mosul, via phone, summer 2008. Note that the conflict in Mosul is between the Arab Sunni and the Kurds—not Arab Sunni and Shi'a, so sectarian tensions were likely not in play.

[35] Interviews with NP leaders and their MNF-I partners, Iraq, February 2009.

Members of the IPS are locally recruited and are, in general, the least capable of the ISF we consider in this analysis. The IPS consists of many different types of police units (e.g., Emergency Response Units and regular police) and is numerically the largest force in Iraq. Under the Provincial Powers Law in the 14 provinces in which elections were held in 2008, the IPS should report to the governor, who is responsible for provincial security.

An important consideration is the tension between the ethnosectarian makeup of a unit and the desires of its leaders. The commands of a leader can often override the religious, tribal, or ethnic character of the people serving under him. However, this is not always the case, and it is difficult to discern this balance.

The analysis up to this point has frequently noted the importance of projected improvement in the ISF in the next three years and beyond. Given that the ISF will be at once an essential pillar and potential problem for Iraq's security and stability during the drawdown and after the U.S. withdrawal, the U.S. approach to the ISF is critical. In essence, the United States must seek to improve both the *capability* and the *character* of the ISF, the former to deter and defeat threats to the state, the latter so that the ISF do not themselves pose a threat to the state and so that other major actors, especially the Sunni and the Kurds, will not feel the need to prepare to defend themselves. Both purposes should inform U.S. strategy, programs, and presence with the ISF while and after U.S. forces depart.

Strengthening ISF fighting capabilities and the security ministries' ability to man, train, and equip the ISF during the drawdown and after the withdrawal will reduce the previously identified dangers of potential violence by extremists and mainstream armed opposition groups (i.e., JAM, the SoI, and the *Peshmerga*). However, it could also increase the dangers of growing GoI authoritarianism and ISF abuse, politicization, or intervention. There are two ways to guard against the latter dangers while also addressing the former ones. The first is to redouble efforts to instill and institutionalize professionalism in the ISF, including the following features and values: civilian oversight, apolitical conduct, merit over personal ties, representative and nonsectarian composition and leadership, stewardship of public resources, regard for the population's safety and rights, intolerance for abusive conduct, the creation of good institutional practices to support these features and values, and, if need be, refusal to be used for partisan purposes. Many reports indicate that progress toward these goals has slipped in recent years—a worrisome trend.[36] Interviews indicate that the "new" Iraqi leaders—field-grade officers and some brigadiers—are more accepting of a professional force that is loyal to civilian leadership, whereas the "old guard," which has taken control of the MoD since the advent of the al-Maliki government, retains much of the conspiratorial nature that led to coups in the past. A culling of leaders who are problematic may be necessary in the future to ensure the loyalty and professional nature of the ISF, and

---

[36] Interviews with U.S. and Iraqi experts, December 2008–February 2009.

the Iraqi Army in particular. Exercising care so that such a culling does not become an ethnic or sectarian purge would be important.

The second way to improve capabilities without engendering fear and possible reactions from main opposition groups is to influence ISF development to produce forces that can contain and defeat extremist threats while not posing a threat to legitimate political actors. The ISF clearly need the capability to counter the sort of large-scale insurgency waged from 2003 to 2007. At a minimum, this means that the ISF should be able to defeat any insurgent force and exert control over all provinces other than those of the KRG. This level of capability should be attained, with limited U.S. support (e.g., ISR and air power), by the end of the Security Agreement.[37]

The most sensitive issue for reasons of Iraqi sovereignty, Arab-Kurdish relations, and regional peace, is the capabilities of the ISF vis-à-vis Iraqi Kurdistan. The Kurds agreed to remain in post–Saddam Hussein Iraq on the understanding that they would be neither controlled by Baghdad nor attacked by Baghdad's army. The Transitional Administrative Law provided safeguards in both respects, but the constitution provides less clear assurances. It does codify the Kurds' right to maintain their own internal security forces (i.e., the *Peshmerga*), and it does place limits on the powers of the Iraqi prime minister to make unilateral decisions. However, these safeguards could, along with the Kurds' sense of security, be undermined if the GoI were seen to be heading in an authoritarian direction and if the ISF were to acquire offensive capabilities that the Kurds believe would be used to attack the Kurdish provinces. (Current GoI plans that concern the Kurds include the intent to purchase M1A1 tanks and F-16 aircraft.[38]) This creates a tension that the MNF-I currently mitigates through its good offices as honest broker, but this role is not one that the ISF can assume after withdrawal. Indeed, this may currently be the MNF-I's most important function.

In acting as honest broker for the ISF and Kurdish forces in contested areas, U.S. forces provide an objective source of information and help defuse potential conflicts.[39] To replicate this critical function and so lessen the chance of confrontation between the ISF and the *Peshmerga*, there is no substitute for a third entity trusted by both that can remain in the contested areas of Iraq for a relatively long time. Given current conditions in Iraq, this entity would need to be a military presence in at least the near term. Whether it came from the United States or elsewhere, it would require a new agreement with the GoI and acquiescence from the KRG. It could involve embedding personnel, including senior officers, with the ISF and the *Peshmerga* to act as monitors and honest brokers, or it could be a stand-alone presence accessible to both groups. Such an external presence would not need the ability to intervene between warring

---

[37] U.S. Department of Defense, 2008.

[38] Interviews with Iraqi leadership and Multi-National Security Transition Command–Iraq staff, Iraq, February 2009; interview with KRG representative, Iraq, February 2009.

[39] Interviews with MNF-I personnel, Iraq, February 2009.

factions; rather, its role would be to moderate disputes before they become violent. Its mission would be to foster transparency, build confidence, and guard against miscalculation. Its presence would be contingent on mutual restraint on the part of the ISF and the *Peshmerga*. The main issues involving control of Kirkuk and other contested areas along the Kurdish-Arab divide are unlikely to be fully settled by 2011. Therefore, absent some new agreement between the United States and Iraq that extends the stay of U.S. military forces, the need for such a third-party presence is likely to persist beyond the departure of the last U.S. military forces from the country.

In sum, the long-term U.S. defense relationship with Iraq—and between the U.S. military and Iraqi state forces (i.e., the ISF and the KRG)—would have three missions:

- capability building (through training, equipping, and enabling)
- character building (through partnering and institution building)
- confidence building (through transparency, moderation, and restraint).

We do not believe that fulfilling these missions will require a U.S. military combat force, except in areas in which there are ongoing combat operations (e.g., Mosul today, but hopefully not by December 2011). Rather, it will require well-prepared and well-placed relatively senior professionals at every level, development of long-term relationships with Iraqi counterparts, and some U.S. or third-party presence along the Kurdish-Arab divide after 2011.

Direct Threats to U.S. Personnel

Having discussed the stability and security of Iraq, we turn now to the violence and instability that could directly threaten U.S. personnel, including departing forces, remaining forces, and civilians who have depended mainly on U.S. forces for their security. Although extremists pose less of a danger to Iraq's stability than would a violent breakdown of the political order, they are more likely to attack U.S. forces and other personnel than to throw Iraq back into large-scale violence. At the same time, if any of the main opposition groups and the GoI enter hostilities, U.S. personnel could be endangered during the drawdown and after the withdrawal.

Extremists

AQI. Jihadis would like to spin the U.S. drawdown as their victory and take credit for it. Attacks on departing forces would add credence to this claim in some media. This threat is confined primarily to the northern part of the country because AQI now operates mainly in Ninewah province, especially Mosul, although it has cells in the Tigris River Valley, Diyala province, and Baghdad. U.S. forces and equipment exiting northern Iraq, whether by northern or southern routes, may have the most exposure to AQI attacks.[40] The primary AQI threats remain suicide bombs and roadside bombs (i.e., IEDs), and some such attacks seem likely.

Although AQI may experience some tactical success against departing U.S. troops and remaining U.S. military and civilian personnel, it is unlikely to be able to sustain repeated attacks over time. Moreover, it has other targets and bigger problems in Iraq, such as the GoI, the ISF, the SoI, and Shi'a in general. AQI is unlikely to pose a major threat to or to disrupt drawdown operations. However, U.S. military and civilian personnel remaining in Iraq in advisory and development roles, for example, may be more exposed than departing forces as intelligence and protection resources decrease compared with when troop levels were high. An attack against remaining U.S. personnel that results in many casualties or the capture of U.S. personnel could have strategic effects, most notably a sharp drop in the U.S. public's support for ongoing activities in Iraq.

Shi'a Special Groups. The Iran-backed Special Groups pose the greatest direct threat from Shi'a extremists to U.S. forces in Iraq. Attacks on U.S. forces by the Special Groups, which peaked in mid-2007, rely on indirect fire, IEDs, car bombs (known as vehicle-borne IEDs), and assassinations of key individuals. The majority of Special Group activities are concentrated in and around Baghdad, with substantial activity also noted in al-Kut, Hillah, Karbala, Dhi Qar, Maysan, and Basra.[41] The groups tend to consolidate their positions in rural areas outside of the cities as opposed to trying to control urban territory.[42] The Special Groups suffered significantly from ISF offensives in Basra, Dhi Qar, Maysan, Baghdad, and Karbala in 2007–2008. A surge of anti-Iranian sentiment among Iraqis has led many Shi'a to inform on the whereabouts of the Special Groups. However, in view of the groups' ambiguous relationship with the Sadrists, who have moved toward greater political participation, and in light of the apparent decline of the quantity of Iranian technology being provided to the Iraqi insurgency, the access and capabilities of such groups have become highly uncertain.

Iran's support for the Special Groups appears to have fallen, and Tehran may well have calculated that Iranian interests are now best served by an orderly drawdown of U.S. forces from Iraq. This does not mean that Iranian troublemaking can be written off, however. The Iranian Revolutionary Guard Corps's role as mediator and guarantor of the March 2008 ceasefire between JAM and the ISF in Basra demonstrated Iran's

---

[40] Note that because most U.S. soldiers will likely fly out of Iraq and their equipment will be moved on FB trucks, there will be few long tactical movements for AQI or other extremists to target.

[41] One facilitation route into and out of Baghdad operates between Sadr City, Shaab, and Ur, northeast Baghdad, into Diyala province. Another runs from Aamel, Byaaa, and Abu Disher, south Baghdad, into the provinces of Babil and Wasit. Weapon caches discovered along Highway 8 between Diwaniyah and Baghdad indicate that Highway 8 is a principal supply route for the Special Groups in central Iraq; in the south, Highway 7 is a critical supply route between Dhi Qar and al-Kut.

[42] Ahmed and Cochrane, 2008, p. 5.

ability to control Special Group actions, indicating that it is capable of renewing Special Group attacks in Iraq at any time. Additionally, any renewal of JAM operations in south and central Iraq would undoubtedly increase the possibility of the Special Groups renewing operations as well.[43] The Special Groups may also want to claim credit for driving out the occupier and may therefore stage attacks for propaganda purposes.

In any case, the Special Groups have the potential to pose a real threat to U.S. personnel, including withdrawing forces (who will be particularly vulnerable to IEDs), residual forces, and civilians. In particular, the relative isolation of U.S. personnel in Talil and the fact that Dhi Qar serves as a vital strategic base and supply route for the Special Groups should be a consideration in the structuring of the drawdown.

Main Opposition Groups

The Shi'a. JAM is unlikely to resume widespread attacks on U.S. troops during the drawdown if U.S. forces and the ISF do not put pressure on it. Due to its experience with the lethality of U.S. forces, JAM will likely wait out the U.S. drawdown before resuming overt military activities, if it does so at all. At the same time, the Sadrists' current commitment to engaging in the political process may not be firm, and al-Sadr is supposedly forming a new, more capable, militia.[44] For the moment, however, the Sadrists appear to be engaging in the political process.

If it did resume violence, JAM could target U.S. troops in Baghdad and the southern provinces, such as Basra, Maysan, Dhi Qar, and Karbala, although U.S. troops are required by the Security Agreement to be out of all Iraqi cities by July 2009. The relative strength of the Sadrists in Dhi Qar following the 2008 provincial elections, when they came second after al-Da'wa, could also contribute to an inhospitable environment in that province, particularly if al-Sadr renews public calls for attacks on U.S. forces. In the event of hostilities, JAM could try to interdict U.S. transport lines running from Baghdad to Kuwait using IEDs and explosively formed penetrators (EFPs), a particularly deadly type of IED. Finally, residual U.S. forces and civilians may present a softer and more inviting target. If hostilities resume, JAM might kidnap U.S. civilians or soldiers for propaganda and political purposes, as did a JAM splinter group run by a close al-Sadr associate in Karbala in 2006.[45] Iran may try to restrain or encourage JAM violence to suit its own needs. However, large-scale attacks seem unlikely, as uninterrupted U.S. departure is in Iran's and al-Sadr's interests.

---

[43] According to some sources, 5,000 JAM or Special Group fighters retreated to Iran after the Basra offensive in spring 2008 to regroup and retrain, leaving open the possibility that they could return to Basra and Maysan (Chon, 2008).

[44] "Al-Sadr Forms 'Promised Day Brigade,' Says Brigade to Fight 'Occupation,'" 2008.

[45] A splinter group of JAM run by Qays Kazali captured and killed five U.S. soldiers from a provincial police site in 2006.

ISCI's armed wing, the Badr Corps, has access to sophisticated Iranian rockets, EFPs, rocket-propelled grenades (RPGs), and, possibly, surface-to-air missiles. Although it might use force against other Shi'a parties and reportedly has regularly used it against the Sunni, it is very unlikely that the Badr Corps would engage U.S. forces in the absence of U.S.-Iranian hostilities.

In the worst-case scenario, U.S. troops based in Baghdad and the southern Shi'a provinces would face attacks by conventional Shi'a militia units wielding rockets, IEDs, mortars, and RPGs. In such a situation, U.S. troops could find themselves between warring Shi'a groups, such as ISCI and JAM, and would then face the risk of attacks if they attempted to enforce peace or were seen as favoring one party over another. However, this situation is unlikely.

The Sons of Iraq. Although they fought one another fiercely during the Sunni insurgency of 2003–2007, Sunni insurgents and U.S. forces have since developed a mutually beneficial relationship. This has reduced dramatically the threat of mainstream Sunni violence against departing U.S. forces or remaining military and civilian personnel. It would take an adverse turn of events to alter this situation, but the possibility cannot be excluded. For example, if the Sunni believed they were under GoI repression or ISF assault with U.S. backing, or if they came under concerted assault from Shi'a militias (as was the case in 2006–2007), the SoI could target U.S. forces and personnel. Although such developments may be unlikely, it should be understood that any occurrence of Sunni violence against U.S. personnel that elicits a forceful U.S. response could lead to renewed Sunni-U.S. hostilities. In sum, a direct threat from nonextremist Sunni to U.S. departing or remaining forces or civilians is improbable but not out of the question, and such a threat could get out of hand.

Hostilities Between the ISF and the *Peshmerga*. Neither the ISF nor the *Peshmerga* pose a direct threat to U.S. forces or personnel, but conflict between the two could put Americans at risk. This risk would not come from attacks on withdrawing forces; rather, it would result from a failure of mediation along the Arab-Kurdish seam in northern Iraq.

A Summary of Potential Threats to U.S. Forces and Personnel

There is a high probability of direct attacks on withdrawing U.S. forces by extremist groups that have the most to gain from being seen as hastening the drawdown: AQI and the Shi'a Special Groups. AQI is particularly dangerous in the areas between the north and the southern Baghdad belt; the Special Groups from Baghdad to the south. AQI would favor suicide bombs. The Special Groups would rely mainly on roadside bombs. Both could attack remaining military and civilian personnel given an opening to do so.

Neither AQI nor the Special Groups has the capability to sustain attacks or seriously disrupt the U.S. drawdown. To the extent that they expose themselves, both are vulnerable to high losses from U.S. forces and the ISF. Both could threaten remaining U.S. military and civilian personnel in specific areas.

JAM is unlikely to attack U.S. forces as they withdraw and would be exposed to defeat if it attempted such attacks on a significant scale or in a sustained way. Other main opposition groups are even less likely to target U.S. forces.

Hostilities between KRG and GoI forces could threaten any Americans caught in the middle, such as embedded advisors and civilians. At the same time, U.S. advisors to one or both forces could serve to build confidence and avert conflict.

An Assessment of Drawdown Options in Light of Dangers to Iraq's Security and U.S. Personnel

The analysis thus far suggests that the effects of withdrawal will depend on the details of the drawdown and the measures taken during the drawdown and after the withdrawal to reduce risks. Some key observations are presented in this section.

The likelihood and severity of extremist (i.e., AQI and Special Group) violence are in important ways insensitive to the speed of U.S. drawdown. In contrast, because the presence of U.S. forces has helped to moderate the behavior of the main opposition groups and their forces (i.e., al-Sadr and JAM, the Sunni and the SoI, and Kurds and the *Peshmerga*) and of the GoI and the ISF, the speed of the drawdown could affect the decisions and actions of these organizations if mitigating measures are not in place. Moreover, because these actors control significant armed power, the decision to pursue violence by one or more of them would be more consequential for Iraq's security and U.S. interests than would extremist violence. It follows that drawdown planning should be shaped by how withdrawal could affect these actors' choices.

Rapid drawdown would likely not increase the danger of JAM violence, as JAM may find that it is already overmatched by the ISF and that reverting to violence would entail major political costs. It follows that a rapid drawdown from predominantly Shi'a areas—from the regions south of Baghdad—would not markedly increase insecurity and instability in these parts of Iraq. Moreover, early drawdown from the Shi'a south could be welcomed by al-Maliki and al-Da'wa, who could claim yet another success. Finally, with a moderate to high risk of direct attack on U.S. forces in areas where the Special Groups operate, there could be a security advantage in leaving soon.

A slower drawdown would be indicated for Sunni and mixed-Arab areas. The SoI now have more trust in the U.S. military than in the GoI and the ISF. Rapid U.S. departure could make them feel, and actually be, vulnerable to government neglect or, even worse, oppression. Moreover, assuming that the Sunni realize that the ISF are steadily gaining a fighting advantage over Sunni fighters, they will be less inclined to resort to force with the passage of time. U.S. forces could leave western Iraq, which is largely Sunni, fairly rapidly without endangering stability. A more gradual departure of

U.S. forces from mixed Sunni-Shi'a areas could provide the time needed to settle the future of the SoI, promote Sunni-Shi'a reconciliation, and leave the ISF strong enough to effectively counter a new insurgency. The most important of these mixed-Arab areas are Baghdad and its belts. Some small number of U.S. forces should remain there for some time.

The greatest threat to stability would be a Kurdish-Arab conflict, which could arise from a potentially dangerous combination of unsettled issues, including the explosive Kirkuk; continued Kurdish encroachment in contested areas; Kurdish–al-Da'wa animosity and marginalization of the Kurds in the GoI and the ISF; Sunni-Shi'a Arab rapprochement; a tipping of Kurdish strategy from that of Talabani (who advocates active participation in the central government) to that of Barzani (who prioritizes security in Kurdistan). If the Kurds also conclude that their political and military position vis-à-vis the GoI and the ISF will deteriorate in the years ahead, eventually leaving Kurdistan vulnerable, they could deduce that the next few years present the best, and last, opportunity to obtain what territory they must—i.e., Kirkuk and other disputed areas—to secure the long-term freedom, safety, and prosperity of Iraqi Kurds. The departure of U.S. forces from contested areas in the north could leave the Kurds feeling less secure yet less constrained. Accordingly, maintaining a significant U.S. presence in this area for some time, while building up a robust embedded presence in both the ISF and the *Peshmerga*, would be prudent. Some such arrangement, whether U.S. or third party, will probably be needed beyond 2011.

During the drawdown, several key events will help shape how security and stability mature. The principal of these will be national elections, currently anticipated to occur in December 2009. Getting a new government elected and seated without unrest is a critical task. It is possible that some level of U.S. combat power will be needed to ensure an orderly transfer of power. However, the importance of the elections is tempered by the fact that, barring a major change in U.S. policy, U.S. forces will depart in all but their entirety during the first 18 months of the new government, while the ethnosectarian struggle will continue for a very long time. Other key events include a scheduled census in mid-2009 that will help resolve such Arab-Kurdish issues as the percentage of the budget that goes to the KRG and a mutually acceptable Article 140 resolution process. Also, the Iranian election in mid-2009 could affect Tehran's approach to Iraq. This set of issues is discussed in the next chapter.

Together, all of these factors suggest a need for a time-tailored drawdown: first from the Shi'a south and the Sunni west; then from the mixed center in and around Baghdad, leaving a few forces in key areas; and finally from the contested north and the few places in Baghdad where forces remain. As noted in the discussion of dangers, maintaining a presence through either embedded personnel or a stand-alone entity to act as an honest broker and mediator will likely prove more critical in the north than large numbers of combat forces. Arguably, combat forces play a more critical role in contested areas around Baghdad and in Mosul (due to the lingering AQI presence);

nonetheless, they must be out of all Iraqi cities in mid-2009. Maintaining some forces as a deterrent in mixed areas until the new government is established seems wise.

This discussion implies that forces in the south and west could be extracted as soon as feasible. Forces in and around Baghdad and the north could be extracted gradually, with the pace governed to some extent by such events as continued Sunni-Shi'a (i.e., SoI-GoI) progress. When combat forces are removed from the center and the north in particular, a significant training and advisory mission should replace them. Noncombat forces would remain through the Security Agreement timeframe (and perhaps longer if the U.S. administration and the GoI so desire).

This plan implies that a very quick drawdown corresponding to the 12-month option would (1) leave critical areas in the north and center uncovered during a period of transition and (2) leave the United States unable to help ensure a peaceful transfer of power early in 2010. On the other hand, the training, advising, and mediating missions currently performed by MNF-I will be the most important going forward, particularly in light of the fact that major tensions between ethnic and sectarian groups (to say nothing of political groups) will continue long after the Security Agreement expires. Furthermore, the costs associated with maintaining such a large force for a longer period are substantial. Finally, the potential for Iraqis and their leaders to view a large presence for a longer period as backtracking on U.S. commitments and offending Iraqi sovereignty argues for not leaving the drawdown of combat brigades to the last possible moment. Therefore, a drawdown option that permits a reasonable period to accomplish the training, advising, and mediating missions and provides some flexibility for the United States both to assist Iraq as it transitions to a new government and to develop the ISF seems to be the best option.

CHAPTER FIVE

Regional Effects[1]

Iraq's neighbors (see Figure 5.1) know now that the United States will withdraw its forces from Iraq, and they have begun to assess how the withdrawal will affect their national interests. Regional players may also be calculating, as the United States is, what contingencies may occur in Iraq as a result of the withdrawal, and they may be considering how they might take advantage of possible developments and contain adverse impacts. In our judgment, key regional actors' interests and likely strategies are not closely related to alternative drawdown timetables, but rather to the withdrawal itself and the nature of the United States' follow-on relationship with Iraq.

Iran, Saudi Arabia, Syria, and Turkey, four of the six states bordering Iraq, have cultivated—and will likely continue to cultivate—proxies inside Iraq. In some cases, these countries have also supported and will likely continue to support Iraqi exile groups that may have a role in affecting developments in Iraq. Moreover, Syria hosts over 1 million Iraqi refugees. Most importantly, elites in each of these countries believe that their national interests will be affected in important ways by developments in Iraq. Compared with other regional actors, therefore, these four countries have both higher *motivations* to intervene and greater *capabilities* to do so. To the extent that Jordan and Kuwait intervene in Iraq, we expect such intervention to largely align with U.S. interests. That said, because the drawdown could exacerbate the Iraqi refugee challenge within Jordan, we consider that potential risk in Chapter Six, Risk Mitigation.

Israel also has a strong interest in Iraq's future because of the effect the U.S. withdrawal could have on Iran's behavior and because Israel considers its security to be affected by the power and influence of the United States in the region. So, Israel has an important interest in the potential outcomes of U.S. withdrawal from Iraq, although it does not have much ability to directly affect developments in country.

Finally, over time, the Iraqi armed forces could become the strongest military in the region. Countries bordering Iraq—first Iran and then Kuwait, for example—could

---

[1]   In addition to the authors listed on the cover, the following individuals contributed to the writing of this chapter: F. Stephen Larrabee, Jeffrey Martini, K. Scott McMahon, Alireza Nader, Charles Ries, Ghassan Schbley, and Frederic Wehrey.

Figure 5.1
Iraq and Its Neighbors

SOURCE: CIA map, provided by the University of Texas Libraries.
RAND *MG882-5.1*

feel threatened as a result, making this a development that needs to be monitored. Two factors ameliorate this problem:

- For about a decade, Iraqi forces will lack a robust power-projection capability that would allow them to invade a neighboring country and sustain an occupation.
- Effective offensive cross-border operations will, for the foreseeable future, depend on U.S. materiel and supporting personnel. The requirement for this support will serve as a strong restraint on (highly unlikely) cross-border aggression on the part of Iraq against its neighbors.

This chapter presents (1) the main goals and interests of key regional players with the capacity to affect events in Iraq and (2) how these countries (and groups based in these countries) may respond (for good or ill) to three of the most worrisome possible adverse developments in Iraq identified in Chapter Four: an outbreak of Arab-Kurdish violence, the reignition of the Sunni insurgency, and Shi'a militancy or fissures. Regional or country-specific strategies the United States may employ are discussed in the next chapter. Specific risks to U.S. forces during the drawdown that may be aggravated by forces from outside Iraq (and the distinctions between drawdown options in that respect) were discussed in Chapter Four.

Iran

Iran is likely to continue to meddle in Iraq both during the drawdown and after the withdrawal of U.S. forces. It certainly has a strong and oft-expressed view that the government in power in Baghdad should be supportive of and friendly toward Tehran, and as the drawdown proceeds, Iran will assuredly work hard to ensure that the Iraq that emerges is not hostile to Iran or Iranian interests.

The U.S. invasion of Iraq has resulted in geopolitical benefits for Iran. Once confronted on its western flank by Ba'athist Iraq, Iran now faces a Shi'a-dominated Iraqi government that is friendly and considerate of Iran's security, political, religious, and economic interests. To varying degrees, Iran protected and nurtured the sympathetic Iraqi political parties, such as al-Da'wa and ISCI, that now dominate the central government, many provincial councils, and the security forces. The removal of the Ba'athist regime in Iraq facilitated the completion of an Iranian arc of influence that runs from Iraq through Syria, Lebanon, and Gaza. Thus, at first glance, the U.S. military's withdrawal from Iraq may enable the Islamic Republic to consolidate primacy not only in the northern part of the Persian Gulf region but also in the Arab Levant. Yet, the reality is much more complex. Although Iran's ultimate objectives are unclear, Iraq may not be as tractable as Iran first assumed, even without a sizable U.S. force presence.

Iran's central goals are to

- preserve the *velayat-e faqih* [rule of the supreme jurisprudent], the Islamic Republic's political/ideological foundation, in the face of internal social, political, and economic pressures
- deter threats to its national security from any quarter
- have a say in all regional issues that are perceived to affect these preceding two objectives.[2]

---

[2] See, for example, Green, Wehrey, and Wolf, 2009; Wehrey et al., 2009a; Wehrey et al., 2009b.

A relatively stable, Shi'a-ruled, and friendly Iraq will allow Iran to pursue these goals with greater ease. From Iran's point of view, the drawdown is the denouement of the U.S. project in Iraq: Having failed to reshape the Middle East, the United States must withdraw its troops, leaving Iran's sense of geopolitical power and purpose intact. The Iranians expect the drawdown will continue, not create, the expansion of Iranian regional influence that is already in motion.

Overt Iranian Military Intervention

The U.S. withdrawal from Iraq is unlikely to lead to overt Iranian military intervention. Iran and Iraq appear to have settled disputes regarding the Shat al-Arab waterway, which historically has been a great source of tension between the two nations. In any case, the two countries would be loath to repeat a conflict like the disastrous Iran-Iraq War of 1980–1988, which led to hundreds of thousands of casualties on both sides.

Covert Iranian Actions and Links to Regional Proxies

U.S. military sources have connected Iran to the funding, training, and arming of Shi'a insurgent groups, such as JAM and the so-called Special Groups. Iran's support to such groups reflects its military doctrine of using proxy insurgent/terrorist groups (including Hezbollah and Hamas) elsewhere to advance its interests. In addition, these proxy groups give Iran a retaliatory capability outside its borders in the event of a U.S.-Iranian military conflict. Despite this threat, Iran has often used its proxy relationships in a measured and pragmatic manner.

Iran has restrained proxy attacks on U.S. forces in Iraq in the past year. The use of EFPs supplied by the Iranian Islamic Revolutionary Guard Corps to Shi'a insurgents in Iraq has declined significantly.[3] Iran was also instrumental in arranging the ceasefire between Muqtada al-Sadr and the Iraqi government in 2008 following the departure of Sadrist and Fadila militias from Basra after an offensive by the ISF.[4] Iran may have taken these steps not only to stabilize the security situation in Iraq[5] but also to demonstrate that it is willing to reduce tensions in response to or prior to U.S. de-escalatory measures, such as the Security Agreement between the United States and Iraq, which stipulates that Iraq will not be used as a base for attacks against "other countries."[6] Nevertheless, Iran will no doubt continue to train and arm Iraqi Shi'a militias in order to preserve its retaliatory capability against U.S. forces.

---

[3]   Morgan, 2008.

[4]   Levinson, 2008.

[5]   Zavis, 2007.

[6]   Agreement Between the United States of America and the Republic of Iraq on the Withdrawal of United States Forces from Iraq and the Organization of Their Activities During Their Temporary Presence in Iraq, signed in Baghdad on November 17, 2008.

The Counterweights of Arab Nationalism and Iraqi Shi'ism

Traditional Arab nationalism and Iraqi Shi'ism will serve as counterweights to Iranian influence in Iraq and other Arab states in the Persian Gulf region.

Much has been made of the link between the Shi'a of Iraq and other Arab states of the Gulf region and the Shi'a of Iran. However, common religious beliefs do not necessarily make for a common culture, much less shared political objectives. More importantly, Iraqi Shi'a leader Grand Ayatollah Ali al-Sistani continues to espouse the quietist approach to politics, which holds that the clergy should remain independent of politics, whereas the clerical communities of the holy Iranian city of Qom cleave to the activist concept of *velayat-e faqih*. This is more than just a difference over a fine point of theology: The quietest approach rejects the political philosophy underlying the Iranian state.

Al-Sistani is arguably the most popular *marja-e taghlid* [source of emulation] in the Shi'a world. Most Arab Shi'a, including those of the Persian Gulf region, look to al-Sistani for guidance, not to Iranian Supreme Leader Grand Ayatollah Ali Khamenei or the *marja* of Qom.[7] In fact, Shi'a quietism has enjoyed a renaissance in Iran since Saddam's fall; al-Sistani is by some accounts one of the most popular *marja* in Iran,[8] probably in part because he is not associated with the perceived corruption and abuses of Iran's ruling clergy.

Tehran has attempted to ameliorate the Persian/Arab divide and the unpopularity of *velayat-e faqih* as a governing model by building a pro-Iranian social/religious network throughout southern Iraq. Iranian-funded charities, seminaries, and nongovernmental organizations have proliferated since the 2003 U.S. invasion.[9] In addition, the millions of Iranian pilgrims visiting Iraq's holy shrines have no doubt left a strong Iranian footprint.[10]

However, it remains doubtful whether Iran will be able to replicate the Hezbollah proxy model in Iraq. Hezbollah's success among the Shi'a of Lebanon was enabled by the unique circumstances there: The Lebanese Shi'a were disenfranchised by their own state and at the mercy of foreign powers, and the Islamic Revolution's ideology of "liberation" (in addition to massive economic and military aid) resonated with them. The Iraqi Shi'a, however, have already achieved liberation, and thus are in no particular need of Iran's revolutionary ideology.

Iraqis Avoid Provoking Iran

Unlike their Ba'athist predecessors, leaders of the new Shi'a-dominated Iraq have been careful to avoid any appearance of a threat to the Islamic Republic or to Iran's national

---

7   "Bahraini Shiites Answer Sistani Call to Protest Bombing," 2006.

8   Slackman, 2006.

9   Peterson, 2005a.

10   Saidazimova, 2008.

security. Even though the holy city of Najaf has resumed its historical role as a center of Shi'a theology, it has not become the focus of opposition to Iranian *velayat-e faqih*, as some had predicted before the U.S. invasion. Al-Sistani has maintained cordial and careful relations with Qom and Tehran, and Iran has been respectful (although suspicious) of his religious authority.[11] For its part, Iran has accepted the distinctly Iraqi nature of the Shi'a-dominated government and has supported Iraqi objectives. For example, after fierce criticism at the beginning, Tehran was largely supportive of the Security Agreement in its final form,[12] which was described as a "gift from God" by Khamenei's Islamic Revolutionary Guard Corps representative.[13]

In return, Iraq has adopted policies that meet Iran's most immediate objectives. Iraq has promised that its territory will not be used for an attack on Iran, has agreed to eventually expel the Mujahedin-e Khalq organization (an Iranian opposition group) from its territory,[14] and has opened up Iraq to Iranian trade and economic investment.

Iranian Levers of Influence in Iraq

Iran and Iraq are not equal partners by any means. Iran will continue to see itself as the strongest power in the Persian Gulf region and will maintain enough leverage over the Iraqi central government to successfully pursue Iran's national objectives in Iraq. The divisions within the Iraqi Shi'a community (and Iraq as a whole) and Iran's traditional ties to various Shi'a groups provide ample opportunity for Iranian meddling in Iraqi affairs. To ensure its ability to affect developments in Iraq, Iran has hedged its bets by supporting virtually every major Shi'a party or group in Iraq. Among Tehran's key levers of influence now are

- **ISCI.** Once known as the Supreme Council for Islamic Revolution in Iraq, ISCI was created, nurtured, and guided by Iran during Tehran's long fight against the Ba'athist regime. It is one of the major political parties in Iraq, although it suffered a setback in the provincial elections of 2008. Its losses can be seen as part of a broader trend in the elections: diminishing support for overtly sectarian parties that are perceived to be antinationalist. ISCI has often behaved in a sectarian manner. For example, it has advocated an autonomous Shi'a region in southern Iraq, which may leave that area more susceptible to Iranian influence. Neverthe-

---

[11] Interview with Iran expert, January 2009.

[12] Theodoulou, 2008.

[13] "Namayand e Vali Faghih Dar Sepah: Tavafoghname Amrica va Aragh Az Altaf e Khoda Bood [The Supreme Leader's Representative in the [Revolutionary Guards] Corps: The Agreement Between America and Iraq Is a Sign of God's Grace]," 2008.

[14] "Iraq Accuses MKO of Plotting Attack," 2009.

less, ISCI will continue to be a key player within the Iraqi central government and among the Shi'a religious establishment in Najaf.

However, ISCI has taken some steps to distance itself from Iran. In 2007, it removed "revolution" from its name and indicated that it accepts Ayatollah Ali al-Sistani, and not Iran's Supreme Leader, Ayatollah Ali Khamenei, as its ultimate *marja-e taghlid*. At key moments, ISCI has been a crucial U.S. partner in post–Saddam Hussein Iraq, and it is likely to preserve its ties with Washington even in the face of pressure from Iran, its traditional supporter. More importantly, even though ISCI is a Shi'a sectarian party with strong ties to Iran, it is nevertheless an *Arab* Shi'a party that strives to position itself as distinct from its clerical counterparts in the Islamic Republic. ISCI has worked to strengthen its ties to the Shi'a clerical establishment in Najaf, which has long competed with Qom, the center of Shi'a thought in Iran.

- **Al-Da'wa.** Another Shi'a party with close ties to the Iranian government, al-Da'wa was once the principal Shi'a opposition group to the Ba'athist regime; many members who were fortunate enough to survive during Saddam Hussein's rule, including current Iraqi Prime Minister al-Maliki, ultimately found sanctuary in Iran and Syria. Unlike ISCI, al-Da'wa was founded in Iraq, and its leaders hold mixed views of Iran and its intentions over the years. Al-Da'wa has often splintered, with some factions closer to the Iranian political philosophy than others. Al-Maliki portrays himself and his branch of the party as part of an Iraqi nationalist movement that is independent of U.S. and Iranian influence. In addition, al-Maliki's al-Da'wa is not dominated by the clergy but by technocratic laymen who often advocate a government based on Islamic law but not directly controlled by the clergy.

- **The Sadrists.** The Sadrists, led by Muqtada al-Sadr, are also a powerful force within Shi'a politics and have benefited from Iranian funding and protection at key moments. Al-Sadr and his family have long viewed the al-Hakim family and ISCI as rivals within Shi'a Iraq.[15] They are in turn viewed by the al-Hakims and their supporters in Najaf as religious and political upstarts. Muqtada al-Sadr, revered by the Shi'a underclass, has portrayed himself as an Iraqi nationalist and sought to depict ISCI and al-Sistani as Iranian pawns. Al-Sadr's opposition to the United States, however, has driven him into Iran's embrace several times. He even now is studying Shi'a jurisprudence in Qom, perhaps to return to Iraq as a higher ranking ayatollah as the U.S. drawdown nears completion. Once back in Iraq, al-Sadr may distance himself once again from his Iranian patrons and reassert his

---

[15] Raghavan, 2006. The al-Hakim family rivals the al-Sadr family in that it is one of the dominant Shi'a religious families. Abdul Aziz al-Hakim is the leader of ISCI and a leading Iraqi theologian and politician.

role as a nationalist leader. However, al-Sadr's movement has fractured and his militia, JAM, has been infiltrated by Iran's security apparatus.[16]

- **Special Groups.** Iran has funded and trained Special Groups that appear to be more closely tied to Iran's Revolutionary Guards than to JAM or the Sadrists. Special Groups provide an additional level of Iranian leverage over the Iraqi central government and the mainstream Shi'a parties.[17]

In summary, the Shi'a dominate the Iraqi state today, but ISCI, al-Da'wa, and the Sadrists will continue to vie for power and influence, especially if they no longer face the common threat of Sunni insurgents. Iran, which has been supportive of all three, can continue to try to broker power among them, relying on its proxy forces to intervene in Iraqi developments when necessary.[18] The victory of al-Da'wa in the January 2009 Iraqi local elections has been reported as Iran's loss.[19] The Iraqi people's sense of nationalism and religious/ideological independence may lead them to select a path that is free of Iranian domination. But, having placed bets on all the primary horses in Iraqi Shi'a politics, the Iranians stand to do well whatever the outcome of the election.

U.S. withdrawal removes one constraint on the exercise of such proxy power, but even among groups Iran has long supported, Iraqi nationalism and Arab sensitivities will limit Iranian leverage.

Saudi Arabia

Saudi Arabia's primary concern when looking at Iraq is the potential challenge to Saudi security from a spillover or "demonstration effect" of developments in Iraq on various Saudi population segments. Much of this concern is rooted in the Saudi regime's (possibly inflated) estimation of its own domestic vulnerabilities and, in particular, its historical fear of aggrieved constituents being mobilized by ideological forces and events *outside* the kingdom. In the past, the Saudi regime has feared Nasserism emanating from Egypt, Marxism from South Yemen, revolutionary Shi'ism from Iran, militancy in Palestine and Lebanon, and Osama bin Laden's brand of jihadism. Halting the spread of Iranian influence is currently one of Riyadh's primary concerns.[20]

---

[16] Tavernese, 2006.

[17] Hess, 2008.

[18] Iran can also play a similar role in the Kurdish north, although its ties to the PUK and the rival Kurdish Democratic Party are more tenuous and opportunistic when compared with its ties to the Shi'a parties.

[19] Daniel, 2009.

[20] For background on the Saudi threat perception of Iran and U.S. efforts to harness this hostility, see Wehrey et al., 2009a; al-Zaydi, 2007; Gause III, 2007; Slackman and Fattah, 2007; Solomon, 2007; Wright, 2007; La Franchi, 2007; Gwertzman, 2007.

Risks to Saudi Arabia from the New Iraq

For Saudis appraising a postdrawdown Iraq, the spillover risks of the situation in Iraq can be grouped into the following categories:

- **Shi'ism/sectarianism.** Saudi officials appear to recognize that most Saudi Shi'a are not susceptible to Iranian agitation. That said, the Saudi regime has long feared that the political empowerment of Iraqi Arab Shi'a, whether through Iraqi elections or the reemergence of Najaf as a center for Shi'a learning, could inspire greater demands for political rights and cultural autonomy by the Shi'a of Saudi Arabia.[21] The fear of Shi'a activism is especially pronounced among the Saudi clerical establishment, not simply for doctrinal and theological reasons but because recognition of Shi'a jurisprudence and religious rights would undermine the privileges salafi clerics have enjoyed in their symbiotic relationship with the royal family.

- **Localism/federalism.** Similarly, members of the al-Saud ruling family are worried by the federal model of government emerging in Iraq, not only because it might enable Iran to consolidate its influence in the Iraqi south but also because of its implications for Saudi unity. Saudi Arabia itself is composed of provinces, each possessing its own traditions, identity, and history, and each suffers varying degrees of marginalization from the central Najd region. While these divisions should not be overplayed, there is still a fear in Riyadh that provincial autonomy in Iraq will produce a similar trend in Saudi Arabia, diluting the traditional dominance of Najd and weakening Riyadh's ability to maintain centralized control over Saudi political life.[22]

- **Tribalism.** The Saudi leadership sees the Awakening Councils as a double-edged sword; it supported the movement as a force against AQI, but it is concerned that the broader phenomenon of tribal empowerment in Iraq may animate tribal activism in Saudi Arabia.[23] Powerful Saudi tribes have at times challenged the al-Saud for increased economic rights or political privilege, and some of these tribes, such as the Shammar, Unayza, Harb, Shararat, and Banu Khalid, have branches and subclans in Iraq.[24] Riyadh has therefore been pushing for the integration of the Awakening movement into the ISF, not solely as a test of good faith for the al-Maliki regime but also to temper the principle of tribal autonomy itself.

- **Jihad.** The regime fears the reemergence of AQI because of the close ideological and inspirational linkages that existed between this entity and al-Qaeda on the Arabian Peninsula (QAP), which waged a campaign on Saudi soil from 2003 to

---

[21] See Wehrey, 2007.

[22] In a March 2007 interview, a salafi cleric in Riyadh indicated that "centrifugal forces in Iraq have threatened Saudi unity."

[23] Interview with an Emirati analyst in the UAE, March 2007.

[24] Interview with a Saudi analyst of jihadism, Riyadh, March 2007.

2007 and has shown possible signs of reactivation.[25] Thus, Riyadh has strong incentives to staunch the flow of Saudi jihadi volunteers into Iraq. Nevertheless, if there were renewed sectarian strife in Iraq, hard-line currents in the Saudi regime may calculate that tacitly allowing an influx of jihadis into Iraq may deflect pressure away from the royal family and therefore be worth the risk of blowback.

- **Iranian influence.** The Saudi policy calculus in regard to Iraq is informed by the idea of Iraq as a contested arena in a larger regional struggle with Iran.[26] Although Saudi officials have long accused the United States of "handing" Iraq to Iran, Riyadh has been surprisingly passive in countering Iranian influence in Iraq.[27] Recent events, however, may have convinced the Saudis that Iranian influence is not as broad-ranging as previously assumed and that it is worth attempting to bring the al-Maliki government "back to the Arab fold."[28] These signals include al-Maliki's resolve in quashing Iranian-backed Special Groups in mid-2008, the ratification of the U.S.-Iraqi Security Agreement despite extensive Iranian lobbying against it, and the defeat of ISCI candidates in the January 2009 Iraqi provincial elections.

- **A resurgent Iraq.** In the longer term, the Saudis also fear future challenges from a reconstituted Iraq. In the Saudi popular imagination, Iraq has long been viewed as the "Prussia of the Arab East"—a militaristic, authoritarian state with the tendency to threaten its neighbors by virtue of its traditionally strong military, capable technocracy, and industrial base. Saudi proregime media sources, such as the editor of *Asharq al-Awsat*, reacted strongly against the proposed sale of U.S. F-16 aircraft and M1A1 tanks to Iraq in the fall of 2008.[29] A noted proliferation scholar has argued that the development of a capable Iraqi Air Force with long-range strike assets would be one more factor compelling Riyadh to think seriously about acquiring a nuclear deterrent.[30] Thus, the Saudi leadership will be watching

---

[25] Abu Musab al-Zarqawi himself called for attacks on the al-Saud, while in Saudi Arabia, QAP commanders frequently framed their operations as a "second front" in the Iraq jihad, often emulating the tactics and style of their counterparts in Iraq.

[26] For background on this relationship, see Wehrey et al., 2009a.

[27] Interview with Saudi think-tank scholars, Jeddah, Saudi Arabia, March 2007. According to one Gulf commentator (al-Qassemi, 2008),

> The Gulf states may continue to lament the fact that Iran is interfering in the internal issues of Iraq as they persist with their policy of two steps forward, two steps back. In fact, it is only natural that Iran steps up to assume a role in its western neighbour that is at risk of falling apart to its detriment. The GCC [Gulf Cooperation Council] countries must immediately awaken from their state of suspended animation . . . .

[28] Al-Rasheed, 2009; al-Qassemi, 2008.

[29] Al-Humayd, 2008b.

[30] Bahgat, 2006.

the rebuilding of the ISF carefully, both for evidence of sectarianism and Iranian influence and in terms of its future power-projection capability.

Saudi Levers of Influence

Support to Iraqi political actors, work by Saudi charities and religious organizations, media coverage, economic aid, and diplomacy, described below, have been the preferred Saudi instruments of influence in Iraq thus far, although funding and support to Sunni militias have been hinted at:[31]

- **Iraqi political actors.** Inside Iraq, Saudi Arabia has developed ties to such Sunni parties as Harith al-Dhari's Association of Muslim Scholars, an offshoot of the Muslim Brotherhood; the Islamic Iraqi Party; and the Tawaffuq bloc.[32] Among Shi'a parties, Riyadh has seen the utility of backing actors who have a nationalist focus, using tribal intermediaries who have both Shi'a and Sunni branches.[33] In January 2006, King Abdullah II met with Muqtada al-Sadr, and it is conceivable that Riyadh would have an interest in backing more-moderate wings of the Sadrist trend to balance the power of ISCI as a counter to Iranian influence.[34]
- **Economic aid and trade.** In principle, Riyadh could use its financial resources and potential trade flows to affect events in Iraq. In reality, this lever has rarely been used. At the October 2003 Madrid Donors' Conference, Saudi Arabia pledged $500 million from the Saudi Development Fund. Yet, as of early 2008, only 17 percent of this amount had been delivered.[35] Saudi Arabia is also among the few remaining countries not to have concluded a debt reduction package with the Iraqis.[36]
- **Media.** Satellite TV is one area in Iraq where Saudi Arabia enjoys an asymmetric advantage over Iran; the Saudi controlled al-Arabiya network enjoys far greater popularity among Iraqi viewers than does Iran's Arabic-language station,

---

[31] The clearest articulation of this option came in November 2006 from Nawaf Obaid, then an advisor to Prince Turki al-Faysal. In an op-ed, Obaid warned of massive Saudi intervention to protect Iraq's Sunni from "being butchered" (Obaid, 2006).

[32] Meijer, 2005. Riyadh has also tried to cultivate Iraqi exile politicians, but these individuals have not enjoyed a high degree of resonance in Iraqi politics. Such Iraqi figures as Ghazi al-Yawar and Iyad Allawi were residents in the kingdom for many years; Yawar is a member of the Shammar tribe and a distant relative of King Abdullah.

[33] Interview with a Saudi analyst, Riyadh, March 2007.

[34] Norton, 2007.

[35] M. Kelly, 2008.

[36] While Saudi Arabia made an offer in 2007 consistent with Paris Club terms, soon afterward, visiting Iraqi finance officials were kept waiting for days by Saudi officials and no agreement was reached. Large differences between the two countries remain on even how much Saddam-era debt Iraq has with Saudi Arabia (Mufson and Wright, 2007).

al-Alam.[37] Riyadh has used this medium to provide a platform for its Iraqi partners and Saudi clerics, often to the dismay of rivals Iraq and Iran, who have accused it of inflaming sectarianism.[38] More recently, Saudi TV has given air time to salafi clerics to issue fatawa banning jihad in Iraq and to dampen sectarianism.[39] In policy terms, therefore, Saudi media can be both instruments of escalation and venues for reconciliation.

- **Diplomacy.** Another Saudi approach to Iraq is to use its leadership in diplomatic forums such as the Arab League, the GCC, and the Organization of Islamic Conference to highlight Iranian misdeeds in Iraq.[40] Saudi Arabia has also welcomed Egyptian involvement in Iraq and has coordinated closely with Jordan on both Iraq diplomacy and broader regional initiatives. According to one interlocutor, the Jordanians have been the "brains" behind many Saudi initiatives, while Riyadh has provided the "muscle" (i.e., money).[41]

That said, as long as violence in Iraq after the U.S. drawdown remains limited to fringe groups, the Saudis are unlikely to provide lethal support to Sunni militias. But in the event of the politicization of the ISF or serious threats to the Sunni minority as a resurgence of violence emerges from government-affiliated groups, the Saudis would be more likely to support Sunni militias. The Saudis can also be expected to lead active diplomacy through Arab institutions and even engage in a diplomatic boycott of the Iraqi government if one of the more-dire scenarios within Iraq unfolds.

Syria

Syria does not have Iran's or Saudi Arabia's wherewithal to fill the vacuum left by withdrawing U.S. forces, but its policies will affect the future stability of Iraq. With its shared border with Iraq, its ties to resistance groups inside Iraq, and its hosting of important Iraqi exile communities (including high-level Ba'athists and members of the former regime's officer corps), Syria has the instruments it needs to promote its interests in Iraq. Like Iran, Syria has a foreign policy tradition of using local proxies and exile groups (e.g., sponsoring Palestinian groups and Hezbollah in Lebanon and hosting Hamas leaders in Damascus).

---

[37] See "BBC Monitoring: Iran Media Guide," 2007.

[38] Abu Nasr, 2007.

[39] "Iraq, Saudi to Monitor Sectarian Fatwas," 2007.

[40] For example, Saudi Arabia met with Egypt and other moderate Arab states in Abu Dhabi to condemn Iranian involvement in Gaza following an Islamic summit in Doha earlier in January 2009. Saudi Arabia perceived this involvement as an Iranian bid to weaken Arab unity (al-Humayd, 2009).

[41] Interview with a Jordanian analyst, Amman, Jordan, March 2008.

Although Syria certainly possesses the *capability* to intervene in Iraq's internal affairs, its *motivation* to do so will depend on the development of the internal security situation in Iraq, the orientation of the regime in Baghdad, and Damascus's assessment of its broader foreign policy interests.

Syrian Interests in Iraq

Syria's main interests in Iraq are to (1) ensure the security of its own regime and (2) take opportunistic advantage of its influence in Iraq as a point of leverage in its dealings with third parties, notably the United States and Iran.

Syria's preeminent concern is to prevent the reemergence of a resurgent, militarily capable Iraq that could threaten Syria's own security, as was the case prior to the Iran-Iraq War. Indeed, it was the threat of Iraqi expansion that provided the initial impetus for the Iranian-Syrian alliance in that conflict. Of second-order importance, Syria also has an interest in cultivating enough influence in Iraq to strengthen its hand in its negotiations with the United States over such issues as Syria's role in regional affairs, economic sanctions, and the Middle East peace process. Becoming a "player" in determining the future of Iraq affords Damascus additional leverage in its pursuit of Syria's other strategic interests.

Given this backdrop, Damascus can be expected to resist measures that leave Iraq

- strong enough to pose a threat to Syria's national security
- stable enough to prevent penetration from Syria and its proxies.

Damascus is restrained by two important countervailing considerations. First, it does not want a central government in Iraq that is so weak as to invite Kurdish separation. Second, it does not seek an Iraq that is such a breeding ground for insurgents that it creates the potential for blowback that threatens Syria's own security.

In summary, Syria is likely to calibrate its intervention in Iraq to support the emergence of a government in Baghdad that is strong enough to hold the country together but not so strong as to pose a regional threat or resist pressure from Syria.

Instruments of Syrian Influence in Iraq

Syria has three important instruments for pursuing its interests in Iraq. The first is the 385-mile shared border that enables it to exercise some control over the flow of insurgents into Iraq. A second important lever of influence is the proxy groups Syria is cultivating inside Iraq and through which it seeks to influence the future trajectory of the country. The third instrument is Syria's hosting of important exile groups that can be allowed to plan operations in Iraq.

Based on such intelligence as the documents and computer data captured in a U.S. military raid at Sinjar, which is in western Iraq along the Syrian border, U.S. military officials believe that at least 90 percent of the foreign fighters who enter Iraq do so via the Syria-Iraq border.[42] And foreign fighters continue to play a destabilizing role in Iraq. Given the weakening of the insurgency caused by the creation of the *Sahwa* councils and the JAM ceasefire, AQI elements in northern Iraq have become the largest source of violence in the country. Syria's commitment to border control is a principal lever by which it can work either to stabilize or destabilize security in Iraq.

Syria has hosted a variety of groups that act as proxies for its intervention in Iraq. These range from Sunni political groups that represent irreconcilable factions of the Ba'ath Party to the Association of Muslim Scholars.

Syria also hosts a number of less well-known but still-important exile communities that could be used to influence events in Iraq. These include a large contingent of lower-level Ba'ath Party leaders who could influence the future stability of Iraq. Syria is also host to an important exile community of military officers from the former regime. One such figure is Misha'n al-Jabouri, a member of the Front for the Salvation of Iraq, an important exile community of military officers from the former regime. The importance of this community is not lost on the political leadership in Baghdad, which in 2009 opened an office in Damascus in a thus-far unsuccessful effort to persuade these officers to return to Iraq. The Iraqi government estimates that there are 23,000 soldiers from the former regime, including 9,000 officers, residing in Syria, Jordan, and other nearby countries.[43] These individuals constitute an obvious security risk to Iraq and, as such, are a logical instrument of leverage for states, such as Syria, that have an interest in exercising influence in Iraq.

The Degree of Syrian Intervention in Iraq

The most important variable that will condition how Syria intervenes in Iraq is the composition and orientation of the Iraqi regime. Damascus would be inclined to work against a government in Baghdad that aligns itself with the U.S.-led Persian Gulf security order and builds a strong external defense capacity while ignoring Syrian security interests.

Damascus will also be looking at Baghdad's responsiveness to Syria's economic interests. On this front, Syria has shown great interest in the reopening of the oil pipeline that runs from Kirkuk to the Syrian port city of Baniyas. This pipeline would provide Syria with both low-cost fuel and a significant source of revenue from transit fees for use of the pipeline. Once rebuilt, the pipeline could serve as a constraint on Syrian behavior to be used as needed by Baghdad. Not coincidentally, Iraq's foreign minister

---

[42] Oppel Jr., 2007.

[43] "Wizārat al-Difā' al-'Iraqiyya Tatrāja': Ijrā'āt 'Awdat Muntasibī al-Jaysh al-Sābiq La Tashmul Fadā'yī Sadam [The Iraqi Ministry of Defense Retreats: Measures to Return the Members of the Former Army Do Not Include Saddam's Fadayin]," 2009.

specifically mentioned the potential of reopening the pipeline in his February 2009 comments on the improvement in Iraqi-Syrian relations.[44]

A second variable that will impinge on Syria's intervention in Iraq is the degree to which the West accommodates Syria's interests in other regional issues. Specifically, if Syria perceives the West as seeking to impose further limits on Syria's role in Lebanon, or if Syria sees no path to reclaiming the Golan Heights, Damascus will be more inclined to intervene in Iraq as a way of demonstrating its importance to regional stability and thereby increase its leverage in the settlement of these outstanding issues.[45] This follows a historical pattern in which Syria prefers horse trading to ideological principles in the conduct of its foreign policy.

Finally, Syria's posture with respect to Iraq will also be shaped by Damascus's relationship with Tehran. Although Syria is a pivotal ally of Iran, it is Iran and not Syria who is the dominant power in the regional system. However, when it comes to intervening in Iraq, Syria is well positioned to channel support to irreconcilables within Iraq's Sunni Arab community, thereby providing Damascus a means to demonstrate its indispensability to Tehran and ensure that its prerogatives are reflected in how these two states coordinate their approach to regional affairs.

Turkey

One imperative drives Turkish policy toward Iraq: to maintain Iraq as an integral state with a strong central government and thereby prevent the emergence of an independent Kurdish state. Turkish officials regard an independent Kurdish state as posing an existential threat to Turkish security because it would be expected to exacerbate separatist pressures among Turkey's Kurdish community, which makes up about 20 percent of Turkey's population and which has shown increasing signs of discontent and restlessness. Thus, Turkish external policy and internal policy are closely linked and mutually reinforcing. The two policy strands meet with respect to the Partiya Karker Kurdistan [Kurdistan Worker's Party] (PKK), a Kurdish terrorist group that seeks an independent Kurdish state and that has a presence in the mountains of northern Iraq. Turkey is

---

[44] "Zebari: al-'Iraq Lam Ya'ud Lub'a bi Yad Amirika . . . wa Hunāk Nufudh Irani Lakn Laysat Hunāk Imlā'āt [Zibari: Iraq Is No Longer a Puppet in America's Hand . . . There Is Iranian Influence but Not a Filling [of the Vacuum]]," 2009.

[45] Syrian President Bashar al-Asad stated as much during the February 2009 visit of a U.S. congressional delegation to Damascus, noting, "If they want to talk about peace, there will be no progress without us" ("Akkad anna al-Salām Muftāh al-Istiqrār fi al-Sharq al-Awsat . . . al-Asad Yabahath wa Wafd al-Kungris al-'Alāqāt: Ishārāt Ijābīya min al-Idāra wa Nantazhir al-Wāqi' [He Confirmed That Peace Is the Key to Stability in the Middle East . . . al-Asad and the Congressional Delegation Discuss the Relationship: Positive Signs from the Administration and We Are Waiting on Real Events]," 2009).

sensitive to anything that might increase the PKK's political authority, recruiting base, and potential for acting against Turkish interests at any point in the future.

Outsiders have suggested that Turkey can make progress on the PKK problem only through a direct dialogue with the KRG leadership in northern Iraq. In the past, Turkey has been unwilling to engage in formal discussions with KRG leaders because it feared this would enhance the KRG's independent status. However, the government of Turkish Prime Minister Recep Tayyip Erdogan has recently and quietly sought to initiate an informal dialogue with the KRG. In October 2008, Murat Ozcelik, Turkey's special envoy to Iraq, and Ahmet Davutoglu, Prime Minister Erdogan's main foreign policy advisor, met with KRG President Barzani in Baghdad. This was the first high-level contact between Turkish officials and Barzani in four years, and it could eventually pave the way for a broader accommodation between Ankara and the KRG.

Such an accommodation would benefit both sides. Turkey and the Iraqi Kurds have much in common. Both are predominately Sunni, secular, and pro-Western. Neither wants to see an Iraq dominated by the Shi'a and closely allied with Iran. The economies of the two entities are closely linked and highly interdependent. Some 1,200 Turkish companies are currently operating in northern Iraq, mostly in construction but also in oil exploration. They have generated over $2 billion in trade and investment.[46]

On the other side of the dialogue, the KRG's future—particularly its economic future—is to a large extent dependant on the quality of the relationship it is able to establish with Turkey. Although the KRG has substantial oil wealth, it needs the capability to extract and transport its oil to Western markets. An existing oil pipeline runs from northern Iraq to the Turkish port of Ceyhan on the Mediterranean. This corridor is the most efficient and cost-effective means to get Iraqi (and someday Kurdish) oil to European markets. Thus, both sides have strong incentives to find a political accommodation over the long run. However, any serious rapprochement between Ankara and the KRG would require the KRG leadership to crack down on the PKK, which Barzani has so far been unwilling to do.

The Turkish government generally supports the U.S. withdrawal of combat forces from Iraq. However, it prefers that the drawdown occur gradually and that it not lead to increased sectarian violence or an increase in the political influence of the Iraqi Kurds. It regards the maintenance of an integral Iraq with a strong central government as the best means of containing Kurdish nationalism and preventing the emergence of an independent Kurdish state on Turkey's southern border.

If unprovoked, Turkey is unlikely to undertake direct military intervention in Iraq beyond that which it is already conducting. The most likely provocation would be a miscalculation by the PKK or by the KRG about the degree of PKK provocation that Turkey will tolerate without triggering a military intervention.

---

[46] Barkey, 2007.

Of equal or greater consequence would be decisions by an element of leadership in the Kurdish region that sought to take advantage of any destabilization that was taking place in Iraq to assert greater control than is currently provided by the Iraq constitution. For example, this situation could arise if the KRG were to try to incorporate Kirkuk into the KRG's territory.

Israel

Israel is not a key player with respect to the U.S. drawdown from Iraq, yet the departure of U.S. forces from Iraq poses a number of risks to Israeli security. Israelis are most worried about the prospect of an enhanced Iranian regional presence. They are also concerned that U.S. withdrawal from Iraq could allow for the spread of terrorism that in turn could threaten the stability of Jordan, both because of the potential for jihadi violence there and because of the strain posed by Jordan's Iraqi refugee population, which numbers in the hundreds of thousands.

Israel has long been concerned about Iranian regional ambitions and hostility toward the Jewish state, but the aftermath of the Iraq War has enhanced Israeli concerns over Iranian regional influence, particularly given the belligerent rhetoric of Iranian President Mahmoud Ahmadinejad and the continuing standoff over Iran's nuclear program. The U.S. drawdown from Iraq can be expected to reinforce Israeli alarm about expanding Iranian influence, but such concerns have posed an increasing challenge to Israel since the United States removed the Iraqi buffer against Iran in 2003.[47] Israeli strategic analysts worry that if Iran were to acquire a nuclear weapon capability, such a capability could lead to even more dangerous behavior by Iranian proxy actors, such as Hezbollah, while constraining Israel's freedom of action to operate against such groups.

From the perspective of many Israelis, the erosion of and limitations on U.S. power are serious strategic consequences of the Iraq War. Moreover, many Israelis also feel that the utility of the U.S. presence in Iraq is declining. But in the view of some Israelis, Iran's growing influence, including in Arab-Israeli affairs, is occurring regardless of whether the U.S. forces are present on the ground in Iraq or not. As a consequence, some Israeli analysts see a number of opportunities in the U.S. departure. Some Israelis believe that the improved security conditions in Iraq in 2008–2009 have provided both an opportunity for the United States to depart Iraq with enhanced credibility and an opening for the United States to focus on other regional issues of greater concern to Israel (especially Iran). Most Israelis expect increased U.S. engagement and dialogue with Iran in

---

[47] It is important to note, however, that some analysts question the extent to which Iraq actually served as a buffer against Iran prior to 2003, as international sanctions severely limited Iraqi power and capabilities to effectively "balance" Iran after the 1991 Gulf War. See Eisenstadt, 1996.

the Obama administration, and some see the U.S. drawdown in Iraq as useful for that dialogue, but most prefer a defined timetable for talks on the nuclear issue.[48]

Effects of the Drawdown on Iraq's Relations with Regional Powers

Serious Challenges Remain

The Middle East will continue to face a number of serious challenges after the United States withdraws from Iraq. Most of these challenges are largely independent of the pace of the drawdown of U.S. forces from Iraq. This includes the growing rise of Iranian influence, a serious concern for key U.S. allies in the region, that has occurred in large part because of the removal of Saddam Hussein from power.

There are no strong indicators that point to terrorism being a serious threat to regional stability as a result of the withdrawal. Indeed, the salafi-jihadi threat is already in decline because "Iraq fatigue" has set in, and many of the most dangerous actors have already moved to other parts of the region, particularly the Afghanistan-Pakistan border area. A U.S. drawdown may even improve the prospects for more-extensive regional and international cooperation on both counterterrorism efforts and efforts to build a broader regional security system. The withdrawal could also improve the prospects for greater regional support, particularly from wealthy Persian Gulf states, by, for example, encouraging such states to provide financial support to international organizations that assist Iraqi refugee populations across the region, particularly in Jordan and Syria.

Military Intervention by Iraq's Neighbors

To the extent that destabilizing scenarios in Iraq lead to intervention by Iraq's neighbors, we find an important distinction between the types of intervention the United States can expect. Although any Turkish intervention, should it occur, would likely be overt, conventional, and specific to the Kurdish question, the other three critical actors (Iran, Saudi Arabia, and Syria) are more likely to intervene in a manner that is covert, unconventional, and more broadly aimed at cultivating general influence within Iraq.

To reduce the risk of intervention, the prevention of Kurdish separatism is critical. Indeed, the growing Kurdish challenge in northern Iraq has increased military cooperation between Turkey and Iran and has aligned Turkey, Iran, and Syria against this common threat because all three states are concerned about the contagion effects on their own significant Kurdish populations. U.S. policies aimed at coordination with Turkey to suppress the PKK are essential to manage this risk. U.S. attention to the Iraqi political reconciliation process and the depoliticization of the ISF will also serve to reduce the concerns of Iraq's Sunni neighbors, particularly such countries as Saudi Arabia and Jordan, even if a Turkish intervention is more likely to be politically rather than militarily oriented.

---

[48] Interviews with Israeli analysts, Jerusalem and Tel Aviv, January 2009.

The Importance of the Political Process

The nature and future evolution of the Iraqi government and the political reconciliation process in Iraq are more critical than the effects of the drawdown itself. The most critical factor in shaping future regional calculations toward Iraq is how the Iraqi system itself evolves. If the Iraqi state is viewed in the region as developing along sectarian lines, Iraq's Sunni neighbors are likely to be antagonized. On the other hand, if Iraq stays too closely aligned with the United States, the Iranian government may meddle more actively in Iraq. Consequently, the evolution of a politically inclusive yet independent and nationally oriented Iraq (that is stable enough to maintain internal security but not strong enough to threaten its neighbors again) will be most conducive to maintaining a balance within the region and reducing the risk of external intervention.

Maintaining such a balance will be a central consideration informing U.S. security assistance to the Iraqi state and should suggest some caution with respect to developing a too-robust U.S. strategic partnership with the al-Maliki government.

The View from Iraq's Neighbors

The effects of withdrawal for regional states are typically viewed through the prism of their own domestic politics. The significant Kurdish populations in Turkey, Syria, and Iran pose a threat to each country's own domestic stability. If the Kurdish populations within these countries were less marginalized, the cross-border Kurdish threat would not be viewed with the same alarm. Similarly, concerns over the spread of sectarianism worry Arab neighbors because of minority (or in some cases majority) Shi'a populations in their own countries. Ruling regimes typically perceive this group as a challenge to their power, and the group is therefore often marginalized and repressed, whether in the eastern provinces of Saudi Arabia or in small Persian Gulf states, such as Bahrain.

Consequently, as the United States draws down forces in Iraq, U.S. policies should encourage regional allies to get their own houses in order on such issues as political reform, accommodation of minority populations, and adequately dealing with the daunting challenge of Iraqi refugees.

The Possibility of Heightened U.S.-Iranian Tensions

The most serious external threat to Iraqi stability in the context of a U.S. withdrawal would likely result from heightened U.S.-Iranian tensions occasioned by extraneous issues, such as the Iranian nuclear program. Although Iranian and U.S. interests largely align with respect to support for a more or less unified and stable Iraqi state, it is well documented that the Iranians have sought to use levers within Iraq (including lethal force) against the Americans, particularly during periods of high tension between the United States and Iran. A successful drawdown and a stable Iraq are much more likely in the presence of some level of U.S. cooperation with Iran. Reducing tensions through an engagement process, perhaps beginning with the question of Iraqi stability, could reduce Tehran's motivations to continue such dangerous intervention in Iraq or at least increase the costs of doing so.

A U.S. engagement with Iran could thus be a critical element in reducing drawdown risks and enhancing postdrawdown opportunities in the region. Such an engagement should be matched with increasing U.S. security reassurances to both GCC allies and Israel. The establishment of new regional security forums that maintain a balance between accommodating Iran and providing assurances to U.S. regional allies could also contribute to greater regional stability over the long run. Indeed, the U.S. departure from Iraq may provide an opening to launch new cooperative forums, even if regional security cooperation will be difficult and require significant U.S. investment. Conversely, heightened tensions over Iran's nuclear program that lead even to U.S. or Israeli military action could present the most serious challenge to an orderly U.S. drawdown and a stable, peaceful Iraq.

CHAPTER SIX

Risk Mitigation[1]

This chapter develops a set of measures that could be taken with an eye to mitigating risks associated with the drawdown and eventual withdrawal of U.S. forces. For the most part, the risks addressed here do not depend strongly on the pace of the drawdown. The degree of risk to stability in Iraq and in the region does, however, depend on *how* the United States withdraws. Thus, most of our suggested mitigating measures are applicable to all of the drawdown alternatives. In this chapter, we focus on measures that U.S. decisionmakers could take in concert with officials of the GoI and other countries in the region. Measures to ensure an orderly process for the physical removal of U.S. forces and equipment have been addressed in Chapter Three. Finally, there are two issues that will require attention over the long term from Iraqi officials. These are the disposition of the detainees that are being turned over to the Iraqi government and the ongoing problem of vulnerable minority populations in Iraq. These are introduced in this chapter as part of the broader context of the challenge over the long term, although the United States will have only limited instruments with which to influence the resolution of these issues.

The Iraqi Security Forces

For the past two years, the ISF and their U.S. trainers focused largely on increasing end strength so that Iraq would have enough forces to address internal security problems. Training and equipping these forces are moving apace: as of this writing, more than 600,000 Iraqis serve in uniform (see Chapter Four). Though some problems with training and equipping remain, three larger problems that had been lesser priorities are now emerging as key issues.

First, the ISF still lack the support and enabling capabilities they need to operate independently. Few units of the Iraqi Army, the NP, or IPS possess the logistics, intel-

---

[1] In addition to the authors listed on the cover, the following individuals contributed to the writing of this chapter: Nora Bensahel, Audra Grant, Stephen Larrabee, Austin Long, Jeffrey Martini, Olga Oliker, Charles Reis, and Kayla Williams.

ligence, and planning capacities necessary to operate on their own. The Iraqi Army faces additional shortfalls in long-range fires and air support. The ISF still rely heavily on U.S. enablers; they are only slowly starting to build their own capabilities in these areas.

Second, and more important, the ISF generally lack the institutional capacity needed to oversee and sustain themselves. Institutional-capacity development is now the Multi-National Security Transition Command–Iraq's highest priority, but much work remains to be done. The MoD has major institutional gaps that limit its ability to oversee budgeting, procurement, modernization, and the ongoing training and professional development of the Iraqi Army. The MoI faces similar challenges with the IPS, which will be further exacerbated as the provincial powers law takes effect and the governors start exerting local control over local police. Unresolved issues about the extent of national versus provincial control may further limit the institutional capacity of the IPS and could lead to duplicative and dysfunctional management.

Third, the Iraqi Army is the strongest of the various elements of the ISF. As a result, its primary mission during the past few years has been to provide internal security. Although this has been necessary, it is not an appropriate long-term mission for military forces. Assuming that the security situation does not significantly deteriorate and that the capacity of the police continues to grow, the GoI needs to move from the use of military forces to the primacy of police in the provision of internal security.

Risk

The drawdown of U.S. forces from Iraq risks exacerbating each of these problems. First, U.S. forces currently provide some key enablers that the ISF need to operate. All three drawdown options retain some enablers until the end of 2011, so drawdown of combat units will not immediately impede the operations of the ISF. However, the ISF need to prioritize measures to enhance their enabling capabilities now in order for them to be functional once the Security Agreement expires. This process is proceeding slowly at best, which raises questions about whether the ISF—and the Iraqi Army in particular, which requires more enablers and equipment than do police forces—will be capable of operating independently after U.S. forces withdraw. Low oil prices and declining budgets will only prolong the process of developing these enablers, since fewer resources will be devoted to procurement.

Second, U.S. forces currently fill gaps in institutional capacity within the MoD and MoI by embedding advisors in these ministries and providing training and leadership development opportunities. Many of these functions will continue until the end of the Security Agreement, but developing ministerial capacity is a slow process. The prospect of the U.S. forces leaving could, on the other hand, spur the Iraqis to take full responsibility for ministerial functions sooner than if there were no deadline. The departure of U.S. forces would, at a minimum, lead to further capacity declines in the short to medium terms while this transition occurs, and over the longer term, the capabilities, responsiveness, and effectiveness of the ISF could also suffer if some of these capacity gaps simply remain unfilled.

Third, the transition to police primacy could be jeopardized if the previous two risks remain unaddressed. If the lack of enablers prevents the NP and the IPS from improving their operational capability, Iraqi government officials will likely continue to rely on the Iraqi Army to provide internal security. If the MoI forces are not given primacy in internal security, the Iraqi Army will remain responsible for that security.

Mitigating Measures

- Continue to give high priority to strengthening the Iraqi police, to include ensuring that whatever security arrangement governs U.S.-Iraqi relations after 2011 provides for continued U.S. assistance in training and developing this force and in building a strong legal framework.
- Maintain embedded U.S. trainers in the ISF as long as possible. Keeping U.S. trainers embedded would help improve the operations of the ISF even as U.S. forces withdraw.
- Encourage the Iraqi Army to gradually transfer control of operations centers to the IPS. The Iraqi Army currently controls the operations centers that have been established to coordinate ISF activity. Yet, the security situation has stabilized in all provinces except Ninewah, which means that responsibility for internal security should transition away from military forces and toward police forces. As their capacity increases, the NP should be encouraged to take responsibility for the operations centers. Transferring authority for centers other than in Ninewah would also permit the Iraqi Army to focus more on its external defense mission.
- Consider adjusting the terms of the Foreign Military Sales program. The United States currently requires Iraq to pay for all of its Foreign Military Sales purchases up front instead of in installments. This policy exists because missing payments hurts other purchasers of U.S. equipment, and Iraq has a general track record of poor payments. Permitting Iraq to make partial payments in installments to purchase equipment would speed delivery.
- Fund International Military Education and Training (IMET) slots and other military exchanges for Iraqis. The U.S. fiscal year 2009 budget contains no funds for Iraqi military officers to participate in the IMET program. IMET is the main mechanism through which foreign military officers are provided with U.S. training to promote their professional development. IMET and other military exchanges would promote long-term relationships with the United States that could help mitigate some of the risks of ISF sectarianism and partisanship.
- Encourage shifts in the Iraqi Army force structure. The current force structure is composed almost exclusively of light infantry units. The United States should help transform some current infantry units into support units.

- MNF-I could use the time remaining to continue to (1) mediate the transition from a condition in which U.S. forces are the guarantor of security to one in which the GoI assumes that function and (2) help the GoI improve its security capabilities over this period. To do this, U.S. forces could concentrate on building lasting relationships with the Iraqi security ministries and forces. Doing so will allow them to continue both to help Iraq professionalize after U.S. forces draw down (and after the end of the Security Agreement, if the GoI permits it) and to help Iraq do all it can to create self-sustaining indigenous capabilities within the security ministries and forces so that these organizations can continue to serve the Iraqi people after U.S. forces depart.

Creeping Authoritarianism

The centralization of power in the Office of the Prime Minister, including direct authority over important components of the ISF and access to off-budget funds, could tempt the current or future prime minister to consolidate power, thereby undermining democratic institutions and threatening stability. If the prime minister centralized power in his or her hands, key groups, including Kurdish, Sunni, and religiously motivated Shi'a political parties, might be excluded from political decisionmaking, thereby becoming less willing to make compromises in Iraq's national interest. Prospects would dim for bringing reconcilable elements of the Sadrist trend into the political process. Creeping authoritarianism would likely aggravate other risks, including the Arab-Kurdish fault line.

Risk

U.S. influence has held tendencies toward incipient authoritarianism in check. MNF-I and U.S. Embassy Baghdad assistance to ministries and their active involvement in brokering political compromises on the budget, provincial powers, and de-Ba'athification have limited the scope for extraconstitutional or extralegal measures. As U.S. forces withdraw, the prime minister could be tempted to consolidate power by establishing control over counterterrorism forces and off-budget funds.

Authoritarianism poses major risks to the creation of a secure, stable Iraq. A bid for authoritarian power could lead key political actors to revert to violence if they judge participation in the electoral politics to be futile. In the extreme, it could precipitate Kurdish secession and undermine national unity. If an authoritarian government emerges in Iraq while U.S. forces are still supporting the ISF, the United States could be perceived as being complicit in such abuses.

Mitigating Measures

- Clearly and unambiguously oppose indiscriminate, extraconstitutional, or extralegal measures taken or proposed by the prime minister or aides. Avoid personalizing Iraq policy; support constitutional institutions and processes, not individuals. Continue efforts to develop the capacity of the Iraqi government to govern. Focus on ministries and provincial authorities. Remain cognizant of the Tribal Councils, but avoid legitimizing them as an alternative governmental structure. U.S. efforts should further focus on helping Iraq continue to develop a political system seen by all major players as their best option for achieving their interests. A political system that denies any major group the ability to achieve reasonable goals would increase the risk of large-scale conflict.
- Ensure that high-level U.S. visitors meet—and are seen to meet—significant political players in Iraq other than the prime minister, including the members of the Presidential Council (for example, President Talabani and Vice Presidents Tariq al-Hashimi and Adil Abdul Mahdi). These meetings will allow visitors to hear, firsthand, concerns related to power sharing and consultation.
- Do not provide equipment and training assistance to defense and intelligence entities that are directly subordinate to any government official outside the formal ISF structures.
- When providing enabling assistance for operations, including intelligence, air assets, and logistical support, the MNF-I should insist on receiving requests through the duly constituted and authorized chains of command from the MoD and the MoI. Apply similar standards to assistance for the Iraqi National Intelligence Service.

The Arab-Kurdish Conflict

The KRG's aspirations for greater autonomy and its desire to incorporate more territory into the KRG endanger Iraq's unity and could spark serious conflict as U.S. troops draw down or shortly thereafter. The future status of Kirkuk and other disputed territories presents the most serious threat to internal stability to Iraq. KRG *Peshmerga* forces have already forcibly moved into contested areas, e.g., Khanaqin, as have government forces. *Peshmerga* forces are capable, and a KRG effort to take control of some disputed areas by force could be militarily successful.

The KRG effort to expand Kurdish-controlled areas, to obtain more autonomy, and to control oil produced in the KRG and disputed regions threatens the central government and other groups in Baghdad. By the same token, an alliance of Sunni and Shi'a political parties against the KRG would threaten Kurdish leaders and potentially deprive them of a major role in Iraq's national politics.

From the Kurdish leaders' perspective, the ISF's interest in acquiring a power-projection capability, notably strike aircraft, is likely to spark fears that these capabilities could be turned against them.

Risk

The secession of the KRG from Iraq could lead to ethnic cleansing, as many Kurds live outside the KRG's area of control and some Arab Iraqis live within it. Turkey, Iran, and Syria would strongly oppose any KRG moves toward independence. Turkey, and possibly Iran, might step up cross-border incursions. Because of the perceived closeness between the U.S. government and the KRG, many in Iraq and beyond would blame the United States if the KRG were to attempt to secede from Iraq. U.S. relations with Turkey would be severely damaged; efforts to engage Iran and Syria would also be undermined.

An outbreak of violence between Arabs and Kurds may not directly threaten U.S. personnel, except potentially those embedded with the ISF engaged in the conflict. It would, however, likely set in motion a series of retaliatory political and military measures that would undermine the integrity of the Iraqi state.

The drawdown of U.S. forces from Iraq could lead the KRG to decide that its interests are best served by moving into the disputed areas while the ISF are still struggling to operate without key U.S. enablers and before they are strong enough to move against the KRG. The *Peshmerga* may be testing the water with their recent encroachment on some areas outside the KRG.

Mitigating Measures

- Phase drawdown of U.S. combat forces so that those serving near the contested areas are among the last to leave, especially the BCTs serving in Multi-National Division (MND)-North that deter both KRG and central government adventurism.
- Avoid creating expectations that U.S. troops will be deployed in the KRG after December 31, 2011. Clearly state that the United States is committed to the terms of the Security Agreement.
- Explore the possibility of a UN peacekeeping or military observer mission with the ISF and the *Peshmerga* along the Arab-Kurdish divide after the last U.S. troops depart in 2011. Alternatively, consider negotiating arrangements for the United States to continue to perform this role.
- Do not seek to resolve territorial disputes by the end of the Security Agreement period or other external timetable. A stable, sustainable solution to the contested territories can only emerge through a political process driven by the participants; efforts to hasten the resolution of these issues to conform to the U.S. drawdown timetable will weaken the ultimate outcome. The UN has made good progress

in keeping all participants involved in negotiations; these efforts should continue even if they progress slowly. Concerns about U.S. withdrawal may lead the parties to seek agreement more quickly. If so, this should be welcomed.

- Insist that the al-Maliki government respect the provisions of the Iraqi constitution guaranteeing Kurdish autonomy. Continue to pressure the al-Maliki government to include Kurds at all levels and refrain from forming an alliance of Sunni and Shi'a secular parties against the KRG. Encourage the Iraqi government to stay involved in the UN-led process to resolve territorial disputes. If coupled with pressure on the KRG, this will help ensure that all sides understand the importance the United States places on maintaining stability and unity in Iraq. The U.S. government could threaten to limit or withdraw U.S. support to any party that fails to negotiate in good faith.

- Insist that the Tribal Councils not be used as instruments to restrict Kurdish rights and autonomy. The creation of the Tribal Councils is a source of serious concern among the Iraqi Kurds. They fear that the Councils will be used to harm their interests, especially in the Ninewah, Diyala, Tamin, and Saluhdin provinces.

- Continue U.S. pressure on the KRG to work with the UN to resolve territorial disputes and to keep Kurdish territories within Iraq. Inform the KRG that destabilizing actions make U.S. security assurances less, not more, likely. Coupled with pressure on the GoI as a whole, this will ensure that all parties understand the importance the United States places on maintaining peace, stability, and unity.

- Continue to assign responsibility for dealing with Arab-Kurdish disputes to a senior deputy who reports directly to the U.S. Ambassador to Iraq.

- Coordinate U.S. strategy toward the KRG with Turkey and, if feasible, Iran and Syria. All three of these countries have a keen interest in the future of the Kurdish region. Coordinating diplomatic strategies, both as and after the United States withdraws, would help ensure that measures taken by all governments involved are mutually reinforcing. Consultations would help reduce the chances of misunderstandings about U.S. objectives and policies toward the Kurdish region. They would also help maintain good U.S.-Turkish relations regardless of how events in Iraq evolve.

- To mitigate the risk of the Kurdish leaders feeling threatened by strike capabilities that the ISF might acquire, the United States should work with Iraq to modernize its forces based on a clear assessment of needs and through a transparent process that informs all Iraqi, and especially Kurdish, leaders of plans based on these needs. Confidence-building measures to assure Kurdish leaders that these weapons will not be used against them would also be wise.

Turkish Incursion into Northern Iraq

Under pressure from the military and nationalists, the government of Prime Minister Erdogan might launch a large-scale, cross-border incursion into northern Iraq designed not only to weaken the PKK, the Kurdish insurgent group that has attacked Turkish forces, but also to hold and occupy KRG territory to put pressure on the KRG government to crack down on the PKK or to forestall a KRG annexation of Kirkuk.

Risk

The risk that Turkey would take military action if the KRG sought to annex Kirkuk is fairly high. Domestic pressure on Prime Minister Erdogan's government to take military action would be strong, especially from the Turkish military. The responsibility to protect the Turkoman population in Kirkuk would probably be used as a pretext for the intervention.

Mitigating Measures

- Intensify political pressure on the KRG leadership, particularly KRG President Barzani, to crack down on the PKK. Make clear to Barzani that the KRG will pay a high price in terms of loss of U.S. economic and political support unless he takes serious steps to do so.
- Warn Turkey in advance, publicly and privately, that a major cross-border incursion into northern Iraq would have serious consequences for U.S.-Turkish relations, especially military and intelligence. Inform the Turkish government that any incursion would very negatively affect bilateral relations and could jeopardize important Turkish interests.
- Coordinate the U.S. response with key European allies to ensure that the Turkish government clearly understands that a large-scale, cross-border incursion into northern Iraq would have serious negative consequences for Turkey's relations with the European Union, including Turkey's bid to become a member.

Iranian Subversion of the Iraqi Government

Iran may attempt to subvert the Iraqi government as U.S. troops withdraw by encouraging or manipulating pro-Iranian forces in Iraq to step up internal unrest.

Risk

Prime Minister al-Maliki has recently strengthened his political position, but the security situation remains fragile as of this writing. Iran still has a large number of operatives in Iraq.

Mitigating Measures

- Open a dialogue with Iran about Iraq's future. The United States could use the dialogue to make clear its views and concerns and also seek to elicit Iran's assistance in stabilizing Iraq. Bilateral relations with Iran could be made contingent on Iranian behavior in Iraq. Improved relations would provide Iran an incentive to refrain from destabilizing activities.
- Step up surveillance of Iranian operatives and local pro-Iranian forces in Iraq. U.S. forces could strengthen the capability of the Iraqi special forces to track and disrupt Iranian-supported groups and to stop flows of money from Iran to those groups.

A Return to Violence by the Sons of Iraq

The Sunni "Awakening," beginning in late 2006 and gathering steam in 2007, was a key factor in attenuating violence against U.S. forces and the ISF. As part of the Awakening, and on the basis of negotiations with U.S. commanders, local Sunni leaders offered to supply men to staff checkpoints and perform other security-related duties. U.S. forces provided short-term stipends to these people. Over time, these volunteers, many of whom were formerly insurgents, became known as the SoI and grew in number to 100,000 members. In 2008, Prime Minister al-Maliki agreed to bring 10 percent of the SoI into the ISF and to support vocational and other training programs for many of the others. Progress in transitioning SoI groups to Iraqi follow-on programs, including recruitment into the ISF, has been slower and more opaque than expected. However, it does appear that the GoI has picked up the ongoing stipends of most of the operational SoI units. Efforts to place significant numbers of SoI into vocational training programs have not gone well, in part because of logistical hurdles and in part because SoI members have not been enthusiastic about leaving high-prestige (gun-carrying) work for uncertain employment futures.

Risk

The progressive drawdown of U.S. combat forces, when coupled with frustration with the pace of SoI incorporation into Iraqi institutions, could lead some SoI groups to resume the insurgency. The SoI or their leaders may become convinced that, absent U.S. pressure, Baghdad will not honor its promises. They may seek to preempt the strengthening of a Shi'a-dominated ISF that could eventually turn against them. They may become embroiled in conflicts with Shi'a militia or even U.S. forces.

Mitigating Measures

- Pressure the al-Maliki government to meet its commitments to cover the cost of the SoI program and to transition the most capable 10 percent of the SoI into the ISF. Key arguments include the cost-effectiveness of the SoI in consideration of violence forgone and intelligence obtained.
- Look for ways to help SoI train for new economic opportunities while the United States still provides widespread training and assistance programs. Among the opportunities would be giving SoI preference for business development grants and job opportunities in the ITN funded by the Commander's Emergency Response Program.
- Ensure that the leadership and foot soldiers in the SoI are accorded respect and prestige. Forestall destabilizing local measures against SoI and Sunni communities, such as forced disarmament or local discrimination in housing or other benefits.

Detainees

The vast majority of U.S.-held detainees are considered "security detainees." That is, they meet the requirements based on UN Security Council Resolution 1546 and its extensions. They are classified as individuals that may be held for "imperative reasons of security" because they are suspected of taking part in attacks or engaging in other insurgent activities. A small number of these people have been convicted by Iraqi courts (primarily the Central Criminal Court of Iraq) and remain in coalition internment facilities at the request of the Iraqi government because of the limited capacity of Iraqi prisons.

Under Article 22 of the Security Agreement, U.S. forces are required to provide the GoI with available information on all detainees being held. The Iraqi government issues arrest warrants for detainees they wish the United States to turn over to its custody. The remaining detainees must be released. All detainees held by U.S. forces are scheduled to be turned over to the Iraqis or released by December 1, 2009.

Risk

Although the lowest-risk detainees will be the first to be released, a sudden influx of detainees into Iraqi communities could prove destabilizing. Some released detainees may attack Iraqi civilians, security forces, or U.S. forces. Should increased instability and violence directly traceable to released detainees be severe, the timing and pace of detainee releases could be revised at the request of the GoI as provided for in the Security Agreement, prolonging U.S. responsibility for detainees beyond what is expected and possibly slowing the drawdown.

In many instances, the Iraqi criminal justice system lacks the capacity to hold detainees. Therefore, some highly dangerous individuals may be released. Prisoners have reportedly been released in exchange for bribes, and others have escaped. The most dangerous clearly threaten U.S. forces.

Mitigating Measures

- Collect biometric and other information on the most dangerous detainees and on all foreign fighters detained in Iraq. Pass these data to Interpol, U.S. Customs and Border Protection, and other appropriate agencies.
- Provide information on the identities of detainees targeted for release to local ISF weeks in advance of release. In addition to their names, include photographs, other identifying information, and the reasons for their detention. Such information will make the ISF aware of potential threats coming into Iraqi communities.
- Continue efforts to build the capacity and capability of the Iraqi criminal justice system, in partnership with international partners where possible. Traditional Iraqi jurisprudence requires two witnesses or a confession to garner a conviction. Urge the Iraqi government to accept the use of forensic evidence. The Judicial Education Development Institute provides forensics training; this program could be expanded. Using training teams from neighboring countries would reduce language barriers and show that modern forensics is not limited to the West. Although training takes a substantial amount of time, U.S. programs designed to increase the number of judges would also be beneficial.
- The U.S. Department of Justice currently inspects nine Iraqi Ministry of Justice prisons to ensure they meet basic standards. However, only a relatively small number of incarcerated Iraqis are in those U.S.-approved facilities. The U.S. Department of Justice Criminal Division's International Criminal Investigative Training Assistance Program has also run programs to develop a modern Iraqi corrections system. Continue and expand these programs to include MoI and MoD facilities.

Vulnerable Groups, Internally Displaced Persons, and Refugees

After U.S. forces depart, long-term stability in Iraq will require accommodation of vulnerable groups, internally displaced persons, and refugees. Although these problems will persist regardless of the pace or modalities of the U.S. drawdown and eventual withdrawal, there are some measures that can be taken to mitigate their risks.

Groups that may be vulnerable to attack after U.S. forces withdraw from Iraq include

- Iraqis who have been affiliated with the United States or U.S. organizations who may be targeted by extremist groups
- foreign nationals working in Iraq as contractors
- minority groups that have come to rely on U.S. forces for protection from extremists (and in some cases elements of the ISF)
- Palestinian and other refugees who came to Iraq under Saddam Hussein and whose support for the former regime makes them targets for attack
- the Mujahedin-e Khalq, a cult-like dissident group from Iran that was supported by Saddam.

None of these groups has reason to believe that the ISF will protect them. Many directly depend on U.S. forces for security, and others count on the influence U.S. forces exercise over the ISF.

In addition, as many as 2.7 million Iraqis are displaced within Iraq. A large number of minorities in formerly multisectarian areas have relocated to parts of Iraq where they are in the majority. Over two-thirds of the internally displaced are from Baghdad; many of these have relocated within that city. In addition, there are some 2 million refugees, most of whom have fled to Syria or Jordan.

Although displacement rates have slowed, the number of both refugees and internally displaced people facing poverty is rising. Thus far, the vast majority of Iraq's internally displaced persons have avoided camps, but many have not been integrated into host communities. In Syria and Jordan, Iraqi refugees cannot work legally. In Iraq, internally displaced people often experience difficulty finding work, and they report limited access to the public distribution system on which many Iraqis depend for food.

The governments of Iraq, Jordan, Syria, and other states involved in this problem view the displacement as temporary. Few efforts have been made to integrate the internally displaced persons and refugees into the new communities in which they reside. Although the Iraqi government has provided incentives to return and many Iraqis indicate a desire to do so, returnee numbers remain small. The vast majority of those who return home are internally displaced people. Although displacement will persist regardless of when or whether U.S. forces leave, withdrawal may exacerbate the risks posed by displacement.

Risk

As the country seen as responsible for the Iraq War, the United States could be held accountable for any harm that might come to vulnerable groups. Moreover, the United States would be open to accusations that the withdrawal has aggravated the security situation. If the ISF fail to keep these people safe, faith in Iraq's government more broadly would be undermined.

The likelihood that there will be violence against vulnerable people varies from group to group. Some level of violence against minorities living in Iraqi communities, such as the Yazidis and some Palestinian refugees, is fairly likely, as are some attacks against U.S. allies.

If U.S. drawdown is marked by increased conflict, it is likely to spur additional displacement, particularly from the few urban areas that remain ethnically mixed. Efforts to return may spark violence. At present, U.S. forces and oversight help ensure that Iraqi police protect and assist returnees who attempt to return to their homes, even in ethnically mixed areas. With less U.S. oversight, Iraqi police may not be able or willing to respond to problems. Refugees who return to Iraq but cannot reclaim their homes may become displaced within Iraq.

The areas of most concern during the drawdown will be those that remain ethnically mixed and those to which returns are most likely. Baghdad will be particularly vulnerable, as will Diyala and the KRG border regions. The potential situation in Kirkuk presents very high risk, as do those in eastern Mosul, Ninewah, and Diyala. Because a large number of internally displaced persons have sought shelter in the KRG (particularly Dahuk and Erbil), non-Kurdish internally displaced people may be displaced again if Arab-Kurdish violence erupts.

U.S. withdrawal will limit the capacity of the United States and the international community to respond to problems. Many of those involved in development assistance, particularly U.S. government and UN personnel, are constrained by regulations that make them dependent on U.S. forces for security when they move within Iraq. With fewer forces, these people will have less freedom to move.

Because of its impact on Iraq's stability and development, displacement has the potential to undermine U.S. goals for a stable and secure Iraq. The potential disruption in the broader region, particularly Syria and Jordan, would also be detrimental to U.S. interests. Although the displacement problem itself is here to stay whether or not the U.S. withdraws, its effects may be exacerbated by force drawdown if more violence erupts.

Mitigating Measures

- U.S. legislation passed in 2008 requires the appointment of a White House–level Refugee Coordinator who is responsible for addressing the range of refugee issues. The position remained unfilled as of this writing. Filling it would ensure that plans and mechanisms are in place before U.S. forces leave.
- U.S. legislation passed in 2008 directs the U.S. government to develop a database of Iraqis eligible for resettlement to the United States. The U.S. government has the records needed to develop such a database although one had not been set up as of this writing. This database could be set up quickly and would expedite the processing of applications from eligible Iraqis.

- Plan for the rapid evacuation and resettlement of substantial numbers of refugees in the event that violence against these groups rises sharply. Not all refugees would necessarily be resettled in the United States. However, the United States would need to provide the means to evacuate these individuals from Iraq. Planning could take place with international organizations, such as the UNHCR.
- Work with the UNHCR and other organizations to ensure that groups at particular risk, such as the Palestinians, can find new homes.
- Because processing, not absorption capacity, is the bottleneck, increase staff and capacity for refugee and special immigrant visa processing at the U.S. Embassy Baghdad. Interviews with embassy staff indicate that they could substantially increase their throughput with just a few more personnel. Other agencies involved in resettlement, such as the U.S. Department of Homeland Security and the intelligence community, could also make this process a priority.
- Continue to urge the Iraqi government to provide assurances that it will ensure the security of these groups.
- Encourage more regional funding. The United States could make it a priority to involve regional states, particularly Saudi Arabia and other Persian Gulf states, in responding to this crisis. The GCC states could offer direct financial support to the Jordanian government for this purpose. Because the GCC will not be willing to provide this sort of direct assistance to Syria, the United States could also encourage sizable financial contributions to aid the refugees there through the UNHCR and other international organizations. This way, such funds could be justified as helping all fellow Muslims while avoiding directly supporting less-than-friendly governments.
- Work with Syria bilaterally and through international partners. Syria hosts more Iraqi refugees than any other state, with significant strain on its economy.[2] The United States could work cooperatively with Syria and the UNHCR to raise additional funds and to facilitate the ability of the Syrian government to improve social services for the refugee population.
- Continue to provide development and humanitarian assistance in areas from which U.S. forces have withdrawn. Options include lowering and adjusting security requirements, relying on the ISF for security, and hiring private security forces. Survey nongovernmental organizations and contractors to establish what support they do and do not find helpful.
- Accept more refugees in the United States. Over the past year, the United States has greatly increased the number of Iraqis admitted to the United States as refugees. This number, however, continues to fall far short of UNHCR referrals. U.S. refugee resettlement agencies have the capacity to resettle more if asked and resourced to do so.

---

[2] The Office of the UN High Commissioner for Refugees, 2008.

- Pursue and fund creative resettlement solutions. Countries that are not traditional resettlement countries generally lack institutions and procedures for accepting and integrating new residents. Many of these countries might benefit from an influx of educated Iraqis. Funding and technical assistance could make it possible for countries in the Middle East and elsewhere to welcome Iraqi refugees.
- Work with countries of first refuge and the Iraqi government to find durable solutions, not just the return of refugees. The United States could use its influence and assistance, both bilaterally and multilaterally, to help countries hosting Iraqi refugees to find realistic solutions. Assistance with both finding resettlement alternatives abroad and with managing the resource and capacity strains caused by displacement may serve as a means of engaging Syria and supporting Jordan. In Iraq, work with the Iraqi government to provide support not only to the internally displaced persons but also to communities hosting them, creating incentives for effective integration.
- Encourage GoI assistance for the internally displaced populations. The GoI has repeatedly pledged to make displacement issues a priority. Encourage the Iraqi government to back these statements with resources. Also continue to encourage the GoI to provide funds to countries of first refuge and to provide host communities with funding for housing, food, education, social services, and other support.
- Continue to work with the GoI to build capacity to manage displacement. Iraq's Ministry of Displacement and Migration (MoDM) is the key actor in providing for the internally displaced and facilitating returns of refugees. The United States and other international actors should continue to work in concert with the MoDM to help build its capacity to develop and implement effective policies to minimize the damage displacement causes.
- Recognize the long-term nature of the problem and establish mechanisms for international involvement and oversight. Recognize displacement for what it is: a long-term development challenge for Iraq and the region. Adopt long-term assistance and oversight measures to ensure that the GoI is aware of both challenges and expectations before U.S. forces are gone. The United States and the international community must then hold Iraq to its commitments.

The Referendum on the Security Agreement

Should the July 2009 referendum on the Security Agreement fail, the United States would lose the legal authority to continue operating in Iraq. A "no" vote would set in motion the termination of the Security Agreement, giving the United States 12 months to withdraw all personnel. That said, there is little indication that the referendum will take place, let alone take place on schedule. As of this writing, legislation to prepare the framework for the referendum has not begun and is not being pushed by the Iraqi government.

Risk

Iraqi leaders have publicly affirmed that the failure of the referendum would force Iraq to withdraw from the Security Agreement.[3] Article 30 of the Security Agreement requires the GoI to give the United States one year's notice before the Security Agreement is terminated.

Although the consequences of a "no" vote are high, the probability of the Security Agreement referendum actually failing is low. Early polling indicates support for the Security Agreement among the majority of the Iraqi public.[4] The political groups that were the strongest backers of the Security Agreement and have the most invested in making sure the referendum passes—al-Da'wa, ISCI, and the Kurdish political leadership—have demonstrated their ability in the past to mobilize their constituencies at important moments. Finally, it is highly unlikely that the Iraqi ruling coalition would allow a referendum to go ahead without being sure that it would pass. The referendum could be delayed either by deadlock over the format of the vote or by challenging the constitutionality of the legislation.

The Security Agreement referendum could fail, however, if U.S. forces or U.S. contractors were involved in a major incident in which Iraqis were harmed or killed.

Mitigating Measures

- Continue to adhere to both the letter and the spirit of the Security Agreement. Ensure that Iraqis continue to take the lead in operations and that U.S. forces are less visible, especially in urban areas. Publicize base handovers in the media, including on local television. Continue the handover of detainees as specified in the Security Agreement.
- Begin transporting large numbers of tracked vehicles out of the country to ship home. Publicize this on local TV stations.
- Avoid being seen as "slow-pedaling" the transition to Iraqi control or simply recategorizing personnel to comply with the Security Agreement.
- Continue to rigidly enforce measures to prevent another security incident along the lines of the 2005 Haditha killings or the 2007 Blackwater shootings. Continue to

---

[3] "'Ard al-Takhalī 'an Mansibihi Muqābil Inha' Nizām al-Muhāsasat al-Tāi'fiya . . . al-Hashemi: al-Istiftā' 'ala al-Itifāq al-Amnī Wasīla lil Taswīb wa al-Islāh [Offer to Relinquish His Position in Return for Ending the Sectarian Quota System . . . al-Hashemi: The Referendum on the Security Agreement Is a Means of Correction and Reform]," 2008.

[4] For example, a survey of more than 5,000 Iraqis drawn from ten different provinces conducted in November 2008 by the Center for Strategic Studies, the polling unit of the Iraqi *al-Sabah* newspaper, found that 46.1 percent of those polled supported the signing of the Security Agreement, 34.5 percent opposed the agreement, and 19.4 percent were undecided ("Fī Istitlā' Ajrathu al-Sabah Akthariya al-'Iraqiyin ma' Tawqī' al-Itifāq al-Amnī [In a Poll Run by al-Sabah, Majority of Iraqis Support Signing the Security Agreement]," 2008).

communicate to soldiers the volatility of the current Iraqi political climate and the potential consequences of inadvertent harm to Iraqis.

- Communicate the same message to private security contractors operating in Iraq. Underscore the U.S. government's commitment to follow through on the Security Agreement provision that grants Iraq primary jurisdiction over the activities of U.S. contractors.

CHAPTER SEVEN

Conclusion

This report contains many detailed observations about topics related to the eventual withdrawal of all U.S. forces from Iraq. As we began our research, we hypothesized that the effects of the drawdown of U.S. forces on Iraq's internal security and stability and on the region would vary with the drawdown alternative selected. However, we discovered that, with the exception of logistics constraints, the effects were only mildly contingent on the pace of removal of U.S. forces from Iraq. Consequently, this report's major findings and recommendations apply to all alternative drawdown schedules.

Major Findings

Drawdown Timelines

The United States can meet the drawdown timelines for the April 2010, August 2010, and December 2011 drawdown dates. There is risk associated with the April and August 2010 deadlines. We conclude that the very fast alternative of having combat forces draw down by April 2010 is feasible provided that detailed planning precedes execution of the plan. This means that the drawdown must begin no later than August 1, 2009. It is logistically feasible, albeit risky, to remove all combat forces from Iraq in the succeeding nine months provided that detailed planning has been completed and resources are available to execute the drawdown. We also conclude that logistics capabilities are not likely to constrain the planned alternative of drawing down combat forces by August 2010. However, starting the drawdown of approximately six BCTs any later than February 2010 puts drawing down to 50,000 by August 2010 at risk. The more extended drawdown case of December 2011 is logistically feasible. However, we acknowledge that all withdrawal options constitute a large, demanding logistics problem requiring substantial resources.

Arab-Kurdish Armed Conflict

The greatest threat to Iraqi stability and security comes from an Arab-Kurdish armed conflict over contested areas. The potential threat posed by this scenario is high because of the substantial fighting capabilities possessed by each side. The *Peshmerga* are a capable fighting force by regional standards, and they could easily be augmented. The ISF are becoming increasingly capable. Thus, should fighting break out between the two factions, it could easily escalate to what amounts to all-out civil war. There are a number of points of friction between the two sides that could spark an incident, which in turn could lead to major fighting. Turkey could be drawn in; indeed, this is the principal concern regarding the possibility of major armed intervention into Iraq from outside the country.

Iran

Of all of Iraq's neighbors, Iran is the best situated and equipped to promote instability in Iraq. Tehran might view the departure of U.S. forces as an opportunity to exploit instability, and this may lead to more-aggressive attempts to destabilize Iraq. Iran still has client organizations operating in Iraq. There are several counterweights to the possibility that Iran may adopt a disruptive strategy, however: the memory of an eight-year bloody war; the fact that some historical sources of tension between the two countries—e.g., the Shat al-Arab waterway—have been reduced; and Arab nationalism and Iraqi Shi'ism. Thus, although Iran has the capability to destabilize Iraq, its decision to do so will largely be a function of the state of its relations with the United States rather than developments in Iraq.

The Iraqi Security Forces

The development, professionalism, and accountability of the ISF are critical to the country's long-term stability. The Iraqi military and the police are the sine qua non of stability in Iraq, from both the national and provincial perspectives. Great strides have been made, particularly in the Army and the NP. But much remains to be done, and the success of turning these security forces into competent and professional organizations will largely determine the course of stability in Iraq. Competence is the first challenge, and the U.S. training teams and partner units will play a major role. But the Iraqi Army must remain an impartial national force that is not seen as the armed wing of any faction or as an organization that wants to assume power for itself. The police are equally important, and they too must enforce and be perceived as enforcing the rule of law rather than their own agenda or that of any faction.

Reconciliation and Development

The success of the U.S. drawdown will depend on continued efforts by the United States and others to promote reconciliation and development within Iraq. Effective security forces and police are not the only factors that will determine whether the United States is able to meet its interests and goals during and after the drawdown: Continued, robust efforts to promote reconciliation among Iraqi regions, confessions, and tribal and other units of loyalty will be necessary, as will continued efforts to promote economic development. These activities will be expensive, and the United States will need active support from European and other allies, countries in the Middle East, and international organizations. As U.S. forces draw down, however, U.S. leverage over the GoI will decrease, as will the level of physical protection available both to American civilians and contractors who remain in the country and to non-Americans. This factor can condition decisions about drawdown rates and the locus of priorities for withdrawal.

Recommendations

As part of our analysis, we identified measures that would smooth the drawdown of U.S. forces or mitigate some of the potentially detrimental consequences of the drawdown discussed in the preceding chapters. We group those consequences into three risk categories: (1) risks to U.S. forces during the drawdown, (2) risks to Iraqi security and stability resulting from the withdrawal of U.S. forces, and (3) risks to regional political and military stability. The body of the report describes ways to mitigate a number of related issues (e.g., refugees, populations at risk). Below, we summarize mitigation measures in the form of recommendations focused on issues that pose the most risk in the three categories just described.

Arab-Kurdish Conflict

The KRG's aspirations for greater autonomy and its desire to incorporate more territory into its area of control endanger Iraq's unity and could spark serious internal conflict or provoke a response from one of Iraq's neighbors. The future status of Kirkuk and other disputed territories presents the most serious threat to internal stability in Iraq. Consequently, we recommend

- phasing the drawdown of combat forces so that those nearest the contested areas are the last to leave. The United States must be careful not to create false expectations among Kurdish leaders that U.S. troops might remain after December 31, 2011.
- exploring the possibility of a UN peacekeeping or military observer mission to the ISF and the *Peshmerga* along the Arab-Kurdish divide once the last U.S. forces depart in 2011. Alternatively, consider negotiating an extension of the U.S. presence for this purpose.
- coordinating diplomatic strategies for the region with Turkey and, if possible, Iran and Syria.

Iranian Subversion

Iran, operating largely through client organizations or operatives in Iraq, has the capability to cause considerable mischief. Whether it has the wish to do so remains a question. In many ways, its interests align with Iraq's, and it is not clear that Iran would wish to delay the U.S. withdrawal in any case. Consequently, we recommend that the United States

- open a dialogue with Iran, perhaps making bilateral relations contingent on Iranian behavior in Iraq
- increase its surveillance of Iranian-supported groups in Iraq and bolster efforts to disrupt Iranian clients in Iraq by stemming the flow of money to them.

A Return to Violence by the Sons of Iraq

The SoI were instrumental in reversing the spiral of violence in Sunni areas and at one point numbered about 100,000 fighters. They remain numerous and well equipped. Should the SoI become frustrated with the rate and degree to which they are being incorporated into Iraqi society, they have the potential to cause serious destabilization in Iraqi society. Consequently, we recommend that the United States

- employ diplomatic efforts aimed at ensuring that the GoI meets its commitments vis-à-vis the SoI
- seek ways to train the SoI and provide them new economic opportunities
- work with the GoI to forestall any destabilizing local measures, such as forced disarmament or local discrimination in housing or other benefits.

Iraqi Security Forces

In many ways, the future of Iraq rests on the skill of its security forces, particularly the Army and the NP. If they are unable or unwilling to preserve the gains made in security and stability, the country could slide back into chaos. While these forces are much improved, they still have serious shortcomings, especially in such enabling capabilities as long-range fires and air support and logistics. Consequently, we recommend that the United States

- keep U.S. personnel embedded with Iraqi security organizations in the country for as long as possible
- encourage the Iraqi Army to transfer its operations centers to the Iraqi police organizations so that they can assume the internal security duties that are properly their responsibility
- consider recasting its rules on foreign military sales so that the Iraqis do not have to deliver full payment up front, at least as long as oil prices remain low
- consider increasing funding for Iraqi officers to train in the United States as a way of improving the professionalism of Iraqi military leaders
- encourage the Iraqi Army to shift some of its forces from combat units to logistics to begin development of the supply capabilities they sorely need.

The Study's Legislative Background

In October 2007, Senator Edward Kennedy proposed funds in the 2008 Defense Appropriations bill for a federally funded research and development center, such as the RAND Corporation, to prepare an independent study of alternative schedules for the safe and secure withdrawal of U.S. military forces from Iraq.

In May 2008, Senator Kennedy's amendment to provide the funds was included in the Senate version of the Supplemental Appropriations bill. The amendment provided funds for the RAND Corporation to conduct an analysis of plans for the withdrawal of forces in Iraq in 12 months and in 18 months, but it was not included in the final law.

In September 2008, a provision to provide the RAND Corporation with $2.4 million to conduct an assesment of timelines for the withdrawal was enacted as part of the Consolidated Security, Disaster Assistance, and Continuing Appropriations bill.[1] It was strongly supported by Senator Daniel Inouye, Chairman of the Defense Subcommittee of the Appropriations Committee, and Senator Robert Byrd, Chairman of the Appropriations Committee. Senator Byrd described the intent of the study:

> There is funding in this bill to conduct an independent and objective study regarding the withdrawal of our troops from Iraq in the next 12 to 18 months. This bill includes $2.4 million for the Department of Defense to provide to the RAND Corporation to conduct this study. As a Federally-funded research and development center and an independent research arm of the Department of Defense, RAND has access to the Department of Defense information necessary to prepare such plans. . . . This study will assume that the United States will leave a limited number of troops in Iraq to train Iraqis, target Al Qaeda, and protect our mission after the withdrawal of the majority of our forces.[2]

The President signed the legislation into law on September 30, 2008, as P.L. 110-329.

---

[1] See U.S. House of Representatives, Committee on Appropriations, Consolidated Security, Disaster Assistance, and Continuing Appropriations Act, 2009, committee print of H.R. 2638/P.L. 110-329, October 2008, p. 515.

[2] U.S. Senate, *Congressional Record*, 110th Cong., 2d sess., September 27, 2008, p. S9885. The RAND Corporation is a private, nonprofit federally funded research and development center.

Drawdown of Remaining Forces

In addition to timelines for the drawdown of combat units, the alternatives presented in this report include drawdown schedules for the remaining forces (trainers, enablers, and support personnel). Alternative 1 calls for the early drawdown of all combat units, and alternative 2 calls for the early drawdown of all combat units and the transition of mission from combat to a noncombat role before the end of the Security Agreement period. In alternative 3, some combat units remain (along with support forces) to the end of the Security Agreement period in December 2011. This appendix details the size and composition of the force that will remain in Iraq through the end of the Security Agreement period under each alternative. In this appendix, we also discuss the formula by which we calculated the drawdown schedule for the support forces.

Tables B.1, B.2, and B.3 summarize the drawdown schedule for all three alternatives described in Chapter Two. The numbers in these tables were used to generate Figures 2.1, 2.2, and 2.3.

Enablers

Enablers provide critical support to Iraqi forces, such as logistics support, close air support, and ISR. It is likely that the ISF will require this support through the end of the Security Agreement period and beyond.

In alternative 1, the enabling forces are maintained at the initial levels until May 2011 to aid the ISF to the maximum degree before full withdrawal in December 2011. From June 2011, forces draw down linearly to zero in December 2011. In alternative 2, we retain the full complement of enablers (16,500 troops) through April 2010 and then begin to gradually draw them down to 8,000 by September 1, 2010. They remain at this level through the beginning of May 2011 and then draw down linearly through the end of December 2011. The re-roled AABs can provide considerable enabling support, and therefore there is less need for a separate enabling force. In alternative 3, we begin a linear drawdown from February 2010. As in alternative 2, the combat units remaining through the end of the Security Agreement period can provide some enabling support.

Table B.1
Drawdown Schedule for Alternative 1

Personnel	May 2009	Nov. 2009	Feb. 2010	May 2010	Sept. 2010	March 2011	May 2011	Dec. 2011
Combat units	62,000	40,000	20,000	0	0	0	0	0
Support*	60,000	47,000	36,000	24,000	19,000	12,000	9,000	0
Training	3,500	3,500	3,500	3,500	3,500	3,500	3,500	0
Enabling	16,500	16,500	16,500	16,500	16,500	16,500	16,500	0
Total	142,000	107,000	76,000	44,000	39,000	32,000	29,000	0

NOTE: Numbers may not total due to rounding.
* Details of the support forces breakdown are included in Table B.4.

Table B.2
Drawdown Schedule for Alternative 2

Personnel	May 2009	Nov. 2009	Feb. 2010	May 2010	Sept. 2010	March 2011	May 2011	Dec. 2011
Combat units	62,000	55,000	55,000	42,000	0	0	0	0
Support*	60,000	55,000	55,000	38,000	16,000	16,000	11,300	0
Training	3,500	3,500	3,500	3,000	2,000	2,000	1,000	0
Enabling	16,500	16,500	16,500	16,500	8,000	8,000	6,000	0
AABs	0	0	0	0	24,000	24,000	17,000	0
Total	142,000	130,000	130,000	100,000	50,000	50,000	35,000	0

NOTE: Numbers may not total due to rounding.
* Details of the support forces breakdown are included in Table B.5.

Table B.3
Drawdown Schedule for Alternative 3

Personnel	May 2009	Nov. 2009	Feb. 2010	May 2010	Sept. 2010	March 2011	May 2011	Dec. 2011
Combat units	62,000	40,000	40,000	34,000	27,000	13,000	10,000	0
Support*	60,000	47,000	47,000	40,000	31,000	16,000	12,000	0
Training	3,500	3,500	3,500	3,500	3,500	3,500	3,500	0
Enabling	16,500	16,500	16,500	14,000	11,000	6,000	5,000	0
Total	142,000	107,000	107,000	92,000	73,000	39,000	31,000	0

NOTE: Numbers may not total due to rounding.
* Details of the support forces breakdown are included in Table B.6.

Trainers

Based on current U.S. projections of ISF improvements (discussed in Chapter Two), drawdown alternative 2 decreases the total number of troops considered trainers beginning in February 2010. In alternatives 1 and 3, the number of trainers remains at pre-drawdown levels until May 2011. As mentioned in Chapter Two, it is desirable to link the departure of trainers to the competence level of Iraqi forces. However, the data available cannot support such an assessment. Consequently, the departing numbers shown in Figures 2.1, 2.2, and 2.3 in Chapter Two are a "best guess" at a reasonable drawdown schedule for trainers.

The number of trainers in Iraq is approximately 3,500, resident in the MTTs. In alternatives 1 and 3, training forces are maintained at the initial levels through the beginning of May 2011 to provide the maximum number of trainers for the ISF before full departure in December 2011. In alternative 2, the drawdown commences at the beginning of February 2010.

Advise and Assist Brigades

In alternative 2, the drawdown plan presented in Chapter Two calls for a transition force consisting of six AABs starting in September 2010, in addition to a number of enablers and trainers. The drawdown schedule calls for the reduction of two additional AABs from March 2011 to May 2011 and a linear reduction from May 2011 to the end of the Security Agreement period. Although their mission is changed to advising and supporting, these forces retain considerable combat capability and therefore are able to support enabling functions and respond to unforeseen contingencies in addition to providing support to trainers.

Support for Remaining Combat Brigades

The number of support troops required in Iraq and the number of BCTs still in the country are directly linked. For example, medical care for each BCT is provided by echelon-above-brigade medical assets. Therefore, as combat brigades depart, a proportionate number of medical units can also leave. To calculate the required number of support troops that would depart simultaneously with the combat brigades, we used a formula that is based on the direct or indirect relationships that exist between combat brigades, support units, and other organizations in theater.

These estimates are displayed for selected support forces and are portrayed in various categories (e.g., engineering, medical, air support) in Figures B.1, B.2, and B.3. Each figure presents data derived from various support-unit allocation rules developed for each category. The details and impact of these allocation rules are included in

Tables B.1, B.2, and B.3. Each table projects the number of support forces present in Iraq at varying intervals beginning in May 2009 and continuing on through December 2011. The May 2009 starting populations for each category were extracted from unclassified briefings and rounded to the nearest hundred. The figures also portray a trend line that represents the drawdown of combat brigades from Iraq.

The Factors

The first factor calculated in the model for each alternative is the direct relationship between support forces and the combat brigades, the multinational divisions, and the MNC-I. For example, the doctrinal allocation of medical support requires that a forward surgical team of 20 personnel be attached to each BCT to provide immediate trauma care and stabilization of severely wounded personnel. Therefore, as a BCT departs, the formula uses a rule of allocation to subtract 20 personnel each from the medical category, the total support number, and the total population in theater.

The model then calculates the support forces needed to provide area support for facilities and other activities independent of combat brigade support. For example, two security force companies with approximately 110 personnel each may provide the perimeter defense and entrance and egress control for a foward operating base (FOB). Therefore, as the FOB is transferred to the GoI or shut down, the formula uses a rule of allocation to subtract 220 personnel each from the security forces category, the total support numbers, and the total population in theater. The closure rate for bases is approximate. Chapter Three discusses base closure and transfer in more detail.

While direct and indirect relationships are calculated in the model, many other units in the theater of operations are not easily captured with simple projections and need to be weighed in view of combinations of factors. For example, approximately 9,000 MNF-I personnel are assigned to support detention operations. In view of this fact, the formula seeks to conservatively employ rules that determine the use of military police and medical and security forces involved in detention operations. These weighted rules may then combine with the logical assumption that as the BCTs depart, fewer detainees will be captured. Thus, as ongoing releases of detainees continue, the "pond is drained" and a conservative retrograde of all support forces involved in detention operations ensues over time.

Using the Formula

Tables B.4, B.5, and B.6 provide the data produced by applying the formula to alternatives 1, 2, and 3, respectively, giving a general framework of how forces might be configured and arrayed in the theater of operations. Figures B.1, B.2, and B.3 depict these data graphically, If the formula projects that there will be 1,200 medical personnel in theater supporting forces after all BCTs have departed, the model must maintain a logical disposition for medical units to provide suitable levels of support. For example, a portion of the 1,200 may consist of a combat support hospital and a medical logistics battalion.

Neither the projections from the formula nor the allocation of forces shown in the tables is definitive. The situation on the ground and the decisions of the MNF-I commander will determine how all forces will be employed in the theater of operations. Additionally, joint personnel billets, in-lieu-ofs (e.g., Navy units fulfilling Army roles), and special forces units were not calculated due to the complexity involved. Tables B.2 and B.5 and Figure B.2 reflect RAND's interpretation of how the administration's drawdown goals might be achieved.

Table B.4
Projection of Support Units for Drawdown Alternative 1

Unit or Personnel by Type	May 2009	Nov. 2009	Feb. 2010	May 2010	Sept. 2010	March 2011	May 2011	Dec. 2011
Both MNF-I and MNC-I or only MNC-I	2	2	2	2	1	1	1	1
MNDs	4	4	2	0	0	0	0	0
BCTs	14	9	4	0	0	0	0	0
Personnel	142,000	107,000	76,000	44,000	39,000	32,000	29,000	0
Support personnel	60,000	47,000	36,000	24,000	19,000	12,000	9,000	0
Military police[a]	13,500	7,200	4,500	1,800	1,700	900	600	0
Medical[b]	3,500	3,500	3,100	2,700	1,800	1,300	1,300	0
Transport/ quartermaster[c]	5,200	4,700	4,100	3,500	2,800	1,600	1,200	0
Security forces[d]	6,400	5,800	4,700	3,600	3,100	1,800	1,300	0
Engineering[e]	7,800	5,900	3,300	600	400	200	200	0
Air support[f]	8,000	8,000	6,700	5,400	4,200	2,800	2,400	0
Sustainment[g]	8,000	6,000	4,300	2,600	2,200	1,700	1,500	0
Support headquarters[h]	8,000	6,000	4,700	3,400	2,900	1,400	800	0

NOTE: Numbers may not total due to rounding.

[a] Support-unit rules: 1 company per BCT; 0.5 battalions per FOB; 2 brigades per MND or MNC-I.

[b] Support-unit rules: 0.25 Level II companies per FOB; 1 CSH per MND; 1 medical battalion per MNC-I or MNF-I; 0.75 brigades per MNC-I or MNF-I.

[c] Support-unit rules: 0.25 truck companies per FOB; 1 quartermaster company per FOB.

[d] Support-unit rules: 1.25 companies per FOB and BCT; 1 brigade per MNC-I or MNF-I.

[e] Support-unit rules: 1 company per FOB; 1 company per BCT; 1 battalion per MND; 1 brigade per MNC-I or MNF-I.

[f] Support-unit rules: 1 battalion per MND; 4 brigades per MNC-I or MNF-I.

[g] Roll-up of all other units, including corps support for MNF-I.

[h] One brigade plus headquarters per MNC-I or MNF-I.

Figure B.1
Flow of Support Units for Drawdown Alternative 1

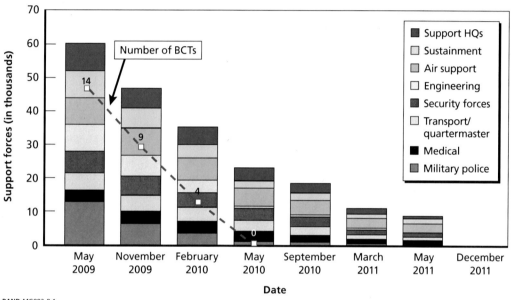

Table B.5
Projection of Support Units for Drawdown Alternative 2

Unit or Personnel by Type	May 2009	Nov. 2009	Feb. 2010	May 2010	Sept. 2010	March 2011	May 2011	Dec. 2011
Both MNF-I and MNC-I or only MNC-I	2	2	2	2	2	1	1	0
MNDs	4	4	4	2	0	0	0	0
BCTs	14	12	12	8	0	0	0	0
AABs	0	0	0	0	6	6	4	0
Personnel	142,000	130,000	130,000	100,000	50,000	50,000	35,000	0
Support personnel	60,000	55,000	55,000	38,000	16,000	16,000	11,300	0
Military police[a]	13,500	11,500	11,500	7,000	900	900	600	0
Medical[b]	3,500	3,500	3,500	2,700	1,700	1,700	1,200	0
Transport/ quartermaster[c]	5,200	4,700	4,700	3,400	1,600	1,600	1,100	0
Security forces[d]	6,400	5,800	5,800	4,200	2,100	2,100	1,500	0
Engineering[e]	7,800	7,100	7,100	4,200	300	300	200	0
Air support[f]	8,000	8,000	8,000	6,400	4,300	4,300	3,100	0
Sustainment[g]	8,000	7,000	7,000	5,000	2,400	2,400	1,700	0
Support headquarters[h]	8,000	7,000	7,000	5,200	2,700	2,700	1,900	0

NOTE: Numbers may not total due to rounding. We recognize that from February 2010 to September 2010, U.S. forces in Iraq will consist of a mixture of AABs, BCTs, and support personnel. However, the exact number of AABs is not known. Therefore, we leave them at zero in this table.

[a] Support-unit rules: 1 company per BCT; 0.5 battalions per FOB; 2 brigades per MND or MNC-I.

[b] Support-unit rules: 0.25 Level II companies per FOB; 1 CSH per MND; 1 medical battalion per MNC-I or MNF-I; 0.75 brigades per MNC-I or MNF-I.

[c] Support-unit rules: 0.25 truck companies per FOB; 1 quartermaster company per FOB.

[d] Support-unit rules: 1.25 companies per FOB and BCT; 1 brigade per MNC-I or MNF-I.

[e] Support-unit rules: 1 company per FOB; 1 company per BCT; 1 battalion per MND; 1 brigade per MNC-I or MNF-I.

[f] Support-unit rules: 1 battalion per MND; 4 brigades per MNC-I or MNF-I.

[g] Roll-up of all other units, including corps support for MNF-I.

[h] One brigade plus headquarters per MNC-I or MNF-I.

Figure B.2
Flow of Support Units for Drawdown Alternative 2

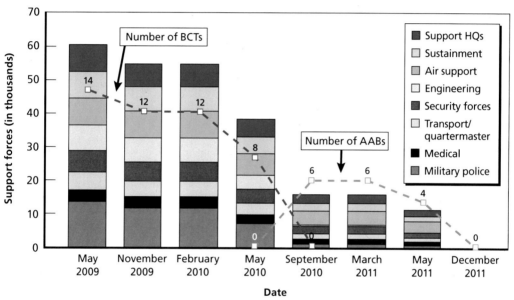

Table B.6
Projection of Support Units for Drawdown Alternative 3

Unit or Personnel by Type	May 2009	Nov. 2009	Feb. 2010	May 2010	Sept. 2010	March 2011	May 2011	Dec. 2011
Both MNF-I and MNC-I or only MNC-I	2	2	2	2	2	1	1	0
MNDs	4	4	4	4	3	2	2	0
BCTs	14	9	9	7	6	3	2	0
Personnel	142,000	107,000	107,000	92,000	73,000	39,000	31,000	0
Support personnel	60,000	47,000	47,000	40,000	31,000	16,000	12,000	0
Military police[a]	13,500	7,200	7,200	6,200	4,800	2,400	1,900	0
Medical[b]	3,500	3,500	3,500	3,000	2,300	1,200	900	0
Transport/ quartermaster[c]	5,200	4,700	4,700	4,000	3,100	1,600	1,200	0
Security forces[d]	6,400	5,800	5,800	5,000	3,900	1,900	1,500	0
Engineering[e]	7,800	5,900	5,900	5,000	3,900	2,000	1,600	0
Air support[f]	8,000	8,000	8,000	6,800	5,300	2,700	2,100	0
Sustainment[g]	8,000	6,000	6,000	5,100	4,000	2,000	1,600	0
Support headquarters[h]	8,000	6,000	6,000	5,100	4,000	2,000	1,600	0

NOTE: Numbers may not total due to rounding.

[a] Support-unit rules: 1 company per BCT; 0.5 battalions per FOB; 2 brigades per MND or MNC-I.

[b] Support-unit rules: 0.25 Level II companies per FOB; 1 CSH per MND; 1 medical battalion per MNC-I or MNF-I; 0.75 brigades per MNC-I or MNF-I.

[c] Support-unit rules: 0.25 truck companies per FOB; 1 quartermaster company per FOB.

[d] Support-unit rules: 1.25 companies per FOB and BCT; 1 brigade per MNC-I or MNF-I.

[e] Support-unit rules: 1 company per FOB; 1 company per BCT; 1 battalion per MND; 1 brigade per MNC-I or MNF-I.

[f] Support-unit rules: 1 battalion per MND; 4 brigades per MNC-I or MNF-I.

[g] Roll-up of all other units, including corps support for MNF-I.

[h] One brigade plus headquarters per MNC-I or MNF-I.

Figure B.3
Flow of Support Units for Drawdown Alternative 3

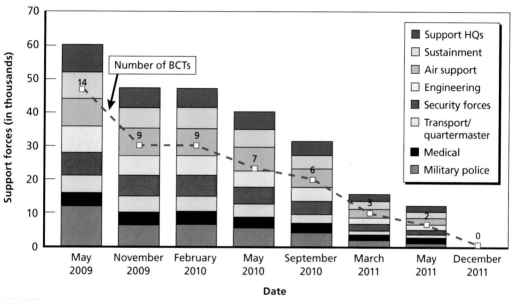

Economic and Advisory Issues Involved in a Drawdown of U.S. Forces from Iraq

Introduction

As U.S. forces draw down from Iraq, the stability and future course of Iraq will depend on more than the ability of the ISF to maintain internal and external security. It will also depend on Iraq's ability to pay for reconstruction and government services, revive its oil sector, improve the operations of its government at all levels, and expand its non-oil economy. All of these will be challenges. The subsequent sections focus on (1) the Iraqi budget and the oil sector, since oil export revenues provide the vast majority of the GoI's revenues; (2) U.S. assistance programs, since these may help the GoI improve its performance and the functioning of the Iraqi economy; and (3) international payment obligations, such as debt service, since large international payments may impair the GoI's ability to fund reconstruction and government services. Each of these sections contains an introduction to the problem, a statement of the risks to Iraq and to U.S. interests, and possible measures for mitigating these risks.

Such mitigation will take place under three sets of policy guidance and constraints: the Obama administration's plan for drawing down all U.S. combat brigades by August 31, 2010, and leaving a residual force of 35,000–50,000; the Security Agreement, signed by the United States and Iraq on November 17, 2008, which calls for all U.S. troops to exit Iraq by December 31, 2011; and the Strategic Framework Agreement (SFA), also signed by the United States and Iraq on November 17, 2008, which specifies nonbinding goals and an implementation structure for cooperation in seven areas (political and diplomatic, defense and security, culture, economy and energy, health and environment, information technology and communications, and law enforcement and justice).[1] The Security Agreement in particular signals a changing relationship

---

[1]   Obama, 2009a; Agreement Between the United States of America and the Republic of Iraq on the Withdrawal of United States Forces from Iraq and the Organization of Their Activities During Their Temporary Presence in Iraq, signed in Baghdad on November 17, 2008; Strategic Framework Agreement for a Relationship of Friendship and Cooperation Between the United States of America and the Republic of Iraq, signed in Baghdad on November 17, 2008.

between Iraq and the United States because it emphasizes the sovereignty of Iraq. This changing relationship includes a more limited U.S. ability to influence Iraqi actions. As a result, the United States will need more Iraqi concurrence and participation in advisory and assistance programs than in previous years—a good assistance strategy in any case.

The Iraqi Budget and Oil

Continued stability in Iraq as the United States draws down its forces will depend in part on improvement in the ISF, reconstruction spending, and the improvement of GoI services. These will in turn depend on GoI expenditures. Iraq's budget depends almost entirely on oil exports.[2] These in turn depend on the price Iraq can get for its exports, the amount of oil it can produce, and the integrity of its export infrastructure. Prices have fallen dramatically since the summer of 2008, with the weekly average price for Basra light crude peaking at $133 per barrel in early July 2008, bottoming at $31 per barrel at the end of December 2008, and then rising to almost $66 as of June 2009. Production in the southern fields, the country's main oil fields, is declining in the absence of adequate field-development investment. Furthermore, the underwater feeder pipelines to the al-Basra Oil Terminal, Iraq's main export terminal, are thought to be seriously degraded. If a catastrophic failure occurs, Iraq will have few short-term options for moving the al-Basra terminal's export volumes to market.[3] In addition, the effort to modernize Iraq's oil laws has stalled over disputes between the Arabs and the Kurds. In the absence of new oil laws, contracting efforts have not yet been success-ful in bringing in new technology or investment to rehabilitate old fields and open the many unexploited new fields.

Recent Budget Developments

The drop in oil prices has already had an effect on Iraqi budget planning. Iraq approved $72 billion in spending in 2008 through both a regular and a supplemental budget, up sharply from 2007; that total included $11 billion in security spending and $21 billion for capital spending (including reconstruction).[4] However, the 2009 budget, approved in early March 2009 by the Council of Representatives and ratified by the Presidency Council in April 2009, includes a spending plan that, at $58.6 billion, is almost 20 per-cent lower.[5] Despite this reduction in spending, expected revenue from oil is down so

---

[2]   International Monetary Fund, 2007, 2008a, and 2008b.

[3]   Dombey and Hoya, 2008.

[4]   U.S. Department of State, 2008.

[5]   All 2009 budget figures are from Special Inspector General for Iraq Reconstruction, 2009b.

much that the budget projects a deficit of $15.9 billion. Approved after several rounds of cuts, the budget was first proposed in 2008 at $79.8 billion.

The approved 2009 budget consists of an operating budget of $46 billion and a capital budget of $13 billion.[6] It provides about $9.1 billion for the MoD and the MoI combined, about 17 percent less than the amount provided for in the base and supplemental 2008 budgets.[7] Such a level of security spending will force Iraq to make painful choices between COIN and external defense missions, and it will fund lower-than-expected security-force manpower levels. In addition, the budget assumes an oil price of $50 per barrel and exports of 2 million barrels per day (mbpd), both optimistic assumptions.[8] Since 2003, Iraq has never had a full quarter in which exports averaged 2 mbpd or more. Although production averaged 2.4 mbpd in 2008, exports averaged 1.8 mbpd during the same period.[9] Iraq received an average of about $92 per barrel for its exports in 2008, but in 2009 (through the end of March), it has received only $36 per barrel. However, the price of oil has started to rise. The price for Basra light crude, which constitutes the majority of Iraq's exports, registered less than $40 per barrel through most of January 2009, but rose to almost $66 in the second week of June 2009. In addition, the futures price Brent crude oil, to which Basra light trades at a 5–10 percent discount, was above $71 per barrel for the July 2009 through December 2009 contracts on the New York Mercantile Exchange as of the second week of June 2009 and was above $75 for all of 2010 and 2011.[10]

Risk

The threat posed by decreased oil revenues to Iraqi economic stability is real. Iraq's revenues will be sharply lower in 2009 than the record income levels obtained in 2008, and they may be constrained farther into the future. Production from the major southern oil fields is declining because of natural reductions in production and because of oil-field management problems.[11] Between 2004 and 2008, revenue from crude-oil exports averaged 89 percent of total GoI revenue.[12] Based on this proportion and assuming a more realistic export level of 1.8 mbpd, Iraq would need to receive $79 per barrel in order to run a balanced budget of $58.6 billion, the level approved for 2009. This would also mean a per-barrel price for Brent crude in the $80s.

---

[6] Iraqi Council of Representatives, 2009. Iraqi dinar values are converted at the rate of 1,170 dinars per U.S. dollar, the rate for most of February 2009 according to Central Bank of Iraq, 2009.

[7] RAND communication with U.S. government officials, March 2009.

[8] Abdul-Zahra with Yacoub, 2009; Special Inspector General for Iraq Reconstruction, 2009b.

[9] Data from Special Inspector General for Iraq Reconstruction, various quarterly and semiannual reports to the U.S. Congress.

[10] Prices are for the "Brent Crude Oil—Last Day" contract.

[11] U.S. Department of State, 2008; Special Inspector General for Iraq Reconstruction, 2009a.

[12] International Monetary Fund, 2007, 2008a, and 2008b.

Iraq's vulnerability to this threat is two-fold. First, with decreased revenues, Iraq may not be able to pay fully for what it deems to be its security needs. The level of security spending expected for 2009 will force Iraq to make painful choices between COIN and external defense missions. Second, Iraq may not be able to meet its immediate reconstruction needs and, in particular, may not be able to continue to expand essential services, such as water, sewerage, and electricity. The consequences of each of these vulnerabilities are interrelated and pertain to the United States' medium- and long-term interest in a stable Iraq. Failure to build up the ISF as the U.S. military draws down could lead to a security vacuum and instability. Failure to continue to make gains in public services could lead to poor economic performance, inadequate job creation, and political instability and unrest. An impaired security service might not be able to counter this unrest, leading to greater security threats.

Mitigating Measures

Raising and diversifying government revenues is largely a medium- to long-term proposition that depends on increasing oil production and expanding the non-oil economy and with it the tax base of the government. The United States by itself has few options aside from working with the Iraqis to help them formulate and implement their own policies. Several mitigating measures fall under the category of better budgeting. Two are working with Iraq to (1) set better priorities regarding the use of the more-limited revenues it will have and (2) remove government subsidies or increase their efficiency. Over the longer term, U.S. mitigating measures could include support for increased oil production and improved infrastructure, although limited public U.S. involvement in changing the hydrocarbons regime may ease the political challenges associated with such change. All options for increasing Iraqi oil production successfully are likely to require international private-sector involvement. Measures for expanding the non-oil economy are included in this appendix's section on support for the Iraqi economy and governance.

One mitigating circumstance is that despite the fall in revenues, Iraq does not have an immediate spending crisis. This is because the country has accumulated budget surplus balances due to past high oil prices and an inability to increase spending commensurately, especially for public works projects and especially for budget years 2005–2007. The accumulated budget surplus balance at the end of 2008 totaled $46 billion. However, available reserves could be much lower, even as little as $20 billion, since the accumulated surplus balance includes funds tied to open letters of credit and obligated but not yet spent for capital projects. For example, out of a $21.1 billion investment budget in 2008, Iraq spent $8.5 billion but committed an additional $8.2 billion, leaving a true surplus balance of less than $5 billion.[13] Nonetheless, the overall accumulated true surplus balance could cover the expected gap between 2009

---

[13] Data are from Special Inspector General for Iraq Reconstruction, 2009b, pp. 26, 97.

expenditures and revenue.[14] Trouble may start in 2010 if the accumulated balance is spent down in 2009, and this problem is likely to become even more serious in 2011, when Iraq has to begin making payments on its international debt.

Better Budgeting. A number of measures by the United States can improve Iraq's budget in the short to medium terms. We first list those that can be implemented over a shorter timeframe and are politically easier to implement; these measures are followed by those that will require a longer time to implement and may be more politically difficult:

- **Work with Iraq to help it better set priorities.** U.S. advisors can work with Iraq to better prioritize the ways in which its more-limited revenues are used. For example, in the security realm, this would involve keeping Iraqi defense expenditures focused on immediate COIN and internal security needs and deferring most purchases of external defense–related weapon systems.
- **Support technical assistance to improve systems for budgeting and expenditures.** Steps include working with Iraq to make sure it fully utilizes its new Financial Management Information System, which will help it track its expenditures, and helping it complete a government-employee census, which will help remove "ghost employees" (employees that exist in name only and are used to funnel money from the government illicitly) from the payrolls. Both of these reforms would reduce opportunities for corruption and ensure that a greater proportion of public spending is used as intended.
- **Work with Iraq to make support for the poor more efficient.** The Public Distribution System—a publicly provided food basket—is costly and inefficient;[15] proposed efforts to monetize it and replace it with a social safety net could be accelerated. Direct income support would better target resources to the poor.
- **Encourage Iraq to remove or reduce government subsidies.** The Iraqis have already demonstrated their ability to remove subsidies: In 2006 and 2007, they lifted price controls and subsidies on some key refined oil products under the first International Monetary Fund Stand-By Arrangement.[16] However, many subsidies remain. Electricity from the public grid is essentially free, for example, and a metering effort and gradual increases in rates to full-cost recovery levels could provide capital for expansion and maintenance of the system, which would enable the Ministry of Electricity to provide more-reliable electricity for more hours than it now does. Many Iraqis are already paying for electricity through neighborhood generators, so moving away from free electricity should not be totally alien, and if

---

[14] For example, one report states that the balance in the Development Fund for Iraq at the end of October 2008 was $24 billion (International Monetary Fund, 2008b).

[15] International Monetary Fund, 2008b.

[16] International Monetary Fund, 2007.

public supply increases, such a change could even reduce their overall electricity costs. In addition, U.S. advisors can work with Iraqis on the writing of privatization laws and on embarking on a privatization of government-owned industrial assets to raise capital and end subsidies to enterprises that could be private.

Expanding Oil Production and Exports. In the longer term, Iraqi revenues can be boosted through the rehabilitation of existing oil fields and the development of new ones. Foreign investment and expertise will be required for this—by one estimate, $75 billion of investment is needed to raise output from current production of about 2.4 mbpd to the Ministry of Oil's goal of 6 mbpd in 2017.[17] The main question is how best to create the incentives for that involvement, given oil market and Iraqi political realities. For several years, the United States has favored a program that includes a new law governing exploration, production, and foreign participation; a new law on sharing oil revenue throughout the country; a new law creating an Iraqi National Oil Company out of the numerous operating companies currently existing within the Ministry of Oil; and a new law turning the Ministry of Oil into a regulatory ministry rather than an operating ministry.[18] None of these laws has been passed, however, and the most important—the law on exploration, production, and foreign participation—has been stalled largely due to constitutional disagreements between the KRG and the central government.

However, Iraq may be able to attract substantial foreign participation without these laws, and U.S. advocacy to complete the legislative program may actually have been counterproductive. In the absence of legal reform, the Ministry of Oil has begun two bidding rounds for technical service contracts, funded by the Iraqi budget, to allow foreign companies to both rehabilitate currently producing fields and open new fields.[19] Because of the terms being offered, it is unclear whether these bidding rounds will be successful. Even if they are, it is unclear whether the now-constrained Iraqi budget can afford the expense. In most cases, significant incremental production may be at least two years away. There should be little expectation of substantially increased production or export volumes during the three-year term of the Security Agreement.

The United States can pursue several mitigating measures when it comes to the hydrocarbon sector. We first list those likely to prove the least costly (because, for example, they use existing U.S. staff); these measures are followed by those that are likely to prove more costly (because, for example, they require additional staff or active military operational involvement). To minimize Iraqi political sensitivity to its involvement, the United States may wish to maintain a low profile in pursuing any of these measures:

---

[17] U.S. Department of Defense, 2008.

[18] U.S. Department of State and Broadcasting Board of Governors Office of Inspector General, 2009.

[19] U.S. Department of State, 2009.

- **Provide assistance to Iraq's own short-term effort.** First and most immediately, the U.S. government can provide technical assistance to a short-term oil-sector recovery plan developed by a new committee that is chaired by Deputy Prime Minister Barham Salih and includes former oil ministers Thamer Ghadban and Ibraham Bahr al-Uloum.[20]

- **Assist with contracting for international participation.** The U.S. government can provide contracting experts (or can help the Ministry of Oil assess such experts that it would directly employ) to (1) help structure the technical service contracts and other possible arrangements in a way that increases the likelihood that international oil companies will agree to them and (2) improve other conditions that would allow the bidding rounds to succeed and new investment to start flowing.

- **Continue and expand U.S. technical and security assistance regarding infrastructure integrity.** U.S. military and civilian agencies are providing assistance to the Ministry of Oil and the Iraqi military regarding maintenance, protection, and rehabilitation of current oil facilities to ensure that pipelines and export terminals do not fail and thereby further reduce Iraq's revenues.[21] Examples of such assistance include direct financing, connecting ministries with companies capable of carrying out ministry infrastructure plans, and facilitating agreements between ministries.[22] Assistance in planning and contracting for infrastructure repairs should continue, especially those that increase export redundancy (such as rebuilding the north-south Iraq Strategic Pipeline or the underwater feeder pipelines to the al-Basra offshore terminal). Although the Iraqi Navy will have taken over point security for the smaller of the two southern export terminals, Khawr al-Amayah Oil Terminal, by spring 2009, the Iraqi Navy does not have the capability to take over perimeter security for that terminal or point and perimeter security for the more important nearby al-Basra Oil Terminal. The U.S., British, and other navies should therefore continue to provide security and training assistance.[23]

Pursuing Economic Development. The longest-term solution to Iraq's revenue problems is economic growth and diversification. The next section discusses U.S. assistance programs regarding political and economic development.

---

[20] "Iraq Considers $200 Million Plan to Reverse Oil-Output Decline," 2009.

[21] Special Inspector General for Iraq Reconstruction, 2009a.

[22] Special Inspector General for Iraq Reconstruction, 2008 and 2009a.

[23] Marsden, 2009; Watkins, 2008.

Support for the Iraqi Economy and Governance

The United States has an interest in a stable Iraq with a functioning government and economy. The SFA is tangible evidence of this interest and of the U.S. commitment to helping Iraq achieve stability and a functioning economy. Beyond that agreement, there are several reasons why governance and the economy remain U.S.—rather than just Iraqi—interests. Continued dysfunctional governance, continued low employment, and continued lack of economic diversification may lead to instability and degrade the security environment during the drawdown, endangering U.S. troops and putting political and security gains at risk.

Risk

The likelihood of poor governance and mediocre economic performance as the United States draws down is very high, potentially harming the broader U.S. interest in a more peaceful and prosperous Iraq. The U.S. civilian-led PRTs have provided an important bridge between provincial and tribal leaders and the central government.[24] U.S. civilian and military advisors have helped the Iraqis plan their budgets, run their procurement systems, and even improve interministerial communications. In addition, U.S. military operations and various aid and reconstruction programs employ as many as 100,000 Iraqis, and the drawdown could cause instability in local areas where this employment is concentrated.[25]

Mitigating Measures

The United States will have only limited tools with which to influence Iraq. First, the money available for physical reconstruction projects is nearly depleted,[26] and funding for advisory programs is declining (and, unless additional funding is appropriated, will mostly run out in 2010). Second, staffing and organization is not ideal for stabilization and reconstruction operations.[27]

As a result of limited tools and the need for Iraqi concurrence and participation, the U.S. government should better align the goals of its assistance programs with the resources available, and it should work, to the extent possible, within the new committees established under the SFA as a means of engaging the Iraqis.

---

[24] U.S. Department of State, 2008.

[25] For example, Joint Contracting Command–Iraq/Afghanistan reported that as of January 2, 2009, 76,000 Iraqis were employed with the U.S. contracting workforce (Special Inspector General for Iraq Reconstruction, 2009a).

[26] Special Inspector General for Iraq Reconstruction, 2009a.

[27] Bensahel, 2008; and Bensahel, Oliker, and Peterson, 2009.

- **Align ends and means.** The U.S. government now has less leverage in the form of money to give than it did in 2003–2008, and Iraq now places a higher value on sovereignty than it did before. Therefore, any programs will need Iraqi buy-in and must be conducted in coordination with the Iraqis. Before the U.S. fiscal year 2010 budget is completed, U.S. and Iraqi political and economic leaders should review areas where Iraq needs assistance, revise the U.S. assistance strategy to improve the match between goals and resources, and plan to keep essential programs well-funded over several budget cycles while retaining the flexibility to move money to meet changing conditions. Such a program review might show that all current U.S. programs are essential, but it is likely that some programs will be identified as outmoded and that new programs will be found to be necessary. In addition, such a program review could increase the probability of buy-in from the U.S. Congress and from the Iraqis.
- **Work through the SFA.** The mechanism for aligning U.S. and Iraqi goals should be the committees established under the SFA, which the Iraqis are coming to view as the main bilateral planning document. These committees just started to meet in February 2009. Using them successfully will involve ensuring that they are properly staffed on both the Iraqi and U.S. sides and that they garner appropriate attention from top officials in the U.S. mission.

The following mitigation measures can form the basis of a joint U.S.-Iraqi effort to bring about further positive evolution in governance and the economy. The first four measures address more-immediate issues or could affect stability during the drawdown. The last four have longer-term outlooks or could help reduce the U.S. effort while still maintaining an advisory and assistance program for Iraq:

- **Adopt a hold-steady approach.** The U.S. military drawdown will breed greater uncertainty regarding security, stability, governance, and the economy. In the absence of a full review of assistance efforts, U.S. civilian advisory capabilities should be maintained at current levels or even increased to backfill some functions led by the MNF-I. One example of such a function is the Energy Fusion Cell, which is situated in the International Zone and works with the U.S. Embassy Baghdad's economic section, the U.S. energy attaché, and international donors to support Iraq's ministries of oil, electricity, and interior.[28] Maintaining (or increasing) U.S. civilian advisory capabilities will necessarily involve the hiring of special staff rather than drawing on scarce Foreign Service generalists. The authority for hiring such special staffers, known as 3161s, is due to expire in spring 2010, when the Iraq Transition Assistance Office sunsets;[29] such authority should be extended

---

[28] Special Inspector General for Iraq Reconstruction, 2009a.

[29] Bush, 2007.

through the end of the Security Agreement. Besides maintaining capabilities, the United States will have to ensure that security is maintained for assistance providers.

- **Pay particular attention to Iraqi budget execution.** Although improved, the Iraqis' ability to spend their entire federal budget in the year of its allotment is still hampered by the inexperience of many government workers, a

> lack of understanding of the budget process at all levels of the GOI, frustration with and misunderstanding of the roles of the MOF [Ministry of Finance] and MOP [Ministry of Planning and International Development], confusing rules for attaining and using letters of credit, lack of automated reporting systems, centralized management of budget spending authority, security issues, and the lack of qualified contractors.[30]

Additional problems at the provincial level include "insufficient training, a shortage of certified accountants, and a lack of clear guidance from Baghdad."[31] In some cases, budgeting, procurement, and related financial transactions have been facilitated through the U.S. Treasury–led civilian-military Public Finance Management Assistance Group. These facilitating efforts should remain in place at least through the end of the Security Agreement, especially since it is increasingly likely that Iraq will face severe budget pressures in 2010 or 2011.

- **Maintain the PRTs.** In the wake of January 2009's provincial elections, many new provincial councils and governors have little or no governing experience and will be called on not only to learn how to govern but to implement a new provincial powers law. These elections took place in 14 provinces and excluded the disputed province of Kirkuk and the three provinces that constitute the Kurdistan region. National elections scheduled for the end of 2009 may further change the dynamics between the central government and the provinces. Therefore, the PRTs should be maintained as the military draws down, and PRT security should be made a priority mission for the remaining forces. (Expansion of the PRTs may be an option to make up for advisory and assistance tasks the military was performing.) It is notable that PRTs in Karbala and Najaf have been effectively secured even with limited U.S. forces in the provinces. Particular attention should be paid to regions that are economically important—such as Basra—or that face a higher risk of instability—such as those in the north, where Arab-Kurdish tensions may be high. Specialized economic- and political-development staff should be added where needed, and every effort should be made to continue to incorporate such staff from friendly countries and international organizations (especially UN agencies) to internationalize the effort.

---

[30] U.S. Department of Defense, 2008, p. 9.

[31] U.S. Department of Defense, 2008, p. 3.

Even without the changes resulting from elections and the new provincial powers law, assistance to provinces would remain important for several reasons: The Iraqis have committed to a federal system, provincial self-government is new and unusual, and greater skills are needed at the provincial level to make sure the central government spends money where it is most needed in each province. Beginning in 2006, all Iraqi government operational expenses, including salaries for provincial employees and Provincial Council members, are budgeted and controlled centrally for the 15 provinces outside the Kurdistan region. In addition, national ministries carry out their own capital and reconstruction projects (for example, repairing electricity, water, and oil and gas infrastructure) throughout the country, except in the Kurdistan region. The 15 provinces receive a capital budget they can use for provincial reconstruction projects with the approval of the Provincial Councils. Coordinating the provincial and national budget streams can be challenging even for well-trained, experienced government officials. Budgeting in the Kurdistan region works differently. The KRG receives 17 percent of both the national capital and operating budgets, with small adjustments, which, with the approval of the region's parliament, it uses within the region.

- **Recognize that different parts of Iraq will require different levels of U.S. assistance during the drawdown.** There are two geographic aspects to supporting the Iraqi economy and governance during the drawdown. First, there are Iraqi areas that may exhibit greater ethnic or sectarian tensions as drawdown occurs. A greater PRT or other assistance presence can help mediate between provincial and central authorities and help stave off dramatic economic problems. Second, there are Iraqi areas where the withdrawal from coalition bases and programs could lead to thousands of Iraqis losing their jobs. Although approximately 6 million people in Iraq are currently employed, the loss of even a few thousand jobs could breed instability if it is geographically concentrated. If the jobs are base-related and the bases are shifting from U.S. to Iraqi control, then assistance programs should be instituted to help shift the employment to the Iraqi base. If the job losses are related to the end of a U.S. assistance program or the closure of a coalition base that is not being transitioned to the Iraqis, then the U.S. government could provide direct assistance to those affected by its drawdown to smooth their transition to a postdrawdown Iraq. Options include lump-sum payments to the people losing their jobs, unemployment payments for a period, and job-training programs and small-business assistance to help those losing their jobs find or create new employment.
- **Continue to include the oil sector in U.S. assistance planning.** This sector will remain the main source of Iraqi government funding. See "The Iraqi Budget and Oil," above.
- **Shift from stabilization programs to longer-term development programs.** Although there is still a need for short-term projects to bring stability to areas

where violence has declined but not disappeared, Iraq's long-term economic health and the growth of a private sector will depend on the development of a legal and regulatory framework that supports business development and finance. This argues in favor of programs that will help Iraq (1) revise its laws and regulations regarding starting, operating, and closing a business; (2) build up the financial sector to provide working capital and other types of business financing; and (3) accede to the World Trade Organization, which requires changes in a country's legal and regulatory framework. Iraq has started to recognize these needs, with Planning Minister Ali Baban calling in February 2009 for new banking and capital markets laws and other legislative changes.[32]

- **Train the trainers and facilitate the hiring of outside experts.** Although past U.S. assistance efforts have involved funding for reconstruction, assistance programs have evolved toward capacity building and training.[33] This evolution toward capacity building and training should continue along two paths. The first is training Iraqis to be trainers. Assistance in this form is cheaper and will increase the human capital of Iraqis. The second is helping the GoI pay for its own expert advisors, capital improvements, and reconstruction costs, which will increase the likelihood that the advice, goods, and systems purchased will be those that the Iraqis actually want and will maintain. The type of help U.S. officials can provide in this area includes assistance in writing statements of work and solicitations and in evaluating proposals from potential vendors.

- **Internationalize assistance.** Attempts to internationalize assistance have been made before. These include the International Reconstruction Fund Facility for Iraq, now coming to a close; the International Compact for Iraq, which continues; and two Stand-By Arrangements with the International Monetary Fund. As an executive director at the International Monetary Fund and the World Bank, the United States should work with these institutions to maintain or increase their involvement with Iraq. The World Bank in particular could increase its in-county presence to assist the Iraqis in accessing its credit windows and to provide advisory services. It should also attempt to bring in additional international aid agencies beyond those already involved and consider including them under the U.S. security umbrella, if they request such help. Bringing in more agencies may require heightened diplomatic effort on the part of the United States, but their involvement can help reduce the burden on U.S. departments and agencies.

Even with a strong advisory and assistance program, progress in developing the private Iraqi economy is likely to be slow. Few oil-rich developing countries have robust

---

[32] Ketz, 2009.

[33] Interview with then-Ambassador Ryan Crocker, in Special Inspector General for Iraq Reconstruction, 2009a, pp. 5–6.

democracies and large private sectors. In the broadest terms, (1) state-controlled oil revenues tend to make rulers less responsive to the population because their countries' taxation needs are lower than those of non-oil countries and (2) large, resource-fueled public sectors crowd out the private sector and raise the cost of doing business.

International Payments

Iraq faces substantial international payment obligations that could hamper its ability to fund economic development, reconstruction, and government services. There are three streams of such payments: external debt service; payments due on compensation claims pursued within a UN process, stemming from the 1990 invasion of Kuwait and the 1991 Gulf War; and commercial and other claims, pursued outside the UN process, stemming from actions of the regime of Saddam Hussein and that could result in the attachment of Iraqi assets held outside the country.

Debt. Iraq had a sizable external debt burden when Operation Iraqi Freedom began in 2003, most of which was in default. With the involvement of the Paris Club of creditor nations and strong support from the United States, 31 countries had, as of March 2009, reduced their claims on Iraq by 80 percent or more.[34] However, total Iraqi debt outstanding is still estimated at $52 billion–$76 billion, with most owed to Kuwait, Saudi Arabia, and China.[35] Helping reduce Iraq's international debt is a U.S. commitment: Article 26 of the Security Agreement obligates the United States to "support Iraq to obtain forgiveness of international debt resulting from the policies of the former regime."[36]

Compensation Within the UN Process. Pursuant to a UN Security Council resolution, Iraq makes payments to a UN Compensation Fund on claims stemming from the 1990 invasion of Kuwait through an allocation of 5 percent of its exports of oil, oil products, and natural gas. Filed by governments and international organizations, these claims include those arising from individuals who suffered some type of loss or harm stemming from Iraq's invasion of Kuwait; those arising from businesses, other private entities, and public-sector enterprises that claim losses on contracts, the destruction of assets, or other business losses; and those arising from governments and international organizations that incurred losses in evacuating citizens, damage to property,

---

[34] International Monetary Fund, 2008b; National Media Center, General Secretariat for the Council of Ministers, Republic of Iraq, 2009.

[35] U.S. Department of Defense, 2008; Weiss, 2008.

[36] Agreement Between the United States of America and the Republic of Iraq on the Withdrawal of United States Forces from Iraq and the Organization of Their Activities During Their Temporary Presence in Iraq, signed in Baghdad on November 17, 2008.

or damage to the environment.[37] By the end of October 2008, the UN Compensation Commission, which oversees the Compensation Fund, had awarded compensation of $52 billion, half of which Iraq had paid and half of which it still owed.[38]

Other International Claims. Iraq has exposure to commercial and other claims in the United States and around the world. Currently, Iraq's assets are immune from most attachments under several mechanisms. Iraq's oil revenues go into the Development Fund for Iraq, which is largely held in the Federal Reserve Bank of New York. This arrangement is provided for by successive UN Security Council resolutions, the most recent of which applies until December 31, 2009.[39] This resolution directs all nations to provide immunity from attachment for Iraqi oil and gas, oil and gas revenues, and assets and revenues deposited in the Development Fund for Iraq. In the United States, this obligation is implemented under executive orders invoking the International Emergency Economic Powers Act and other laws, and these executive orders also add all accounts held by the Central Bank of Iraq to the protected assets. The original executive order, which others rely on, modify, and add to, is valid for 12 months at a time, and its most recent extension took place in May 2009 and will expire in May 2010.[40] In addition, a 2003 presidential determination makes inapplicable to Iraq 1996 changes to the Foreign Sovereign Immunities Act that had allowed people to sue Iraq for such acts as torture, extrajudicial killing, and hostage-taking.[41] Iraq has been a defendant in lawsuits initiated by U.S. citizens under the 1996 provision, with claims estimated in the billions of dollars, and these plaintiffs had challenged the immunity granted to Iraq by the presidential determination. However, the U.S. Supreme Court ruled in June 2009 that the presidential determination was valid, meaning that these lawsuits could not proceed.[42] Nonetheless, commercial cases and perhaps other cases against Iraq related to the Saddam Hussein era can proceed around the world, putting Iraqi assets at risk of attachment.

Risk

Iraq is scheduled to start servicing its rescheduled international debt in 2011, with a low estimate of expected debt obligations in that year of $2.4 billion.[43] If the budget numbers stay constant, budget execution remains low, and debt forgiveness is not forthcom-

---

[37] United Nations Compensation Commission, undated-a.

[38] United Nations Compensation Commission, 2008.

[39] United Nations Security Council, 2008.

[40] Obama, 2009b.

[41] Bush, 2003; United States Code §1605(a)(7), 2000 (repealed).

[42] Supreme Court of the United States, 2009.

[43] International Monetary Fund, 2008b. This amount is equivalent to about 4 percent of the proposed 2009 budget and more than 20 percent of the proposed 2009 security budget.

ing from the remaining sovereign creditors, either debt service could be substantially higher as a proportion of actual expenditures or Iraq could default. Compensation to the UN fund would amount to an additional $1.6 billion annually, assuming oil exports of 1.8 mbpd and a price received by Iraq of $50 per barrel. Iraq's exposure to lawsuits is impossible to predict at this time.

The main threat posed by high levels of international payments is that Iraq will have fewer resources to pay for its reconstruction, improvement of government services, and security. High levels of debt and the risk of having assets seized could harm Iraq's ability to borrow on international capital markets when its own revenues are insufficient to support reconstruction, improvement of government services, and adequate security. In addition, enhancing Iraq's ability to rebuild itself and achieve a functioning economy is a U.S. goal under the SFA.[44]

Mitigating Measures

One way to mitigate all of these problems is to make more aid available to Iraq, through either bilateral or multilateral mechanisms. Whether this can be done will depend entirely on (1) how high a value countries place on security and stability in Iraq and (2) whether they believe aid can help achieve these goals. Large flows of inward foreign investment, such as for oil exploration and development, would also reduce the burden of international payments that Iraq will owe. However, Iraq's ability to attract such flows will depend on the business environment it creates and the ability of private investors to earn profits and recover their capital. Some relevant measures for improving the business environment were included in our discussion about shifting from stabilization programs to longer-term development programs. The measures below specifically address debt, compensation, and other claims.

Debt. Achieving debt reduction with Iraq's remaining sovereign creditors will be difficult. The key countries are China, Kuwait, and Saudi Arabia. Although a memorandum of understanding with China was signed, no final agreement had been reached as of the end of 2008, and total debt stock is estimated at $8.5 billion.[45] The total stock of debt with Kuwait and Saudi Arabia is under dispute, but has been estimated variously at $8 billion–$27 billion for Kuwait and $15 billion–$50 billion for Saudi Arabia.[46] Both countries have discussed forgiving Iraqi debt at various times, and neither is demanding payment or servicing in the short term.[47] The Kuwaitis are constrained in what they can do in debt reduction by the need to take any resulting agreement

---

[44] Strategic Framework Agreement for a Relationship of Friendship and Cooperation Between the United States of America and the Republic of Iraq, signed in Baghdad on November 17, 2008.

[45] International Monetary Fund, 2008a and 2008b.

[46] El Gamal, 2008; Weiss, 2008; and interviews with a knowledgeable former U.S. government official, January 2009.

[47] El Gamal, 2008.

through their parliament, which remains hostile to Iraq. The following list presents potential mitigating measures:

- **Give priority to debt reduction with China but continue to address Saudi Arabia and Kuwait.** Iraq may have leverage with China because it signed an important oil production–sharing agreement with a Chinese state oil company in August 2008.[48] The U.S. and Iraqi governments should give priority to completing debt reduction with China, and the United States and key allies should support diplomatic engagement by the Iraqis in Beijing. However, Saudi Arabia and Kuwait should remain on the debt-reduction agenda. Although Saudi Arabia reportedly has pledged to cancel 80 percent or more of Iraqi debt, and although Kuwait's government reportedly has said it will not allow the debt to become a burden on Iraq,[49] a commitment not to collect debt is not the same as formal debt forgiveness, and Iraq's standing in international credit markets could remain impaired. With 31 creditor countries having signed agreements to reduce claims on Iraq and an additional two having concluded negotiations but not yet signed formal agreements as of March 2009, a coordinated diplomatic effort could move this issue forward (although considerable diplomatic effort has already been made).
- **Consider supporting the establishment of special debt facilities that help Iraq if it cannot access international capital markets.** Should Iraq not resolve its debt issues and subsequently have trouble accessing international capital markets, countries willing to lend to Iraq could set up their own debt facilities or arrange lending through multilateral institutions.

Ultimately, none of these measures may prove necessary. If enough banks and investors are willing to lend money to Iraq, resolving remaining debt and reparations issues may be unnecessary. Nonetheless, the situation bears continued monitoring because it could impinge on U.S. goals for Iraq and Iraqi internal stability.

Compensation. The dollar amount of the compensation set-aside has decreased with the fall in oil prices. Nevertheless, contributing 5 percent of all Iraqi oil, oil products, and natural gas export earnings to the Compensation Fund remains a burden. Therefore, a mitigating measure is to

- **Consider working to change the proportion.** Changing the proportion of oil revenue that Iraq must deposit in the UN Compensation Fund would require the agreement of the Governing Council of the UN Compensation Commission, which is made up of the same countries that are members of the UN Security

---

[48] Kurtenbach, 2008.

[49] El Gamal, 2008.

Council.[50] Therefore, any change in the 5-percent allocation would require a diplomatic effort by the United States and countries sympathetic to Iraq and, in all likelihood, acquiescence by the government of Kuwait (but not necessarily by the Kuwaiti parliament).

Other International Claims. Ultimately, Iraq will need to resolve claims against it so that it no longer needs its assets to be shielded. Having immunity from attachment may hinder Iraq's ability to access international capital markets, since creditors will find it difficult to enforce their claims. However, a number of steps are available if the United States is interested in continuing to shield Iraqi assets, especially given current U.S. obligations under the UN Security Council resolution:

- **Continue immunity from lawsuits against Iraq in the United States.** The U.S. Congress may be able to remove the immunity that the Supreme Court ruling affirmed. The administration should work with Congress to ensure this immunity remains in place. At the same time, U.S. and Iraqi government officials should work on a sovereign-to-sovereign basis to resolve the claims of U.S. citizens, as is normally done when sovereigns are immune from lawsuits.
- **Extend the UN Security Council resolution.** Through 2009, the United States should coordinate with Iraq and allies regarding whether there should be a new effort in the UN Security Council to extend the arrangements and protections for the Development Fund for Iraq for another year.
- **Address potential claims and attachment risk in other countries.** Iraq may face claims and attachment risk in other countries. Addressing this is mostly beyond U.S. abilities, but the United States can encourage other countries to extend immunities and can work with Iraq to ensure that it has appropriate legal representation to analyze and address its potential worldwide liabilities.

---

[50] United Nations Compensation Commission, undated-b.

Bibliography

1st Sustainment Command, Theater, *Expendable Retrograde OPT*, December 18, 2008.

3d Sustainment Command, Expeditionary, *ESC Task Org*, December 14, 2008.

"3rd Expeditionary Support Command Concept of Support," undated briefing, presented February 14, 2009.

3rd U.S. Army/ARCENT, *Environmental Standard Operating Procedures*, August 3, 2004.

330th Transportation Battalion, "Proposed JBB/Warhorse/Caldwell Window During 2/3 ACR & 2 SCR Moves," briefing, undated.

Abdul-Zahra, Qassim, with Sameer N. Yacoub, "Iraq Passes Sharply Reduced Budget for 2009," Associated Press, March 5, 2009.

Abu Nasr, Donna, "Saudi Arabia Treads Carefully as It Tries to Douse the Threat of Sectarianism," Associated Press, February 2, 2007.

Agreement Between the United States of America and the Republic of Iraq on the Withdrawal of United States Forces from Iraq and the Organization of Their Activities During Their Temporary Presence in Iraq, signed in Baghdad on November 17, 2008.

Ahmed, Farook, and Marisa Cochrane, "Backgrounder 27: Recent Operations Against Special Groups and JAM in Central and Southern Iraq," Institute for the Study of War, April 2008.

"Akkad anna al-Salām Muftāh al-Istiqrār fi al-Sharq al-Awsat . . . al-Asad Yabahath wa Wafd al-Kungris al-ʿAlāqāt: Ishārāt Ijābīya min al-Idāra wa Nantazhir al-Wāqiʿ [He Confirmed That Peace Is the Key to Stability in the Middle East . . . al-Asad and the Congressional Delegation Discuss the Relationship: Positive Signs from the Administration and We Are Waiting on Real Events]," *Dar al-Hayat* (online), in Arabic, February 19, 2009. As of January 2009: http://www.daralhayat.com/arab_news/levant_news/02-2009/Item-20090218-8b08cb60-c0a8-10ed-0002-75387ba7a63b/story.html

Al-Baghdadi (pseud.), "Al-Qaʾida: al-ʿIraq Jamiʾat al-Irhab [Al-Qaʾida: Iraq Is a University of Terrorism]," in Arabic, April 17, 2008. As of November 2008: http://www.middle-east-online.com/?id=47152

Al-Hashimi, Tariq, Web page, undated. As of February 26, 2009: http://alhashimi.org

Al-Humayd, Tariq, "al-Insihab al-Amriki al-Sakut al-Thani [The American Withdrawal: The Second Defeat]," *Asharq al-Awsat* (London), in Arabic, October 9, 2007.

———, "Betraying the Awakening Council," *Asharq al-Awsat* (London), August 24, 2008a.

———, "La Lil-Taslih al-'Iraq [No to the Arming of Iraq]," *Asharq al-Awsat* (London), in Arabic, September 10, 2008b.

———, "Masrihat Doha [The Theater of Doha]," *Asharq al-Awsat* (London), January 17, 2009.

"Al-'Iraq fi Marhalat ma ba'd al-Sahwāt al-Sunnīya wa al-Tashazhī al-Shī'ī [Iraq [Enters] the Phase of the 'Post-Sunni Awakening' and the Splintering of the Shi'a]," *Dar al-Hayat* (online), in Arabic, June 20, 2008. As of January 2009:
http://www.daralhayat.com/special/features/06-2008/Article-20080619-a0cf9a8a-c0a8-10ed-0007-ae6d46cebd94/story.html

Al-Qassemi, Sultan, "Gulf States May Continue to Ignore Iraq at Their Own Peril," *The National* (United Arab Emirates), June 21, 2008.

Al-Rasheed, Abd al-Rahman, "Khiyar Iraq: Namuthij Iran um al-Khalij [Iraq's Choice: The Model of Iran or the Gulf]," *Asharq al-Awsat* (London), in Arabic, February 19, 2009.

"Al-Sadr Forms 'Promised Day Brigade,' Says Brigade to Fight 'Occupation,'" Al-Amarah Militant News Network, in Arabic, GMP20081114676007, November 14, 2008.

Al-Zaydi, Mishari, "Uhadhir 'an Taqdhi Alihi al-Ama'im [Warning Against the Religious Establishment]," *Asharq al-Awsat* (London), July 19, 2007.

Al-Zhafiri, Ali, "Harith al-Dari . . . I'lān al-Mabādi' bayn Amirika wa al-'Iraq [Harith al-Dari . . . Announcement of Principles Between America and Iraq]," interview with Shaikh Harith al-Dari, al-Jazeera, in Arabic, February 18, 2008. As of January 2009:
http://www.aljazeera.net/Channel/archive/archive?ArchiveId=1086251

"'Ard al-Takhalī 'an Mansibihi Muqābil Inha' Nizām al-Muhāsasat al-Tāi'fiya . . . al-Hashemi: al-Istiftā' 'ala al-Itifāq al-Amnī Wasīla lil Taswīb wa al-Islāh [Offer to Relinquish His Position in Return for Ending the Sectarian Quota System . . . al-Hashemi: The Referendum on the Security Agreement Is a Means of Correction and Reform]," *Dar al-Hayat* (Beirut), in Arabic, December 7, 2008.

Association of Muslim Ulama, "Ma al-Hukm al-Shar'ī fī al-Itifāqīya al-Amnīya bayn al-Hukūma al-Hālīya wa bayn Idārat al-Ihtlāl al-Amiriki? [What Is the Ruling of Shar'ia on the Security Agreement Between the Current [Iraqi] Government and the American Occupation?]," Web page, in Arabic, November 28, 2008. As of January 2009:
http://iraq-amsi.org/news.php?action=view&id=30372&71723067cb6439daca0cb87b985cb1d1

"Badr Corps Statement, April 2008," issued via almejlis.org, April 2008 (OSC GMP20080421676005, April 21, 2008).

"Baghdad: Mapping the Violence," BBC, undated. As of February 11, 2009:
http://news.bbc.co.uk/2/shared/sp/hi/in_depth/Baghdad_navigator/

"Baghdad tatajiha l-tashri'a qanun majalis Isnad al-Asha'ir . . . wast makhawif men tahawliha ila milishiyyat [Baghdad Commences Legislation on a Law for Tribal Support Councils Amidst Fears That They Will Turn into Militias]," *Asharq al-Awsat* (online), in Arabic, November 9, 2008. As of December 2008:
http://www.asharqalawsat.com/details.asp?section=4&article=494091&issueno=10939

Bahgat, Gawdat, "Nuclear Proliferation: The Case of Saudi Arabia," *Middle East Journal*, Vol. 60, No. 3, Summer 2006.

Bahney, Benjamin, and Renny McPherson, "Know Your Enemy," *Washington Times*, November 9, 2008, p. B3.

"Bahraini Shiites Answer Sistani Call to Protest Bombing," *Khaleej Times* (Dubai), February 23, 2006.

Barkey, Henri J., "Kurdistandoff," *The National Interest*, July/August 2007, p. 53.

"BBC Monitoring: Iran Media Guide," OSC IAP20070327950024, March 27, 2007.

BBC Monitoring Middle East, "Iraqi Premier Urged to Stop Support Councils' Work," November 21, 2008. As of March 17, 2009:
http://www.iqpc.co.uk/News.aspx?id=123650356&IQ=government

Bell, Jack, "Memo on Transfer of Property, Notes from CENTCOM J-4 Visit," June 6, 2008.

Bennett, Brian, "Underestimating Al Sadr, Again," *Time*, February 11, 2008.

Bensahel, Nora, "International Perspectives on Agency Reform: Testimony Before the Armed Services Committee, Subcommittee on Oversight and Investigations, U.S. House of Representatives," Santa Monica, Calif: RAND Corporation, CT-298, January 29, 2008. As of May 13, 2009:
http://www.rand.org/pubs/testimonies/CT298/

Bensahel, Nora, Olga Oliker, and Heather Peterson, *Improving Capacity for Stabilization and Reconstruction Operations*, Santa Monica, Calif.: RAND Corporation, MG-852-OSD, 2009. As of May 13, 2009:
http://www.rand.org/pubs/monographs/MG852/

Bowman, Tom, "U.S. Soldiers, Iraqi Police Unite to Redeem Ramadi," *All Things Considered*, February 22, 2007.

The Brookings Institution, "Tracking Reconstruction and Security in Post-Saddam Iraq," updated monthly. As of January 2009:
http://www.brookings.edu/saban/iraq-index.aspx

The Brookings Institution and Human Rights First, *Preparing for the Future: Protecting Iraqi Refugees and Internally Displaced Persons*, The Brookings-Bern Project on Internal Displacement and Human Rights First, January 25, 2008.

Bush, George W., "Suspending the Iraq Sanctions Act, Making Inapplicable Certain Statutory Provisions Relating to Iraq, and Delegating Authorities, Under the Emergency Wartime Supplemental Appropriations Act, 2003," Presidential Determination No. 2003-23 of May 7, 2003, *Federal Register*, Vol. 68, No. 95, May 16, 2003.

———, "Memorandum to the House of Representatives Returning Without Approval the 'National Defense Authorization Act for Fiscal Year 2008," December 28, 2007.

Center for New American Security, *Phased Transition: A Responsible Way Forward and Out of Iraq*, June 1, 2007.

Central Bank of Iraq, "Key Financial Indicators for February 25, 2008 [sic—should read 2009]," spreadsheet, Baghdad, 2009.

Chon, Gina, "Radical Iraq Cleric in Retreat," *Wall Street Journal*, August 5, 2008.

Cochrane, Marisa, "The Battle for Basra," Iraq Report No. 9, Institute for the Study of War, June 23, 2008.

Combat Studies Institute, *Operational Leadership Experiences in the Global War on Terrorism*, October 18, 2007.

Combined Joint Special Operations Task Force–Army, "Request for Forces," briefing, July 9, 2008.

Commonwealth Institute, *Quickly, Carefully, and Generously: The Necessary Steps for a Responsible Withdrawal from Iraq*, Report of the Task Force for a Responsible Withdrawal from Iraq, June 2008, Cambridge, Mass.: Commonwealth Institute, 2008.

Cordesman, Anthony H., *Violence in Iraq: Reaching an Irreducible Minimum*, The Center for Strategic and International Studies, February 25, 2008.

Crane, Keith, briefing slides on the topics of oil, budget, and economic growth, undated.

Daniel, Trenton, "Pro-Iran Party Loses Big in Iraq Local Elections, Returns Show," McClatchy Newspapers, February 5, 2009.

Dombey, Daniel, and Carola Hoyos, "US Warns on Ageing Iraqi Oil Pipelines," *Financial Times*, October 14, 2008.

Dreazen, Yochi J., and Gina Chon, "U.S. Presses Baghdad for Progress in Aiding Once-Restive Areas," *Wall Street Journal*, December 3, 2007, p. A9.

Eisenstadt, Michael, "Target Iraq's Republican Guard," *Middle East Quarterly*, December 1996.

El Gamal, Rania, "Kuwait to Ask MPs to Forgive Iraq Debt," ArabianBusiness.com, August 28, 2008.

Elsea, Jennifer, and Nina M. Serafino, *Private Security Contractors in Iraq: Background, Legal Status, and Other Issues*, Congressional Research Service, RL32419, September 29, 2008.

Fafo, *Iraqis in Jordan, Their Number and Characteristics*, 2007. As of February 16, 2009: http://www.fafo.no/ais/mideast/jordan/IJ.pdf

Fagen, Patricia Weiss, *Iraqi Refugees: Seeking Stability in Syria and Jordan*, Georgetown University Institute for the Study of Migration and Center for International and Regional Studies, Washington, D.C., 2007.

Ferris, Elizabeth, *Regional Dimensions of the Iraqi Displacement Crisis and the Role of the United Nations*, The Brookings Institution, October 25, 2007.

"Fī Istitlāʿ Ajrathu al-Sabah Akthariya al-ʿIraqiyin maʿ Tawqīʿ al-Itifāq al-Amnī [In a Poll Run by al-Sabah, Majority of Iraqis Support Signing the Security Agreement]," *al-Sabah* (online), in Arabic, November 22, 2008. As of January 2009: http://www.alsabaah.com/paper.php?source=akbar&mlf=interpage&sid=73542

Fick, Nathaniel, "Fight Less, Win More," *Washington Post*, August 12, 2007, p. B1.

Finer, Jonathon, "At Heart of Iraqi Impasse, a Family Feud," *Washington Post*, April 19, 2006, p. A1.

Flynn, Michael, Rich Juergens, and Thomas Cantrell, "Employing ISR: SOF Best Practices," *Joint Forces Quarterly*, No. 50, July 2008, pp. 56–61.

Gause III, F. Gregory, "Saudi Arabia: Iraq, Iran and the Regional Power Balance and the Sectarian Question," *Strategic Insights*, February 2007.

Glain, Stephan J., *Mullahs, Merchants, and Militants: The Collapse of Arab Democracy in the Arab World*, New York: Thomas Dunne Books/St. Martin's Press, 2004.

GlobalSecurity.org, "Mujahedin-E Khalq (MEK) Training Camp," last updated January 21, 2007. As of January 2009: http://www.globalsecurity.org/military/world/iraq/mek.htm

Gompert, David C., John Gordon IV, Adam Grissom, David R. Frelinger, Seth G. Jones, Martin C. Libicki, Edward O'Connell, Brooke Stearns Lawson, and Robert E. Hunter, *War by Other Means—Building Complete and Balanced Capabilities for Counterinsurgency: RAND Counterinsurgency Study—Final Report*, Santa Monica, Calif.: RAND Corporation, MG-595/2-OSD, 2008. As of March 24, 2009:
http://www.rand.org/pubs/monographs/MG595.2/

Government of Iraq, Draft of the Law on the Operational Procedures for the Creation of Regions, October 11, 2008.

Green, Jerrold D., Frederic Wehrey, and Charles Wolf, Jr., *Understanding Iran*, Santa Monica, Calif.: RAND Corporation, MG-771-SRF, 2009. As of April 9, 2009:
http://www.rand.org/pubs/monographs/MG771/

Gwertzman, Bernard, "Sick: Alliance Against Iran," Council on Foreign Relations, January 23, 2007.

"Harb Sirrīya 'ala Makhābi' al-Asliha wa Khutūt al-Imdād wa al-Tamwīl . . . al-Qa'ida Tufajjir al-Sirā' Dākhil al-Mudun al-Sunnīya wa Hamas—al-'Iraq Tanshaqq 'an Thawrat al-'Ashrīn [A Secret War over Hidden Arms Caches, Supply Lines, and Financing . . . al-Qa'ida Unleashes Conflict Inside the Sunni Towns and Iraqi Hamas Splits from the 1920 Revolution [Brigades]]," *Dar al-Hayat* (online), in Arabic, March 31, 2007. As of January 2009:
http://www.daralhayat.com/arab_news/levant_news/03-2007/Item-20070330-a443ad44-c0a8-10ed-0090-0556b129d347/story.html

Harib, Sa'id, "Why Does the Gulf Cooperation Council Reject Iraq's Entry?" *Awan Online*, in Arabic, December 18, 2008 ("Gulf Writer Justifies GCC Rejection of Iraq Membership," OSC GMP20081220054009).

"Harith al-Dari . . . I'lān al-Mabādi' bayn Amirika wa al-'Iraq [Harith al-Dari . . . Announcement of Principles Between America and Iraq]," al-Jazeera, in Arabic, February 18, 2008. As of January 2009:
http://www.aljazeera.net/Channel/archive/archive?ArchiveId=1086251

"Hazoor Amrica dar mantagheh ba hadaf moghabaleh ba Enghelab Islami ast [America's Regional Presence Seeks to Fight the Islamic Revolution]," Kayhan News, December 4, 2008.

Headquarters, U.S. Central Command, *Retrograde Concept Plan*, January 7, 2009.

Headquarters, U.S. Department of the Army, Deputy Chief of Staff, G-4, *Contractor-Acquired, Government-Owned (CAGO) Equipment Disposition: Business Case Analysis*, December 1, 2007.

———, "RESET Logistics ROC Drill (Phase 1)," briefing, May 7, 2008.

Henry, Ryan, "Memo on Op Plans," undated.

Hess, Pamela, "US: Quds, Hezbollah Training Militia in Iran," Associated Press, August 15, 2008.

Human Rights Watch, *The Quality of Justice: Failings of Iraq's Central Criminal Court*, December 2008. As of March 23, 2009:
http://www.hrw.org/sites/default/files/reports/iraq1208web.pdf

International Crisis Group, *Shiite Politics in Iraq: The Role of the Supreme Council*, Middle East Report No. 70, November 15, 2007.

———, *Failed Responsibility: Iraqi Refugees in Syria, Jordan and Lebanon*, Middle East Report No. 77, July 2008a.

———, *Oil for Soil: Toward a Grand Bargain on Iraq and the Kurds*, Middle East Report No. 80, October 28, 2008b.

International Monetary Fund, *Iraq: 2007 Article IV Consultation, Fifth Review Under the Stand-By Arrangement, Financing Assurances Review, and Requests for Extension of the Arrangement, Waiver of Applicability, and Waivers for Nonobservance of Performance Criteria—Staff Report; Public Information Notice and Press Release on the Executive Board Discussion; and Statement by the Executive Director for Iraq*, IMF Country Report No. 07/301, August 2007.

————, *Iraq: First Review Under the Stand-By Arrangement and Financing Assurances Review—Staff Report; Staff Supplement; Press Release on the Executive Board Discussion; and Statement by the Executive Director for Iraq*, IMF Country Report No. 08/303, Washington, D.C., September 2008a.

————, *Iraq: Second Review Under the Stand-By Arrangement and Financing Assurances Review—Staff Report; Staff Supplement; Press Release on the Executive Board Discussion; and Statement by the Executive Director for Iraq*, IMF Country Report No. 08/383, Washington, D.C., December 2008b.

"Iraq Accuses MKO of Plotting Attack," Fars News Agency, January 22, 2009.

"Iraq Considers $200 Million Plan to Reverse Oil-Output Decline," Platts.com, February 9, 2009.

"Iraq, Saudi Agree to Monitor Sectarian Fatwas," Associated Press, July 15, 2007.

Iraqi Council of Representatives, "Qanūn Tasdīq Itifāq bayn Jumhuriyat al-'Iraq wa al-Wilayat al-Mutahida al-Amirikiya bi Sha'n Insihāb al-Quwāt al-Amirikiya min al-'Iraq wa Tanzīm Anshitatiha khilal Wujūdiha al-Mu'aqqat fīhi [Law Ratifying Agreement Between the Republic of Iraq and the United States of America Regarding the Withdrawal of American Forces from Iraq and the Organization of Their Activities During Their Temporary Presence in Iraq]," in Arabic, November 27, 2008.

————, "Majlis al-Nuwab Yuqirr Mashrū' al-Muwāzana al-'Āmma li 'Ām 2009 [The Council of Representatives Ratifies the Public Budget Bill for the Year 2009]," in Arabic, March 5, 2009.

Jasim, Hoda, and Rahma al-Salem, "The Awakening Council: Iraq's Anti–al-Qaeda Sunni Militias," *Asharq al-Awsat* (online), December 29, 2007. As of January 2009:
http://www.asharq-e.com/news.asp?section=3&id=11292

Joint Chiefs of Staff, *OIF/OEF Equipment Reset, PDM II Study*, July 8, 2008.

Joint Explanatory Statement to the Consolidated Security, Disaster Assistance, and Continuing Appropriations Act, 2009, H.R. 2638, c. September 24, 2008.

Joseph, Edward, and Michael O'Hanlon, *The Case for Soft Partition in Iraq*, Saban Center for Middle East Policy, Brookings Institution, June 2007. As of January 2009:
http://www.brookings.edu/papers/2007/06iraq_joseph.aspx

Kaplan, Robert D., "It's the Tribes, Stupid!" *Atlantic*, November 2007. As of January 2009:
http://www.theatlantic.com/doc/200711u/kaplan-democracy

Kelly, Matt, "Allies Fall Short on Iraq Aid Pledges," *USA Today*, January 20, 2008.

Kelly, Terrence K., "An Iraqi Modus Vivendi: How Would It Come About and What Would It Look Like? Testimony Presented Before the Senate Foreign Relations Committee," Santa Monica, Calif.: RAND Corporation, CT-303, April 3, 2008. As of March 17, 2009:
http://www.rand.org/pubs/testimonies/CT303/

Ketz, Sammy, "Iraq Seeks to Diversify Revenues: Planning Minister Says Iraq Aims to Boost Farming, Industry, Religious Tourism Amid Tumbling Oil Prices," Middle-East-Online.com, February 23, 2009.

Knickmeyer, Ellen, and Sudarsan Raghavan, "Top Aide to Sadr Outlines Vision of a U.S.-Free Iraq," *Washington Post*, September 12, 2006, p. A18.

Kukis, Mark, "Turning Iraq's Tribes Against Al-Qaeda," *Time*, December 26, 2006.

Kurtenbach, Elaine, "China, Iraq Reach $3 Billion Oil Service Deal," Associated Press, August 28, 2008.

La Franchi, Howard, "As Mideast Realigns, US Leans Sunni," *Christian Science Monitor*, October 9, 2007.

Levinson, Charles, "Iranians Help Reach Iraq Cease-Fire," *USA Today*, March 31, 2008. As of December 2008:
http://www.usatoday.com/news/world/iraq/2008-03-30-iraqnews_N.htm

Levinson, Charles, and Ali A. Nabhan, "Iraqi Tribes Caught Between Rival Shiite Parties," *USA Today*, October 20, 2008. As of December 2008:
http://www.usatoday.com/news/world/iraq/2008-10-19-iraqi-vote_N.htm?loc=interstitialskip

Lischer, Sarah Kenyon, "Security and Displacement in Iraq," *International Security*, Vol. 33, No. 2, Fall 2008.

Long, Austin, "The Anbar Awakening," *Survival*, Vol. 50, No. 2, March–April 2008.

Loven, Jennifer, "Bush Gets Updates on Reconstruction from Team Leaders," *San Diego Union-Tribune*, January 9, 2008.

Lubold, Gordon, "New Look at Foreign Fighters in Iraq: An Analysis Shows That the Bulk of Them Come from Countries Allied with the U.S.," *Christian Science Monitor*, January 7, 2008.

MacFarland, Sean, "Addendum: Anbar Awakens," *Military Review*, May–June 2008.

MacFarland, Sean, and Niel Smith, "Anbar Awakens: The Tipping Point," *Military Review*, March–April 2008.

Mahdi, Usama, "ISCI and the Kurds Fearful of Autocratic Decision-Making by al-Maliki," in Arabic, November 28, 2008. As of March 17, 2009:
http://www.ankawa.com/forum/index.php/topic,243556.0.html

Malkasian, Carter, "A Thin Blue Line in the Sand," *Democracy*, No. 5, Summer 2007.

Mann, Morgan, "The Power Equation: Using Tribal Politics in Counterinsurgency," *Military Review*, May–June 2007, pp. 104–108.

Marlowe, Anne, "In War Too, Personnel Is Policy," *Wall Street Journal*, June 14, 2008, p. 11.

Marsden, Sam, "Naval Training Team to Remain at Vital Iraq Port," Press Association Newsfile, April 2, 2009.

Marsh, Bill, "Iraq Withdrawal: Five Difficult Questions," *New York Times*, July 29, 2007. As of March 23, 2008:
http://www.nytimes.com/2007/07/29/weekinreview/29marsh.html?_r=1&scp=1&sq=Bill%20Marsh:%20Iraq%20Withdrawal&st=cse

"Mashrūʿ al-Islāh al-Siyāsī: Iltizām bi al-Dustūr bidūn Ijtihādāt . . . wa Ihtirām Sultāt al-Hukūma al-Itihādiya wa al-Iqlīm [Political Reform Bill: Commitment to the Constitution Without Interpretation . . . and Respect for the Authorities of the Unified and Provincial Government[s]]," *al-Sharq al-Awsat* (online), in Arabic, November 28, 2008. As of January 2009:
http://www.asharqalawsat.com/details.asp?section=4&issueno=10958&article=496748&feature

"Masihi'un wa mandae'un yandamun ila majlis Isnad Markz Muhafithat al-Basra [Christians and Mandaens Join the Basra Province Support Council]," IraqAlaan.com, in Arabic, December 13, 2008. As of January 2009:
http://iraqalaan.com/bm/Politics/11587.shtml

McCaffrey, Barry R., *Iraq AAR*, November 4, 2008.

McCallister, William, "Sons of Iraq: A Study in Irregular Warfare," *Small Wars Journal*, September 8, 2008.

McCary, John, "The Anbar Awakening: An Alliance of Incentives," *Washington Quarterly*, Vol. 32, No. 1, January 2009, pp. 43–59.

Meijer, Roel "The Association of Muslim Scholars in Iraq," The Middle East Research and Information Project, Middle East Report No. 237, Winter 2005. As of February 20, 2009:
http://www.merip.org/mer/mer237/meijer.html

Military Surface Deployment and Distribution Command, "595th Transportation Terminal Group Port Capabilities: Jordan, Iraq, Kuwait," briefing, undated.

Ministry of Displacement and Migration of Iraq and International Organization for Migration, *Returnee Monitoring and Needs Assessment Tabulation Report*, Baghdad, September 2008. As of February 16, 2009:
http://www.iom-iraq.net/Library/Returnee%20Monitoring%20TABULATION%20REPORT%20September%202008%20English.pdf

"MNC-Kuwait PDSS Brief," briefing, undated.

Morgan, David, "Iran Seen Reining In Actions in Iraq—Officials," Reuters India, December 12, 2008.

Mortenson, Darrin, "The Threat of a Re-Surge in Iraq," *Time*, March 24, 2008.

Mufson, Steven, and Robin Wright, "In a Major Step, Saudi Arabia Agrees to Write Off 80 Percent of Iraqi Debt," *Washington Post*, April 18, 2007, p. A18.

Muhammad, Abu Rumman, "al-'Iraq: Sandūq al-Iqtirā', Marhalīan, Badl Sanādīq Juthath al-Maqtū'a al-Ru'ūs [Iraq: The Ballot Box Replacing Boxes of Bodies with Severed Heads]," *Dar al-Hayat* (online), in Arabic, February 8, 2009. As of January 2009:
http://www.daralhayat.com/opinion/ideas/02-2009/Article-20090207-517599fa-c0a8-10ed-016d-304658aaab05/story.html

Mulrine, Anna, "Putting War Talk on Hold: Why the Pentagon Thinks Attacking Iran Is a Bad Idea," *U.S. News and World Report*, August 18, 2008, p. 20.

Multi-National Force–Iraq, *041030 Final Requisition for AWRAP: TOT REQUIREMENTS; CASPIAN-SDTE; NEA-WD*, undated-a.

———, "Appendix 1 to Annex A [Materiel Disposition Flowcharts]," briefing, undated-b.

———, "Base Return-Closure FEPP Inventory: Economy Formula; Condition Codes FMV Instructions; Transfer Scenario," spreadsheet, undated-c.

———, *Environmental Advisory Reversion of Real and Personal Property at COS XXXXX, Iraq to the Government of Iraq*, undated-d.

———, "Kuwait Arifjan to Buehring Strip Map: From Arifjan to Buehring," briefing, undated-e.

———, "Kuwait Arifjan to KCIA Civilian Strip Map: From Arifjan to KCIA Civilian Flights," briefing, undated-f.

———, "Kuwait Arifjan to KNB & ASP Strip Map: From Arifjan to KNB & ASP," briefing, undated-g.

———, "Kuwait Arifjan to SPOD Strip Map: From Arifjan to Port of Shuaybah (SPOD)," briefing, undated-h.

———, "Kuwait Strip Map: APOD to Camps Commando & Coyote," briefing, undated-i.

———, "Kuwait Strip Map: Master with Photo," briefing, undated-j.

———, *Memorandum of Agreement for Coalition Force Use of Government of Iraq Real Property and Facilities on Camp Ramadi*, undated-k.

———, *Record of Return of Property by and Between Multi-National Force–Iraq (MNF-I) and the Government of Iraq (GoI)*, undated-l.

———, "SSAMCRS-16 Relook," spreadsheet, undated-m.

———, "Support Drawdown," spreadsheet, undated-n.

———, "Truckload Redeployment Analysis Data," spreadsheet, undated-o.

———, *Authority to Transfer U.S. Property in Iraq*, October 20, 2008.

———, *Updated Notice of Return-Contingency Operating Site (COS) Iskandariyah*, January 2, 2009a.

———, "Transfer and Acceptance of Military Real Property," spreadsheet, January 15, 2009b.

———, "Transfer and Acceptance of Military Real Property," spreadsheet, January 26, 2009c.

Multi-National Security Transition Command–Iraq, Command Briefing, February 2009.

"Muthahira Asha'iriyya Ihtijajan 'ala al-Mutammar al-Awwal l-majlis al-Isnad fi al-Diwaniyya [Tribal Demonstration Protesting Against the First Conference of the Support Council in Diwaniyya]," *Asharq al-Awsat* (online), in Arabic, November 10, 2008. As of December 2008: http://www.asharqalawsat.com/details.asp?section=4&issueno=10940&article=494320&feature

"Namayand e Vali Faghih Dar Sepah: Tavafoghname Amrica va Aragh Az Altaf e Khoda Bood [The Supreme Leader's Representative in the [Revolutionary Guards] Corps: The Agreement Between America and Iraq Is a Sign of God's Grace]," Emruz News, December 3, 2008.

National Media Center, General Secretariat for the Council of Ministers, Republic of Iraq, "Iraq to Settle Debts with Tunis," March 23, 2009.

Nawaf, Obaid, "Stepping into Iraq," *Washington Post*, November 29, 2006, p. A23.

Naylor, Hugh, "Syria Is Said to Be Strengthening Ties to Opponents of Iraq's Government," *New York Times*, October 7, 2007.

Negus, Stephen, "Call for Sunni State in Iraq," ft.com, October 15, 2006.

Norton, Augustus Richard, "The Shiite Threat Revisited," *Current History*, Vol. 435, December 2007.

Nuri, Rami, "Ninawa: Tahalafat Sa'aba wa Khiyarat al-Inshiqaq al-Kurdi—al-'Arabi Asa'ab [Ninawa: Alliances Are Problematic and Options for the Kurdish/Arab Schism Are Even More So]," *Dar al-Hayat* (online), in Arabic, March 10, 2009. As of March 17, 2009: http://www.alhayat.com/arab_news/levant_news/03-2009/Item-20090309-ec95b5b8-c0a8-10ed-0042-76fd5c5d7041/story.html

Oaks, David, "Notes from Reposture VTC," October 18, 2007.

Obaid, Nawaf, "Stepping into Iraq," *Washington Post*, 2006.

Obama, Barack, remarks delivered at Camp Lejeune, N.C., February 27, 2009a.

————, "Continuation of the National Emergency with Respect to the Stabilization of Iraq," May 19, 2009b.

Odierno, GEN Raymond, letter to the MNF-I, February 27, 2009a.

————, interview with ABC reporter Martha Raddatz, Baghdad, March 10, 2009b.

The Office of the UN High Commissioner for Refugees, *Assessment on Returns to Iraq Amongst the Iraqi Refugee Population in Syria (April 2008)*, undated-a. As of February 16, 2009: http://www.unhcr.org/cgi-bin/texis/vtx/home/opendoc.pdf?tbl=SUBSITES&id=48185fa82

————, "Cumulative UNHCR Iraqi Submissions Versus Arrivals to the United States (Including Non-UNHCR), 31 October 2008," chart, undated-b. As of February 11, 2009: http://www.unhcr.org/cgi-bin/texis/vtx/iraq?page=statistics

————, *UNHCR's Eligibility Guidelines for Assessing the International Protection Needs of Iraqi Asylum-Seekers*, Geneva, August 2007.

————, "UNHCR Syria Update," November 2008. As of April 14, 2009: http://www.unhcr.org/news/NEWS/4926c9d52.pdf

Ondiak, Natalie, and Brian Katulis, *Operation Safe Haven Iraq 2009*, Center for American Progress, Washington, D.C., January 2009.

Opall-Rome, Barbara, "U.S. to Deploy Radar, Troops in Israel: Move Called Safeguard Against Iran Missile Threat," *Defense News*, August 18, 2008, p. 1.

Oppel, Richard, Jr., "Foreign Fighters in Iraq Are Tied to Allies of U.S.," *New York Times*, November 22, 2007.

Paley, Amit R., "In Iraq, a Prison Full of Innocent Men," *Washington Post*, December 6, 2008, p. A1.

Parker, Ned, "Kurdish Leader Sees Authoritarian Drift in Iraq," *L.A. Times*, January 11, 2009.

Peltz, Eric, "Notes from CENTCOM J-4 Visit," December 19, 2008.

Perry, Walter, "Memo: Joint Staff–RAND Meeting 12/15," December 17, 2008.

Peterson, Scott, "Iran Flexes Its 'Soft Power' in Iraq," *Christian Science Monitor*, May 20, 2005a.

————, "Rumblings of Radicalism in Kurdistan," *Christian Science Monitor*, November 3, 2005b.

Poole, Oliver, "Army Base Stripped Bare Days After Handover," *The Daily Telegraph* (London), August 23, 2006a. As of March 23, 2009: http://www.telegraph.co.uk/news/1527055/Army-base-stripped-bare-days-after-handover.html

————, "Jubilant Iraqi Looters Strip Military Base After British Forces Pull Out," *The Daily Telegraph* (London), August 26, 2006b, p. 18.

"The Princes of Shadows: How to Sponsor Terrorism Saudi Style," Press TV, October 22, 2008.

Proskauer Rose LLP, "U.S. Supreme Court to Hear New Sovereign Immunity Case: Key Issues for Military Contractors and Sovereign/Private Ventures in Iraq and Beyond," Client Alert, January 2009.

"Protesters Demand Basra's Autonomy," Press TV, December 28, 2008. As of January 2009: http://www.presstv.ir/detail.aspx?id=79706&sectionid=351020201

Przeworski, Adam, *Democracy and Markets: Political and Economic Reform in East Europe and Latin America*, Cambridge, U.K.: Cambridge University Press, 1991.

Radi, Ali Muhsin, "Statement Issued by Iraqi Islamic Supreme Council's Culture and Information Bureau on Remarks Attributed to Certain Leaders of Islamic Da'wah Party," Buratha News Agency, September 24, 2008 (translated by OSC GMP20080927649001).

Raghavan, Sudarsan, "Shiite Clerics' Rivalry Deepens in Fragile Iraq," *Washington Post*, December 21, 2006.

Rasheed, Ahmed, "China Starts Iraq's First Foreign Oil Work in Decades," Reuters.com, January 2, 2009.

Ravid, Barak, "NATO Okays Pact to Boost Security, Political Ties to Israel," *Ha'aretz* (Tel Aviv), December 2, 2008.

Ricks, Thomas, "Situation Called Dire in West Iraq: Anbar Is Lost Politically, Marine Analyst Says," *Washington Post*, September 11, 2006, p. A1.

Robertson, Nic, "Sunni Demand Could Unravel Iraqi Government," CNN.com, May 7, 2007. As of February 26, 2008:
http://edition.cnn.com/2007/WORLD/meast/05/07/iraq.sunnithreat/index.html

Robinson, Glenn, "The Role of the Professional Middle Class in the Mobilization of Palestinian Society: The Medical and Agrarian Communities," *International Journal of Middle East Studies*, Vol. 25, No. 2, May 1993, pp. 301–326.

Roggio, Bill, "The Anbar Campaign," *The Long War Journal* (online), August 4, 2005. As of May 30, 2008:
http://www.longwarjournal.org/archives/2005/08/the_anbar_campa_3.php

———, "A Look at Operation Knight's Assault," *The Long War Journal* (online), April 4, 2008. As of March 2009:
http://www.longwarjournal.org/archives/2008/04/a_look_at_operation_1.php

Saidazimova, Gulnoza, "Iran/Iraq: Trade Flow Increases, but Mostly from Tehran to Baghdad," Radio Free Europe/Radio Liberty, March 4, 2008.

Salame, Ghassan, ed., *Democracy Without Democrats? The Renewal of Politics in the Muslim World*, London and New York: Taurus, 1994.

Sanger, David E., "US Rejected Aid for Israeli Nuclear Raid on Iranian Nuclear Site," *New York Times*, January 11, 2009.

Sarsar, Saliba, "Quantifying Arab Democracy: Democracy in the Middle East," *Middle East Studies Quarterly*, Summer 2006, pp. 21–28.

Sayed, A/Rahman, "Against All Odds: Federal Iraq Is to Emerge," Awate.com, August 24, 2005. As of January 2009:
http://www.awate.com/artman/publish/article_4223.shtml

Simon, Steve, "The Price of the Surge," *Foreign Affairs*, Vol. 87, No. 3, May/June 2008.

SITE Institute, "Tactical Withdrawal: Jihadist Forum Member Provides Dialogue with a Soldier of the Islamic State of Iraq from a Paltalk Chat," 2008010801, January 1, 2008.

Slackman, Michael, "Iraqi Cleric Deepens Religious Ties with Iran," *International Herald Tribune*, June 9, 2006.

Slackman, Michael, and Hassan M. Fattah, "In Public View, Saudis Counter Iran in Region," *New York Times*, February 6, 2007.

Solomon, Jay, "U.S.-Arab Alliance Aims to Deter Terrorism, Iran," *Wall Street Journal*, August 9, 2007.

Special Inspector General for Iraq Reconstruction, *Quarterly Report to Congress*, October 30, 2008.

———, *Quarterly Report and Semiannual Report to the United States Congress*, Arlington, Va., January 30, 2009a.

———, *Quarterly Report to the United States Congress*, Arlington, Va., April 30, 2009b.

Strategic Framework Agreement for a Relationship of Friendship and Cooperation Between the United States of America and the Republic of Iraq, signed in Baghdad on November 17, 2008.

Sumaida'ie, Samir Shakir Mahmood, "Iraq: Looking to the Next Five Years," speech at the Woodrow Wilson Center, April 9, 2008. As of February 11, 2009:
http://www.wilsoncenter.org/index.cfm?fuseaction=events.event_summary&event_id=400820

Tavernese, Sabrine, "Cleric Said to Lose Reins of Parts of Iraqi Militia," *New York Times*, September 28, 2006.

Theodoulou, Michael, "Tehran Gives Backing to US-Iraq Agreement," *The National* (United Arab Emirates), December 1, 2008.

Turbiville, Graham H., Jr., *Logistic Support and Insurgency*, Hurlburt Field, Fla.: Joint Special Operations University, undated.

United Nations Compensation Commission, "The Claims," Geneva, Switzerland, undated-a.

———, "The Governing Council," Geneva, Switzerland, undated-b.

———, "Status of Process and Payment of Claims," Geneva, Switzerland, October 30, 2008.

United Nations Security Council, "Resolution 1859 (2008), Adopted by the Security Council at Its 6059th Meeting, on 22 December 2008," 2008.

United States Code, Title 28, Section 1605, General Exceptions to the Jurisdictional Immunity of a Foreign State, 2000 (repealed).

United States Committee for Refugees and Immigrants, *World Refugee Survey 2008–Iraq*, June 19, 2008. As of February 13, 2009:
http://www.unhcr.org/refworld/docid/485f50daa.html

U.S. Army Materiel Command, *AMC Proposed LOGCAP Redeployment*, undated-a.

———, *Proposed Requirement Concept (Joint Logistics Reposture Integration Program)*, undated-b.

U.S. Army and U.S. Marine Corps, FM 3-24S/MCWP 3-335, *U.S. Army/Marine Corps Counterinsurgency Field Manual*, Washington, D.C., December 16, 2006.

U.S. Central Command, *Date Change for USCENTCOM Joint Supply and Maintenance Conference and Final Agenda*, January 2009.

U.S. Department of Defense, *Measuring Stability and Security in Iraq: December 2008 Report to Congress in Accordance with the Department of Defense Supplemental Appropriations Act 2008 (Section 9204, Public Law 110-252)*, Washington, D.C., December 2008.

U.S. Department of Justice, "Fact Sheet: Department of Justice Efforts in Iraq," Washington, D.C., February 13, 2008.

U.S. Department of State, *Report to Congress Submitted to U.S. Policy in Iraq Act, Section 1227(c) of the National Defense Authorization Act for Fiscal Year 2006 (P.L. 109-63), as Amended by Section 1223 of the National Defense Authorization Act for Fiscal Year 2008 (P.L. 110-181)*, Washington, D.C., October 2008.

———, *Iraq Weekly Status Report*, January 7, 2009.

U.S. Department of State and Broadcasting Board of Governors Office of Inspector General, *A Review of U.S. Policy Relative to Petroleum-Sector Contracting in Iraq, Report of Inspection*, Report Number ISP-I-09-28A, March 2009.

U.S. Department of State, Bureau of Near Eastern Affairs, "Section 2207 Report on Iraq Relief and Reconstruction," July 2008.

U.S. Department of State, Bureau of Population, Refugees, and Migration, Office of Admissions, Refugee Processing Center, "Summary of Refugee Admissions as of January 31, 2009," January 31, 2009. As of February 11, 2009:
http://www.wrapsnet.org/WRAPS/Reports/AdmissionsArrivals/tabid/211/Default.aspx

U.S. Department of the Treasury, "Treasury Designates Individuals and Entities Fueling Violence in Iraq," press release, September 16, 2008. As of January 2009:
http://www.ustreas.gov/press/releases/hp1141.htm

U.S. Government Accountability Office, *Securing, Stabilizing and Rebuilding Iraq: Iraqi Government Has Not Met Most Legislative, Security and Economic Benchmarks*, GAO-07-1195, September 2007.

———, *Rebuilding Iraq: DOD and State Department Have Improved Oversight and Coordination of Private Security Contractors in Iraq, but Further Actions Are Needed to Sustain Improvements*, GAO-08-966, July 2008.

U.S. House of Representatives, Committee on Appropriations, Consolidated Security, Disaster Assistance, and Continuing Appropriations Act, 2009, committee print of H.R. 2638/P.L. 110-329, October 2008.

U.S. Marine Corps Center for Lessons Learned, "Interagency Activity in Stability Operations: Lessons and Observations from Commanders, Military and Non-DoD Government Personnel in Iraq," January 5, 2007a.

———, "Company Commanders' Observations: Lessons and Advice from Ground and Logistics Combat Element Company Commanders Who Served in Iraq, 2004–2007," October 18, 2007b.

U.S. Senate, *Congressional Record*, 110th Cong., 2d sess., September 27, 2008, p. S9885.

Visser, Reidar, "The Draft Law for the Formation of the Regions: A Recipe for Permanent Instability in Iraq?" Historiae.org, September 27, 2006. As of January 2009:
http://www.historiae.org/aqalim.asp

———, "The Basra Federalism Initiative Enters Stage Two," *Iraq Updates*, December 17, 2008. As of January 2009:
http://www.iraqupdates.com/p_articles.php/article/41820/refid/RSS-latest-17-12-2008

Vlahos, Michael, "Fighting Identity: Why We Are Losing Our Wars," *Military Review*, November–December 2007, pp. 2–12.

Watkins, Eric, "EA Report Outlines Issues with Iraqi Energy Security, Fragile Systems," *Oil & Gas Journal*, December 15, 2008.

Wehrey, Fred, "Saudi Arabia: Shiites Pessimistic on Reform But Push for Reconciliation," *Arab Reform Bulletin*, Washington, D.C.: Carnegie Endowment for International Peace, June 2007.

Wehrey, Frederic, Theodore W. Karasik, Alireza Nader, Jeremy Ghez, Lydia Hansell, and Robert A. Guffey, *Saudi-Iranian Relations Since the Fall of Saddam: Rivalry, Cooperation, and Implications for U.S. Policy*, Santa Monica, Calif.: RAND Corporation, MG-840-SRF, 2009a. As of March 26, 2009:
http://www.rand.org/pubs/monographs/MG840/

Wehrey, Frederic, David E. Thaler, Nora Bensahel, Kim Cragin, Jerrold D. Green, Dalia Dassa Kaye, Nadia Oweidat, and Jennifer Li, *Dangerous But Not Omnipotent: Exploring the Reach and Limitations of Iranian Power in the Middle East*, Santa Monica, Calif.: RAND Corporation, MG-781, 2009b. As of July 7, 2009:
http://www.rand.org/pubs/monographs/MG781/

Weiss, Martin A., *Iraq's Debt Relief: Procedure and Potential Implications for International Debt Relief*, Congressional Research Service Report for Congress, Order Code RL33376, Washington, D.C., updated on October 2, 2008.

West, Bing, and Owen West, "Iraq's Real 'Civil War,'" *Wall Street Journal* (online), April 5, 2007. As of January 2009:
http://online.wsj.com/article/SB117573755559660518.html?mod=opinion_main_commentaries

The White House, *National Strategy for Victory in Iraq*, November 30, 2005. As of May 30, 2008:
http://www.whitehouse.gov/infocus/iraq/iraq_strategy_nov2005.html#part1

Wilson, Peter, et al., The Evolution of the ISF: Alternative Strategic Options, Santa Monica, Calif.: RAND Corporation, unpublished manuscript.

Wittes, Tamara Cofman, *Freedom's Unsteady March: America's Role in Building Arab Democracy*, Washington, D.C.: Brookings Institution Press, 2009.

"Wizārat al-Difāʿ al-ʿIraqiyya Tatrājaʿ: Ijrāʾāt ʿAwdat Muntasibī al-Jaysh al-Sābiq La Tashmul Fadāʾyī Sadam [The Iraqi Ministry of Defense Retreats: Measures to Return the Members of the Former Army Do Not Include Saddam's Fadayin]," *Asharq al-Awsat* (online), in Arabic, February 16, 2009. As of January 2009:
http://www.asharqalawsat.com/details.asp?section=4&article=507350&issueno=11038

Wright, Robin, "U.S. vs. Iran: Cold War, Too," *Washington Post*, July 29, 2007.

Wong, Edward, and Khalid al-Ansary, "Iraqi Sheiks Call Sunni Leader a 'Thug,'" *New York Times*, November 19, 2006.

Zavis, Alex, "Iran in Deal to Cut Flow of Arms," *Los Angeles Times*, September 30, 2007.

"Zebari: al-ʿIraq Lam Yaʿud Lubʿa bi Yad Amirika . . . wa Hunāk Nufudh Irani Lakn Laysat Hunāk Imlāʾāt [Zibari: Iraq Is No Longer a Puppet in America's Hand . . . There Is Iranian Influence but Not a Filling [of the Vacuum]]," *Asharq al-Awsat* (online), in Arabic, February 17, 2009. As of January 2009:
http://www.asharqalawsat.com/details.asp?section=4&article=507490&issueno=11039